Thesaurus
of
Linguistic
Indexing Terms

Anita Colby
Principal Lexicographer
and
LLBA Staff

sociological abstracts, inc.
P.O. Box 22206
San Diego, California 92192-0206

P
121
.C65X
1992

Library of Congress Catalog Card Number: LC 92-062352
ISBN 0-930710-10-X
Printed and bound in the United States of America

Contents

Acknowledgment

The *Thesaurus of Linguistic Indexing Terms* was developed to assist in retrieving information contained in *Linguistics and Language Behavior Abstracts* (LLBA) and *Second Language Instruction Abstracts* (**SLIA**). With the assistance of Barbara Booth and her lexicography students at UCLA, and David Acheson of the RAND Corporation, Anita Colby of the ERIC Clearinghouse created the hierarchical displays, interrelated the terms, and developed many of the scope notes. This team was supported by the LLBA editorial staff, led by Lynette Hunter, and including Jamie Stidger and Wendy Levin; other participants included Florian Andrade, John Hitchcock, Randy Logsdon, Maria Dalquist and Timothy Francis. Michael Blair, Manager of Indexing and Classification for *Sociological Abstracts*, assisted by interfacing with and coordinating communication among the contributing participants.

The first edition is dedicated to professionals in linguistics, reference and research librarians, and students who may benefit from its use.

Preface to the First Edition

We users of LLBA may not all be fully aware of just how useful a thesaurus can be in connection with increasing the benefits that are available "for the asking" to those who want to use LLBA and its database most wisely.

The *Thesaurus of Linguistic Indexing Terms* can help us broaden our searches, as well as focus them more appropriately. It identifies both the theoretical and the empirical linkages between the particular topic that concerns us and the manifold other topics that are related to it. With the advent of computerized bibliographic retrieval, it is all the more important to give considerable advance thought to exactly what topics and terms should be searched. The *Thesaurus* will be invaluable in this connection.

The *Thesaurus* helps us understand how long a particular term has been used in indexing as well as the various terms that predated it. Accordingly, the *Thesaurus* also makes a contribution to the history of ideas and the history of our various language disciplines.

The *Thesaurus* records how the language sciences are constantly growing, changing, and becoming more complex. Those of us who work in these areas, whether as researchers, teachers, students, or practitioners, must constantly stay abreast of countless ongoing changes in terminology and in the linkages between terms and concepts if our work is not to suffer from datedness and insularity. The *Thesaurus* will be a boon to all of us in this very connection.

The availability of the *Thesaurus* is a very welcome indication of the ongoing maturation of LLBA. Suggestions for its further improvement will be greatly appreciated. As it is intended to be a helpful and stimulating tool, LLBA wants to hear from its readers in order to make it even more useful.

Joshua Fishman

Professor Emeritus
   Social Sciences
   Yeshiva University
Visiting Professor
   Linguistics
   Stanford University
Chairman
   Advisory Board LLBA

Introduction

Linguistics and Language Behavior Abstracts (LLBA) is a compendium of nonevaluative abstracts that reflect the world's literature in linguistics, language acquisition, speech and language disorders, language teaching, and related disciplines. The LLBA database covers journal articles, conference papers, proceedings, books, individual book chapters, and book reviews.

LLBA provides subject access to the literature of its field through its classified organization and through two types of indexing conventions: descriptors, which are chosen from a controlled vocabulary of words and phrases; and identifiers, which are indexing phrases composed in natural language to identify dependent and independent variables, tests or measures, populations, and additional information. The authority file for descriptors was created in 1972 and first used retrospectively for the Cumulative Subject Index to Volumes I-V (1967-1971). Prior to 1992, descriptors consisted of a unique alphanumeric code, the term itself, and in more recent years, occasionally, a See Also reference to another descriptor.

By 1991, the descriptor authority file contained approximately 850 controlled vocabulary terms. These terms formed the basis of this thesaurus. This first edition of the *Thesaurus of Linguistic Indexing Terms* contains 2,632 vocabulary terms, of which 1,376 are Main Term descriptors and 1,236 are nonindexable Use references and discontinued terms. A total of 713 terms from the Descriptor Authority File were retained and incorporated into the thesaurus, some retained in their original form, some retained with new changes in word form, and some terms representing multiple concepts split into two or more new descriptors. Only 137 terms from the Descriptor Authority File were discontinued.

Thesaurus Development

The first step in the Thesaurus Project was the development of a Descriptor Input Form for each of the 850 terms in the Descriptor Authority File. The forms were then grouped into major subject categories, such as Syntax, Language Teaching, and Research Methods. Each term was searched against the database to determine the number of instances of use (postings) since 1973 and the years of first and last usage. Online and manual subject searches were conducted to identify trends in meaning or usage over time. Lexicographic authorities, including other thesauri, dictionaries, and linguistics texts, were consulted to establish preferred word forms, identify synonyms, and gather definitions. Subject terms, language names, personal names, and geographic place names each received special treatment.

Subject Terms

Particular attention was paid to the number of postings and the scope of the concept in selecting subject descriptors. Descriptors with several hundred postings each year were exhaustively analyzed to identify more specific concepts within the broader concept that might be good candidates for new descriptors. Conversely, descriptors with few or no entries in a several year period were merged whenever possible into a more generic term. In general, the objective was to establish many, very specific descriptors in the core areas of language behavior and linguistics, and fewer, more general descriptors in peripheral areas in order to improve subject retrievability in both the printed and online versions of LLBA.

Languages and Language Families

While the Descriptor Authority File only incorporated the most frequently encountered languages, the Thesaurus includes a greatly expanded set of languages and language families. In comparison to other subject terms, a relatively small number of postings were considered sufficient warrant to establish the name of a language family. *Classification and Index of the World's Languages*, by C. F. and F. M. Voegelin, was used as the authority for the form and classification of all non-African languages, and *The Languages of Africa*, by Joseph H. Greenberg, was used as the authority for African languages.

Geographic Place Names

Geographic descriptors include most of the world's countries, the states of the United States, and the provinces of Canada. In addition to assigning geographic descriptors for locations that are the focus of research, the following LLBA indexing practices are noted:

1. Immigrant groups are assigned a geographic descriptor for their place of residence, a "Cultural Group" term for their place of origin, and generally, a language term.

2. To facilitate retrieval, both a state or province and country descriptor may be assigned to the same document.

Personal Names

Personal names were entered selectively, based on frequency of occurrence as the focus of linguistics/language literature. All names are displayed in their fullest form and include dates of birth and death whenever possible.

Thesaurus Structure

The *Thesaurus of Linguistic Indexing Terms* contains an alphabetical listing of Main Term descriptors used for indexing and searching the LLBA database and printed indexes beginning with the January 1992 issue. It also references discontinued terms and codes from the former Descriptor Authority File, which must be used for accessing information prior to 1992. Associated term relationships are displayed under each Main Term. These may include a Descriptor Code (DC), Scope Note (SN), History Note (HN), Used For (UF) and Used references, Broader Terms (BT), Narrower Terms (NT), and Related Terms (RT). Each of these elements of the Thesaurus display is explained below.

Main Terms (MT)

Main Terms appear in boldface letters. Nouns and noun phrases are preferred for Main Terms, with plural word forms used with nouns that can be quantified (Conjunctions, Language Attitudes, Phonation Disorders) and singular word forms used with nouns representing processes, properties, and conditions (Conjugation, Polysemy, Space). The gerund or verbal noun is also used with process terms (Learning, Language Processing).

Main Term descriptors are limited to 60 characters. Punctuation is used minimally. In cases where ambiguity may occur, and to distinguish the meaning of homographs, Main Terms and Use reference terms appear with qualifying expressions in parentheses.

Derivation (Diachronic Linguistics)
Derivation (Morphology)

Creativity (Linguistics)
Creativity (Psychology)

Descriptor Codes (DC)

Descriptor Codes for the terms in the Descriptor Authority File were unique alphanumeric authority numbers. New Descriptor Codes have been assigned to all Main Terms. These five-digit numeric codes are easily distinguished from the former alphanumeric codes. Since a Descriptor Code is a unique number representing a Main Term, it may be used in online searching as an alternative to the Main Term itself.

Frequency (Acoustics)
DC 26100

Scope Notes (SN)

Scope notes are brief statements of the intended meaning or usage of a Main Term. They may provide definitions, user instructions, or both.

Paleography
SN Study of ancient and medieval ways of writing, particularly the decipherment of texts.

Language Usage
SN Patterns in the use of a particular language in speech or writing. For language of use in a particular context, use Language Use.

Auditory Perception
SN Recognition, identification, and understanding of acoustic signals. Not to be confused with Speech Perception.

History Notes (HN)

History Notes link Thesaurus descriptors with the Descriptor Authority File terms used in indexing prior to 1992. They are the key to searching the printed indexes and the online database from 1973 to 1991. History Notes provide the range of years in which a term was in use, its former Descriptor Code, and the word form of the term if it has changed. Often they provide search instructions. History Notes appear for both Main Terms and discontinued terms.

History Notes are standardized according to the disposition of or action taken on the former Descriptor Authority File term. Examples of several types of History Notes are given below.

Ear Preference
HN Formerly (1981-1991) DC ea2.

This term was used in indexing between 1981 and 1991 and was retained in the Thesaurus in its exact form. The History Note refers to the former Descriptor Code assigned to the term.

Grammatical Relations
HN Formerly (1988-1991) DC re9c, Relation (Grammatical).

The History Note refers to the former descriptor Relation (Grammatical), which was used in indexing between 1988 and 1991. The inverted form has been replaced by a direct entry form.

Hearing Conservation
HN Formerly (1973-1991) included in DC he2, Hearing Conservation and Improvement

The History Note documents a "term split." In this case, the two concepts Hearing Conservation and Hearing Improvement had been present in the Descriptor Authority file as a single term. Each was established as a single descriptor in the Thesaurus.

Indo-Iranian Languages (1973-1991)
HN DC in2, deleted 1992. See now Indic Languages or Iranian Languages.

Discontinued terms appear with "see now" notes pointing to Thesaurus descriptors that are taking the place of the discontinued term. This type of History Note is used when two or more descriptors are referenced.

Trigrams (1973-1991)
HN DC tr6.
Use Nonsense Syllables

"Use" references direct the indexer or searcher from non-preferred synonyms or variant expressions to preferred Main Terms. When terms from the Descriptor Authority File were downgraded to the status of Use references, the History Note records the former Descriptor Code.

Used For (UF)

Terms referenced by the Used For designation are non-preferred terms. They include synonyms and variants of the Main Term and specific terms indexed under a more generic descriptor. Often they include discontinued terms from the Descriptor Authority File; these appear with a qualifying range of years indicating their period of active use in indexing. For every Used For term, a reciprocal Use reference is generated, pointing to the preferred Main Term.

Native Language
UF First Language
Mother Tongue

Auditory System
UF Air Conduction
Auricle
Bone Conduction (1973-1991)
Ear
Hearing Structures
Inner Ear (1973-1991)
Middle Ear (1973-1991)
Outer Ear, Pinna, Auricle (1978-1991)
Pinna

Surgery
UF Mastoidectomy (1973-1979)
Operations (Surgery)
Stapedectomy (1973-1991)
Surgical Treatment (1973-1991)
Tympanoplasty (1973-1991)

Use

"Use" references direct the user from synonyms and other non-preferred expressions to the Main Term. They are the reciprocal entries of terms referenced by the Used For designation. Discontinued terms appearing as Use references are shown with a qualifying range of years of active use and History Notes recording the former Descriptor Code.

Point of Articulation
Use Place of Articulation

Memory Trace Theory (1973-1991)
HN DC me4
Use Memory

Broader Terms (BT) and Narrower Terms (NT)

Broader Terms indicate the more general class or classes to which the Main Term logically belongs. Narrower terms indicate the more specific sub-classes of the Main Term. The Broader/Narrower Term relationship is reciprocal; for every Broader Term reference there is a corresponding Narrower Term reference.

Second Language Instruction
BT Instruction

Instruction
NT Second Language Instruction

Broader Term/Narrower Term relationships create thesaurus hierarchies, sequences of class relationships that may extend upward more generally or downward more specifically through several levels. At any point in the hierarchy, Broader Term/Narrower Term designations refer upward or downward only to the next most general or specific level. However, by tracing these references, a complete hierarchy or "family tree" can be approximated.

Broader	Languages
	.African Languages
	..Congo Kordofanian Languages
	...Niger Congo Language
	....Benue Congo Phylum
	.....Bantoid Languages
Narrower	......Swahili

Note: Searching a Broader Term in the LLBA online database will not automatically retrieve abstracts representing the concepts of its Narrower Terms *unless those Narrower Terms have also been assigned to the documents in indexing* (e.g., searching Niger Congo Languages will not automatically retrieve Swahili).

Related Terms (RT)

Terms designated within a Main Term display as Related Terms bear a close conceptual relationship described by the Broader Term/Narrower Term relationship. Related Terms are always entered reciprocally. They should be considered for use as other appropriate search terms.

Refugees
RT Foreigners
    Immigrants
    Migrants

Search Guidelines

Until you become familiar with the Thesaurus and its indexing vocabulary, your success in searching the LLBA database and printed indexes will be aided if you follow the steps outlined below. A basic point to remember is that you may need to search *different* or *additional* terms to capture the literature added to the database before 1991.

1. Make a list of words or phrases that clearly and briefly describes your research topic. The first few times, you may find it helpful to do this on paper.

2. Locate the descriptors (Main Terms) most specifically describing your topic. Carefully review Scope Notes for indexing instructions and the intended meaning of terms. Check the Broader Terms, Narrower Terms, and Related Terms to identify any other descriptor pertinent to the topic. These will help you to broaden or narrow the focus of your search. Then check History Notes and Used For references to identify corresponding terms for searching prior to 1991. In the example below, you would need to search Statistical Analysis for materials indexed in 1992 and thereafter, but you would need to add the terms Experimental Data Handling and Stochastic Models to capture the materials indexed in 1991 and before.

Statistical Analysis
HN Formerly (1988-1991) DC st2a.
UF Experimental Data Handling (1973-1991)
    Statistical Methods
    Stochastic Models (1973-1991)

Keep in mind that information pertinent to your research may be indexed under a broader descriptor. Specific articles indexed under narrower concepts may also be directly applicable.

3. Repeat step 2 for other terms you have identified as appropriate to your topic. You should end up with two lists of terms, one for searching prior to 1991 and another for searching after 1991.

4. Turn to the annual cumulative indexes of LLBA or access the LLBA database through Dialog or BRS.

Searching the Printed Indexes

Begin with the Subject Index section of individual issues or annual cumulative indexes published in 1992 or thereafter. Consult several or all of the Thesaurus descriptors you have listed; then focus your search on those descriptors found to be the most productive for your topic. Usually these will represent the most concrete or central aspect of the topic.

Examine the entries under the descriptors to locate pertinent material, noting the abstract accession numbers. Follow up by reading the abstracts and obtaining journal citations in the Main Section.

Then turn to the annual indexes published prior to 1992. Repeat the steps outlined above, using the Descriptor Authority File terms referenced in History Notes and discontinued Used For terms. In a comprehensive search, be alert to the range of years during which the terms were in use.

Searching Online

Frequently, Main Term descriptors in the Thesaurus are identical to one of the component words in a former descriptor. However, even if there is only a slight variation in form, both forms must be searched as well as any discontinued terms appearing as Used For references. This should be expressed as an "OR" statement (use the appropriate commands and protocols of your online service):

Animal Communication OR Animal Communication and Vocalization OR Species Specific Communication

Keep in mind that both old and new index terms can be combined flexibly with words in titles, identifier phrases, and abstracts in search strategies. Online search capabilities give you powerful tools for precision and recall retrieval.

Sample Thesaurus Entries

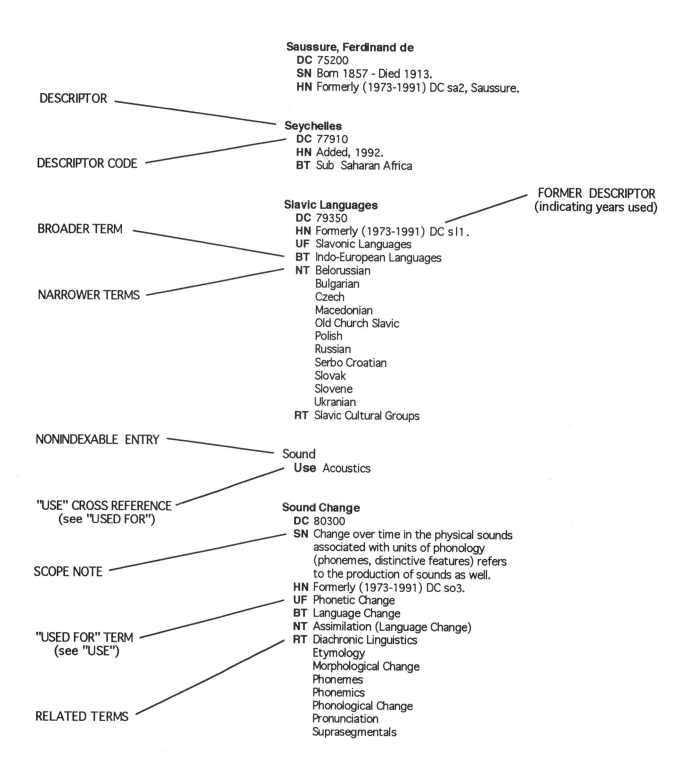

DESCRIPTOR

DESCRIPTOR CODE

BROADER TERM

NARROWER TERMS

NONINDEXABLE ENTRY

"USE" CROSS REFERENCE
(see "USED FOR")

SCOPE NOTE

"USED FOR" TERM
(see "USE")

RELATED TERMS

FORMER DESCRIPTOR
(indicating years used)

Saussure, Ferdinand de
DC 75200
SN Born 1857 - Died 1913.
HN Formerly (1973-1991) DC sa2, Saussure.

Seychelles
DC 77910
HN Added, 1992.
BT Sub Saharan Africa

Slavic Languages
DC 79350
HN Formerly (1973-1991) DC sl1.
UF Slavonic Languages
BT Indo-European Languages
NT Belorussian
       Bulgarian
       Czech
       Macedonian
       Old Church Slavic
       Polish
       Russian
       Serbo Croatian
       Slovak
       Slovene
       Ukranian
RT Slavic Cultural Groups

Sound
  Use Acoustics

Sound Change
DC 80300
SN Change over time in the physical sounds
       associated with units of phonology
       (phonemes, distinctive features) refers
       to the production of sounds as well.
HN Formerly (1973-1991) DC so3.
UF Phonetic Change
BT Language Change
NT Assimilation (Language Change)
RT Diachronic Linguistics
       Etymology
       Morphological Change
       Phonemes
       Phonemics
       Phonological Change
       Pronunciation
       Suprasegmentals

Alphabetical List
of
Terms

Ablative Case
Use Case

Aboriginal Australians
DC 00050
HN Added, 1992.
BT Australian Cultural Groups
RT Indigenous Populations

Abure
Use Akan

Academic Achievement
DC 00070
HN Added, 1992.
UF Educational Attainment
Scholastic Achievement
RT Achievement Tests
Education
Educational Activities
Learning
Students
Tests

Accelerated Speech
Use Speech Rate

Accent (Second Language)
Use Foreign Accent

Accent (Vocal Stress)
Use Stress

Accentuation
DC 00080
HN Added, 1992.
UF Stress Assignment
Stress Placement
RT Intensity (Acoustics)
Intonation
Phonology
Pitch (Acoustics)
Rhythm
Sentences
Stress
Suprasegmentals
Syllables
Words

Acculturation
DC 00090
SN Psychological and social adjustment
to a new culture, often following im-
migration.
HN Added, 1992.
RT Cross Cultural Communication
Cultural Background
Cultural Change
Cultural Differences
Cultural Factors
Cultural Groups
Culture
Immigrants
Indigenous Populations
Language Contact
Language Culture Relationship
Migrants
Refugees
Second Language Learning

Accusative Case
Use Case

Achievement Tests
DC 00100
SN Tests measuring a person's current
knowledge, abilities, or skills.
HN Formerly (1973-1991) DC ac1a,
Achievement Testing.
BT Tests
RT Academic Achievement
Aptitude Tests
Language Tests
Reading Tests
Writing Tests

Acoustic Phonetics
DC 00150
SN The branch of phonetics that studies
the physical nature of speech
sounds.
HN Formerly (1973-1991) DC ac2.
BT Phonetics
RT Acoustics
Auditory Perception
Distinctive Features
Distortion of Speech Signal
Formants
Frequency (Acoustics)
Fundamental Frequency
Intensity (Acoustics)
Signal Detection
Sound Spectrographs
Speech
Speech Synthesis
Voice Recognition

Acoustic Stimulation
Use Auditory Stimulation

**Acoustic Theory of Speech Produc-
tion (1973-1991)**
HN DC ac3, deleted 1992. See now
Acoustics or Acoustic Phonetics.

Acoustics
DC 00200
HN Added, 1992.
UF Sound
Sound Transmission
Sound Waves
NT Psychoacoustics
RT Acoustic Phonetics
Auditory Perception
Auditory Stimulation
Distortion of Speech Signal
Formants
Frequency (Acoustics)
Fundamental Frequency
Hearing
Intensity (Acoustics)
Noise
Signal Detection
Silence
Sound Spectrographs

Acquired Dyslexia
Use Dyslexia

Acronyms
DC 00230
HN Added, 1992.
BT Lexicon
RT Morphology
Terminology
Word Formation
Words

Acrostics
Use Word Games

Active Voice
Use Voice (Grammatical)

Adamawa Eastern Phylum
DC 00250
HN Added, 1992.
UF Adamawa Languages
Gbaya
Sango
Ubangian Languages
BT Niger Congo Languages

Adamawa Languages
Use Adamawa Eastern Phylum

Address Forms
DC 00260
HN Added, 1992.
UF Forms of Address
RT Cultural Factors
Interpersonal Behavior
Interpersonal Communication
Kinship Terminology
Politeness
Pronouns
Registers (Sociolinguistics)
Sociolinguistics

Aden
Use Republic of Yemen

Adjectives
DC 00350
HN Formerly (1973-1991) DC ad1, Ad-
jective.
BT Form Classes
RT Adverbs
Articles
Case
Comparison
Determiners
Gender (Grammatical)
Nouns
Number (Grammatical)
Quantifiers
Semantic Differential

Adolescent Language
DC 00400
HN Formerly (1973-1991) DC ad2.
BT Language
RT Adolescents
Adult Language
Age Differences
Child Language
Oral Language

Adolescents
DC 00450
HN Added, 1992.
UF Teenagers
Youth
RT Adolescent Language
Children
High School Students
Junior High School Students
Secondary School Students
Young Adults

Adult Child Interaction
DC 00470
HN Added, 1992.
UF Child Adult Interaction
BT Interpersonal Behavior
NT Parent Child Interaction
RT Adults
Age Differences
Baby Talk
Children
Dyadic Interaction
Interpersonal Communication
Linguistic Accommodation
Maternal Speech
Parents
Registers (Sociolinguistics)
Sex Differences
Socialization
Student Teacher Relationship

Adult Illiteracy
Use Adult Literacy

Adult Language
DC 00500
HN Formerly (1973-1991) DC ad3.
BT Language
NT Maternal Speech
RT Adolescent Language
    Adults
    Age Differences
    Child Language
    Oral Language
    Young Adults

Adult Literacy
DC 00550
HN Added, 1992.
UF Adult Illiteracy
    Illiterate Adults
BT Literacy
RT Adults
    Basic Writing
    Functional Literacy
    Literacy Programs
    Reading Ability

Adults
DC 00600
HN Added, 1992.
NT Elderly
    Young Adults
RT Adult Child Interaction
    Adult Language
    Adult Literacy
    Parents

Adverbs
DC 00650
HN Formerly (1973-1991) DC ad4, Adverb.
BT Form Classes
RT Adjectives
    Comparison
    Verbs

Advertisements
DC 00670
HN Added, 1992.
UF Commercials
RT Business
    Mass Media
    Persuasion
    Political Discourse

Aeolic
Use Ancient Greek

Aerodynamics of Speech
Use Air Flow

Affect
Use Emotions

Affective Meaning
Use Connotation

Affixation
Use Affixes

Affixes
DC 00750
HN Formerly (1973-1991) DC af1, Affix.
UF Affixation
    Bound Morphemes
    Infixes
BT Morphemes
NT Prefixes
    Suffixes
RT Agreement
    Conjugation

Affixes (cont'd)
RT Derivation (Morphology)
    Form Classes
    Incorporation (Grammatical)
    Inflection (Morphology)
    Morphology
    Morphophonemics
    Reflexivity
    Roots (Morphology)
    Word Formation

Afghanistan
DC 00800
HN Added, 1992.
BT Middle East

Africa
DC 00830
HN Added, 1992.
NT North Africa
    Sub Saharan Africa
RT African Cultural Groups
    African Languages

African Americans
Use Black Americans

African Cultural Groups
DC 00850
HN Added, 1992.
BT Cultural Groups
NT North African Cultural Groups
    Southern African Cultural Groups
RT Africa
    African Languages
    Arab Cultural Groups

African Languages
DC 00900
HN Added, 1992.
BT Languages
NT Afroasiatic Languages
    Congo Kordofanian Languages
    Khoisan Languages
    Nilo Saharan Languages
RT Africa
    African Cultural Groups

Afrikaans
DC 00950
HN Added, 1992.
UF Cape Dutch
    Taal
BT Germanic Languages
RT Dutch

Afroasiatic Languages
DC 01100
HN Formerly (1973-1991) DC af2, Afro-Asiatic Languages.
UF Erythraic Languages
    Hamito-Semitic Languages
    Semito-Hamitic Languages
BT African Languages
NT Berber Languages
    Chadic Languages
    Cushitic Languages
    Egyptian Coptic
    Semitic Languages

Age Differences
DC 01150
HN Formerly (1973-1991) DC ag1, Age Differences in Language.
UF Developmental Differences
RT Adolescent Language
    Adult Child Interaction
    Adult Language
    Child Language

Age Differences (cont'd)
RT Elderly
    Maternal Speech
    Sex Differences
    Social Factors
    Sociolinguistics
    Voice Quality

Aged
Use Elderly

Agent Patient Relationship (Grammatical)
DC 01160
HN Added, 1992.
UF Goal Agent Relationship (Grammatical)
    Patient Agent Relationship (Grammatical)
    Recipient Agent Relationship (Grammatical)
BT Grammatical Relations
RT Case Grammar
    Functional Grammar
    Government Binding Theory
    Grammatical Analysis
    Passive Voice
    Predicate
    Semantic Categories
    Subject (Grammatical)
    Syntax
    Thematic Roles
    Verbs

Aggression (Verbal) (1981-1991)
HN DC ag2.
Use Verbal Aggression

Agrammatic Aphasia
Use Agrammatism

Agrammatism
DC 01200
SN Type of aphasia affecting the ability to form normal grammatical constructions, resulting in telegrammatic speech.
HN Added, 1992.
UF Agrammatic Aphasia
BT Aphasia
RT Grammar Instruction
    Language Pathology
    Syntactic Processing

Agraphia
Use Writing Disorders

Agreement
DC 01230
HN Added, 1992.
UF Concord
RT Affixes
    Conjugation
    Functional Grammar
    Gender (Grammatical)
    Generalized Phrase Structure Grammar
    Government (Grammatical)
    Government Binding Theory
    Grammatical Analysis
    Grammatical Relations
    Inflection (Morphology)
    Number (Grammatical)
    Subject (Grammatical)
    Syntax
    Verbs

Aided Recall
DC 01250
HN Formerly (1973-1991) DC ai1.
UF Cued Recall
BT Recall (Memory)
RT Encoding (Cognitive Process)
Recognition
Serial Learning
Unaided Recall

Air Conduction (1973-1991)
HN DC ai2.
Use Auditory System

Air Flow
DC 01300
HN Formerly (1973-1991) DC ai3.
UF Aerodynamics of Speech
Air Pressure Dynamics
Ingressive Air Flow
Intra Oral Air Pressure (1973-1991)
Oral Air Flow
RT Nasalization
Pharyngeal Structures
Phonation Structures
Respiratory System

Air Pressure Dynamics
Use Air Flow

Akan
DC 01350
HN Added, 1992.
UF Abure
Anyi
Baule
Guang
Metyibo
Twi
BT Kwa Languages

Akkadian
Use Semitic Languages

Alabama
DC 01400
HN Added, 1992.
BT Southern States
United States of America

Alaska
DC 01450
HN Added, 1992.
BT United States of America
RT Arctic Regions

Albania
DC 01500
HN Added, 1992.
BT Balkan States
Eastern Europe

Albanian
DC 01550
HN Added, 1992.
UF Gheg
Tosk
BT Indo European Languages

Alberta
DC 01600
HN Added, 1992.
BT Canada

Alcoholism
DC 01650
HN Added, 1992.
BT Disorders
RT Behavior Disorders
Drug Effects

Aleut
Use Eskimo Aleut Languages

Alexia
Use Aphasia

Algebraic Linguistics
Use Mathematical Linguistics

Algeria
DC 01700
HN Added, 1992.
BT Arab Countries
Mediterranean Countries
North Africa

Algonkian Languages
Use Algonquian Languages

Algonquian Languages
DC 01750
HN Added, 1992.
UF Algonkian Languages
Cree
Ojibwa
BT North Amerindian Languages

Aliens
Use Foreigners

Alliteration
Use Phonological Stylistics

Allomorphs
Use Morphemes

Allophones
Use Phonemes

Alphabets
DC 01800
HN Formerly (1973-1991) DC al1, Alphabet.
BT Writing Systems
NT Initial Teaching Alphabet
International Phonetic Alphabet
RT Ideographs
Orthographic Symbols
Orthography
Phonetic Transcription
Written Language

Altaic Languages
DC 01850
HN Formerly (1973-1991) DC al2.
UF Tungus Languages
BT Languages
NT Japanese
Korean
Mongolian Languages
Turkic Languages

Alzheimers Disease
DC 01900
HN Added, 1992.
BT Nervous System Disorders
RT Memory Disorders
Mental Disorders

Amarigna
Use Amharic

Ambidexterity
Use Handedness

Ambiguity
DC 01950
HN Formerly (1973-1991) DC am1.
UF Grammatical Ambiguity
Lexical Ambiguity

Ambiguity (cont'd)
UF Structural Ambiguity
RT Communication
Context Clues
Homographs
Homonyms
Homophones
Meaning
Rhetorical Figures
Semantics
Word Meaning

American Blacks
Use Black Americans

American English
DC 02100
HN Added, 1992.
UF Canadian English
BT English
NT Black English

American Indians
DC 02150
HN Formerly (1973-1991) DC am2, American Indian.
UF Indians (American)
Native Americans
BT Latin American Cultural Groups
North American Cultural Groups
RT Indigenous Populations

American Linguistic Theory (1973-1991)
HN DC am3, deleted 1992. See now specific linguistic theories and theoreticians, or History of Linguistics.

American Samoa
DC 02250
HN Added, 1992.
BT Polynesia

American Sign Language
DC 02350
HN Added, 1992.
BT Sign Language

Amerindian Languages
DC 02400
HN Added, 1992.
BT Languages
NT Central Amerindian Languages
North Amerindian Languages
South Amerindian Languages

Amharic
DC 02450
HN Added, 1992.
UF Amarigna
BT Semitic Languages

Amnesia
Use Memory Disorders

Analogy (Language Change)
DC 02550
SN A mechanism of language change in which a complex structure is constructed on the pattern of existing structures and competes with and often replaces an inherited form.
HN Added, 1992.
RT Diachronic Linguistics
Grammatical Change
Morphological Change

Anaphora
- **DC** 02600
- **SN** The use of one linguistic unit as a substitute for, or to refer back to, a preceding word or phrase.
- **HN** Formerly (1973-1991) DC am7.
- **UF** Antecedents (Grammatical)
- **BT** Reference (Grammatical)
- **RT** Deixis
  Government Binding Theory
  Meaning
  Pronouns
  Reflexivity
  Semantics
  Trace Theory

Anatolian Languages
- **DC** 02650
- **HN** Added, 1992.
- **UF** Hittite
  Luwain
  Lycian
  Lydian
  Palaic
- **BT** Indo European Languages

Anatomical Systems
- **DC** 02750
- **HN** Added, 1992.
- **NT** Auditory System
  Brain
  Oral Cavity
  Pharyngeal Structures
  Phonation Structures
  Respiratory System
  Sensory Systems
- **RT** Biology
  Disorders
  Eye Movements
  Medicine

Ancient Egyptian
- **Use** Egyptian Coptic

Ancient Greek
- **DC** 02800
- **HN** Added, 1992.
- **UF** Aeolic
  Classical Greek
- **BT** Greek

Andean Equatorial Phylum
- **DC** 02850
- **HN** Added, 1992.
- **UF** Andean Languages
  Arawakan Languages
  Aruan Languages
  Cahuapan Languages
  Chapacura Wanhaman Languages
  Equitorial Languages
  Guahibo Pamigua Languages
  Jivaroan Languages
  Macro Tucanoan Languages
  Maipuran Languages
  Pamiguan Languages
  Piaroan Languages
  Salivan Languages
  Tucanoan Languages
- **BT** South Amerindian Languages
- **NT** Quechua
  Tupi Languages

Andean Languages
- **Use** Andean Equatorial Phylum

Andorra
- **DC** 02900
- **HN** Added, 1992.
- **BT** Western Europe

Anglo Americans
- **DC** 02940
- **HN** Added, 1992.
- **BT** North American Cultural Groups
  Whites
- **RT** Asian Americans
  Black Americans
  Hispanic Americans
  Jewish Americans

Anglo Saxon
- **Use** Old English

Angola
- **DC** 02950
- **HN** Added, 1992.
- **BT** Sub Saharan Africa

Animacy and Inanimacy
- **DC** 03100
- **SN** Syntactic and morphological phenomena reflecting a classification of nouns or referents into two basic groups, one characterized by attributions of volition, life, consciousness, or other human qualities (ie, animacy) and the other characterized by the absence of the quality (ie, inanimacy). Also, a semantic feature used to describe or explain the meaning of words or other linguistic units and/or their distribution in the syntax or morphology of a language.
- **HN** Formerly (1973-1991) DC an2, Animate and Inanimate.
- **UF** Animate Nouns
  Inanimate Nouns
- **RT** Nouns
  Semantics

Animal Communication
- **DC** 03150
- **HN** Formerly (1973-1991) DC an1. Animal Communication and Vocalization.
- **UF** Animal Language
  Animal Vocalization
  Species Specific Communication (1975-1987)
- **BT** Communication
- **RT** Interspecies Communication
  Nonverbal Communication
  Origin of Language
  Primates

Animal Human Communication
- **Use** Interspecies Communication

Animal Language
- **Use** Animal Communication

Animal Vocalization
- **Use** Animal Communication

Animate Nouns
- **Use** Animacy and Inanimacy

Annamese
- **Use** Vietnamese

Anomalous Strings
- **DC** 03200
- **HN** Formerly (1973-1991) DC an3.
- **UF** Deviant Sentences
  Nonsense Sentences
- **NT** Nonsense Syllables
  Nonsense Words
- **RT** Error Analysis (Language)
  Grammaticality
  Language Processing

Anomalous Strings (cont'd)
- **RT** Memory
  Phonological Processing
  Phonology
  Psycholinguistics
  Sentences

Anomia
- **Use** Aphasia

Antecedents (Grammatical)
- **Use** Anaphora

Anthropological Linguistics
- **DC** 03250
- **SN** Study of the relationship between language and culture (eg, traditions, beliefs, family structures) in a community, using the theories and methodology of anthropology. Often focuses on cultures with no written language.
- **HN** Formerly (1973-1991) DC an4.
- **UF** Linguistic Anthropology
- **BT** Linguistics
- **RT** Archaeological Evidence
  Componential Analysis
  Cultural Factors
  Diachronic Linguistics
  Ethnographic Linguistics
  Ethnolinguistics
  Kinship Terminology
  Language Culture Relationship
  Linguistic Relativity
  Linguistic Theories
  Origin of Language
  Paleolinguistics
  Social Factors
  Sociolinguistics
  Unknown Languages

Anthroponomastics
- **Use** Onomastics

Anthroponymy
- **Use** Onomastics

Antonyms
- **DC** 03300
- **HN** Formerly (1973-1991) DC an5, Antonym.
- **BT** Lexicon
- **RT** Meaning
  Semantics
  Synonyms

Anxiety
- **DC** 03350
- **HN** Formerly (1973-1991) DC an6.
- **UF** Apprehension
  Writing Anxiety
- **RT** Emotional Disturbances
  Emotions

Anyi
- **Use** Akan

Aphasia
- **DC** 03400
- **HN** Formerly (1973-1991) DC ap1.
- **UF** Alexia
  Anomia
  Dysphasia
  Expressive Aphasia
  Receptive Aphasia
- **BT** Nervous System Disorders
- **NT** Agrammatism
  Brocas Aphasia
  Wernickes Aphasia
- **RT** Brain Damage
  Language Pathology

Aphasia (cont'd)
RT Language Therapy
Learning Disabilities
Memory Disorders
Neurolinguistics
Receptive Language
Speech Pathology
Writing Disorders

Appalachia
DC 03450
HN Added, 1992.
RT Alabama
Georgia (USA)
Kentucky
Pennsylvania
South Carolina
Tennessee
Virginia
West Virginia

Applied Linguistics
DC 03500
HN Formerly (1973-1991) DC ap2.
BT Linguistics
RT Articulation Disorders
Behavioristic Linguistic Theory
Language Planning
Language Processing
Language Teaching Methods
Language Therapy
Lexicography
Linguistic Theories
Metalanguage
Phonation Disorders
Phonological Processing
Second Language Instruction
Second Languages
Speech Pathology
Speech Therapy
Theoretical Linguistics
Translation

Apprehension
Use Anxiety

Aptitude Tests
DC 03600
SN Tests measuring a person's capacity or potential for performance.
HN Formerly (1973-1991) DC ap3, Aptitude Testing.
BT Tests
RT Achievement Tests
Intelligence Tests

Arab Countries
DC 03650
HN Added, 1992.
NT Algeria
Bahrain
Egypt
Iraq
Jordan
Kuwait
Lebanon
Libya
Morocco
Palestine
Qatar
Republic of Yemen
Saudi Arabia
Sudan
Syria
Tunisia
United Arab Emirates
Yemen Arab Republic
Yemen (Peoples Democratic Republic)
RT Arab Cultural Groups
Mediterranean Countries
Middle East
North Africa

Arab Cultural Groups
DC 03700
HN Added, 1992.
BT Cultural Groups
NT Palestinians
RT African Cultural Groups
Arab Countries
Middle East
Middle Eastern Cultural Groups
North African Cultural Groups

Arabic
DC 03750
HN Added, 1992.
BT Semitic Languages

Aramaic
DC 03800
HN Added, 1992.
UF Assyrian
Chaldean
Old Aramaic
Syriac
BT Semitic Languages

Arawakan Languages
Use Andean Equatorial Phylum

Arbitrary Reference
Use Reference (Grammatical)

Archaeological Evidence
DC 03820
HN Added, 1992.
RT Anthropological Linguistics
Diachronic Linguistics
Language Culture Relationship
Nostratic Theory
Onomastics
Origin of Language
Paleography
Paleolinguistics
Proto Indo European
Unknown Languages

Arctic Regions
DC 03850
HN Added, 1992.
RT Alaska
Greenland
Lapland
Northwest Territories
Siberia
Yukon

Areal Linguistics
DC 03900
SN The branch of linguistics that studies the geographical distribution and diversification of languages within a specifiable region.
HN Added, 1992.
UF Geographical Linguistics
Linguistic Geography
BT Linguistics
RT Comparative Linguistics
Dialectology
Indigenous Languages
Language Contact
Language Typology
Linguistic Theories
Regional Dialects

Argentina
DC 03950
HN Added, 1992.
BT South America

Argot
Use Slang

Arithmetic
Use Mathematics

Arizona
DC 04100
HN Added, 1992.
BT United States of America
Western States

Arkansas
DC 04150
HN Added, 1992.
BT Southern States
United States of America
RT Ozark Mountains

Armed Forces
DC 04200
HN Added, 1992.
UF Military Personnel
RT Occupations
Registers (Sociolinguistics)
Slang

Armenia
DC 04240
HN Added, 1992.
BT Commonwealth of Independent States
RT Union of Soviet Socialist Republics

Armenian
DC 04250
HN Added, 1992.
UF Grabar
BT Indo European Languages

Art
DC 04450
HN Formerly (1973-1991) DC ar1, Art as Language.
UF Communicative Function of Art
Fine Arts
Photography
Visual Arts
RT Color
Creativity (Psychology)
Drama
Films
Folklore
Literature
Music
Visual Media

Art as Language (1973-1991)
HN DC ar1.
Use Art

Articles
DC 04550
HN Formerly (1973-1991) DC ar2, Article.
UF Definite Articles
Indefinite Articles
BT Form Classes
RT Adjectives
Determiners
Function Words
Nouns

Articulation
DC 04600
SN The production of distinctive speech sounds by means of specific coordinated movements of the speech tract. Use Phonation for the production of vocal sounds.

Articulation (cont'd)
HN Formerly (1973-1991) DC ar3.
UF Speech Production
RT Articulation Disorders
   Articulatory Phonetics
   Assimilation (Language Change)
   Consonants
   Phonation
   Phonation Structures
   Phonetics
   Place of Articulation
   Pronunciation
   Speech
   Speech Tests
   Vowels

Articulation Disorders
DC 04650
HN Formerly (1973-1991) DC ar4.
UF Dysarthria
   Lisping
BT Disorders
RT Applied Linguistics
   Articulation
   Articulatory Phonetics
   Cleft Palate
   Handicapped
   Phonation Disorders
   Phonetically Balanced Lists
   Speech
   Speech Pathology
   Speech Tests
   Speech Therapy
   Stuttering
   Voice Disorders

Articulation Point
Use Place of Articulation

Articulatory Phonetics
DC 04750
SN The branch of phonetics that studies the physiology of speech sound production (including articulation and phonation).
HN Formerly (1973-1991) DC ar5.
UF Physiological Phonetics
BT Phonetics
RT Articulation
   Articulation Disorders
   Distinctive Features
   Oral Cavity
   Phonation
   Phonation Structures
   Place of Articulation
   Pronounceability
   Pronunciation
   Pronunciation Accuracy
   Radiography
   Singing
   Speech
   Speech Duration
   Speech Rate
   Suprasegmentals
   Voicing
   Whispering

Artificial Intelligence
DC 04800
HN Added, 1992.
UF Expert Systems
RT Cognitive Processes
   Computer Applications
   Cybernetics
   Human Computer Communication
   Intelligence
   Logic
   Natural Language Processing
   Neural Networks
   Semantic Processing

Artificial Languages
DC 04850
HN Added, 1992. Formerly (1973-1991) included in DC sy4, Synthetic Languages.
UF Constructed Languages
BT Languages
NT Computer Languages
   Esperanto
RT Cross Cultural Communication
   Glossolalia
   International Languages
   Language Universals
   Natural Language
   Secret Languages

Artificial Speech
Use Speech Synthesis

Aruan Languages
Use Andean Equatorial Phylum

Asia
DC 04940
HN Added, 1992.
NT Far East
   Middle East
   South Asia
   Southeast Asia
RT Asian Cultural Groups

Asian Americans
DC 04945
HN Added, 1992.
BT North American Cultural Groups
RT Anglo Americans
   Asian Cultural Groups
   Black Americans
   Hispanic Americans
   Jewish Americans

Asian Cultural Groups
DC 04950
HN Added, 1992.
UF Oriental Cultural Groups
BT Cultural Groups
NT South Asian Cultural Groups
   Southeast Asian Cultural Groups
RT Asia
   Asian Americans
   Commonwealth of Independent States

Aspect
DC 05100
SN A category of verb inflection signaling differences in the internal time structure of events (eg, static/dynamic, begun/on-going/complete, repeated). Distinguish from tense, which marks contrasts in external time reference.
HN Added, 1992.
BT Grammatical Categories
RT Auxiliary Verbs
   Mood (Grammatical)
   Morphology
   Syntax
   Tense
   Verbs

Assessment Instruments
Use Measures (Instruments)

Assimilation (Language Change)
DC 05200
SN A process of phonological or phonetic change in which a phonetic feature spreads to adjacent or nearby phonemes, sometimes with elimination of a contrasting feature. In total assimilation, phonemes become identical.

Assimilation (Language Change) (cont'd)
HN Added, 1992.
BT Sound Change
RT Articulation
   Diachronic Linguistics
   Palatalization
   Phonetics
   Phonological Analysis
   Phonological Change
   Synchronic Linguistics

Association (Psychology)
Use Associative Processes

Associative Processes
DC 05300
HN Added, 1992.
UF Association (Psychology)
   Remote Associates
BT Cognitive Processes
NT Free Association
   Word and Letter Association
RT Connotation
   Context Clues
   Context Effects (Perception)
   Generalization
   Information Processing
   Language Thought Relationship
   Learning Processes
   Logic
   Long Term Memory
   Memory
   Paired Associate Learning
   Recognition
   Semantic Processing
   Serial Learning
   Word Recognition

Assonance
Use Phonological Stylistics

Assumptions
Use Presuppositions

Assyrian
Use Aramaic

Athapascan
Use Na Dene Phylum

Athletics
Use Sports

Attention
DC 05350
HN Formerly (1973-1991) DC at1.
RT Attention Deficit Disorders
   Cognitive Processes
   Listening
   Perception

Attention Deficit Disorders
DC 05400
HN Added, 1992.
BT Disorders
RT Attention
   Behavior Disorders
   Emotional Disturbances
   Learning Disabilities
   Nervous System Disorders

Attitude Change (1977-1983)
HN DC at2, deleted 1983. See now Attitudes or Persuasion.

Attitudes
DC 05450
HN Formerly (1982-1991) DC at3.
UF Opinions (1973-1991)
NT Language Attitudes
    Stereotypes
    Teacher Attitudes
RT Beliefs
    Emotions
    Expressive Function of Language
    Judgment
    Semantic Differential
    Sexism
    Social Perception

Audiolingual Language Teaching
DC 05500
SN Foreign-language teaching approach
    that emphasizes the development of
    speaking and listening skills through
    drill and repetition.
HN Formerly (1973-1991) DC au1.
UF Aural-Oral Method of Language
    Teaching
BT Language Teaching Methods
RT Communicative Language Teaching
    Conversation Courses
    Direct Method of Language Teaching
    Language Laboratories
    Second Language Instruction
    Second Language Learning

Audiology
DC 05550
HN Formerly (1973-1991) DC au2.
BT Medicine
RT Audiometry
    Auditory Masking
    Auditory Perception
    Auditory Stimulation
    Auditory System
    Auditory Thresholds
    Hearing
    Hearing Aids
    Hearing Conservation
    Hearing Disorders

Audiometric Tests
Use Audiometry

Audiometry
DC 05600
SN Procedures and tests to assess hear-
    ing acuity and range.
HN Formerly (1973-1991) DC au3.
UF Audiometric Tests
    Hearing Measurment
    Hearing Testing
    Pure Tone Audiometry
    SISI Test
    Speech Audiometry
BT Tests
RT Audiology
    Auditory Masking
    Auditory Perception
    Auditory Stimulation
    Auditory System
    Auditory Thresholds
    Distortion of Speech Signal
    Ear Preference
    Hearing
    Hearing Disorders
    Phonetically Balanced Lists

Audiovisual Language Teaching
DC 05650
HN Formerly (1973-1991) DC au4.
BT Language Teaching Methods
RT Computer Assisted Instruction
    Educational Television
    Language Laboratories
    Language Teaching Materials

Audition
Use Hearing

Auditory Comprehension
Use Listening Comprehension

Auditory Disorders
Use Hearing Disorders

Auditory Evoked Responses
Use Evoked Responses

Auditory Feedback (Delayed)
Use Delayed Auditory Feedback

Auditory Localization
DC 05700
HN Formerly (1973-1991) DC au5.
UF Localization (Sound)
    Sound Localization
BT Auditory Perception
RT Auditory Stimulation
    Hearing
    Psychoacoustics
    Space

Auditory Masking
DC 05750
HN Formerly (1973-1991) DC au6.
BT Masking
RT Audiology
    Audiometry
    Auditory Perception
    Auditory Stimulation
    Auditory System
    Auditory Thresholds
    Hearing
    Noise

Auditory Perception
DC 05800
SN Recognition, identification, and un-
    derstanding of acoustic signals. Not
    to be confused with Speech Percep-
    tion.
HN Added, 1992.
BT Perception
NT Auditory Localization
RT Acoustic Phonetics
    Acoustics
    Audiology
    Audiometry
    Auditory Masking
    Auditory Stimulation
    Auditory System
    Auditory Thresholds
    Delayed Auditory Feedback
    Discrimination Learning
    Distortion of Speech Signal
    Ear Preference
    Hearing
    Hearing Disorders
    Language Processing
    Listening
    Listening Comprehension
    Noise
    Psychoacoustics
    Sound Identification
    Speech Perception

Auditory Stimulation
DC 05950
HN Formerly (1973-1991) DC au7.
UF Acoustic Stimulation
    Aural Stimulation
BT Stimulation
NT Binaural Stimulation
    Monaural Stimulation
RT Acoustics
    Audiology

Auditory Stimulation (cont'd)
RT Audiometry
    Auditory Localization
    Auditory Masking
    Auditory Perception
    Auditory System
    Auditory Thresholds
    Decoding (Cognitive Process)
    Delayed Auditory Feedback
    Frequency (Acoustics)
    Hearing
    Intensity (Acoustics)
    Listening
    Noise
    Psychoacoustics
    Speech Perception
    Visual Stimulation

Auditory System
DC 06100
HN Added, 1992.
UF Air Conduction (1973-1991)
    Auricle
    Bone Conduction (1973-1991)
    Ear
    Hearing Structures
    Inner Ear (1973-1991)
    Middle Ear (1973-1991)
    Outer Ear, Pinna, Auricle (1978-
    1991)
    Pinna
BT Anatomical Systems
RT Audiology
    Audiometry
    Auditory Masking
    Auditory Perception
    Auditory Stimulation
    Auditory Thresholds
    Ear Preference
    Hearing
    Hearing Aids
    Hearing Disorders
    Psychoacoustics

Auditory Thresholds
DC 06150
HN Formerly (1973-1991) DC au8.
UF Hearing Thresholds
    Speech Reception Thresholds
BT Thresholds
RT Audiology
    Audiometry
    Auditory Masking
    Auditory Perception
    Auditory Stimulation
    Auditory System
    Hearing
    Hearing Disorders
    Sound Identification
    Speech Perception

Aural Comprehension
Use Listening Comprehension

Aural Disorders
Use Hearing Disorders

Aural Stimulation
Use Auditory Stimulation

**Aural-Oral Method of Language
Teaching**
Use Audiolingual Language Teaching

Auricle
Use Auditory System

Austin, John Langsham
DC 06200
SN Born 1911 - Died 1960.
HN Formerly (1973-1991) DC au9, Austin.

Australasia
DC 06250
SN Australia, New Zealand, and neighboring islands in the South Pacific Ocean.
HN Added, 1992.
NT Australia
New Zealand
RT Australasian Cultural Groups

Australasian Cultural Groups
DC 06300
HN Added, 1992.
BT Cultural Groups
NT Aboriginal Australians
RT Australasia

Australia
DC 06350
HN Added, 1992.
BT Australasia
NT Tasmania

Australian English
DC 06400
HN Added, 1992.
BT English

Australian Macro Phylum
DC 06450
HN Formerly (1984-1991) DC au9a, Australian Macro-Phylum.
UF Kardutjara
Pama Nyungan
Tiwi
BT Languages

Austria
DC 06550
HN Added, 1992.
BT Western Europe

Austro Asiatic Languages
DC 06600
HN Formerly (1985-1991) DC au9b, Austro-Asiatic Languages.
UF Cambodian
Khmer
Malacca Languages
Mon Khmer Languages
Munda Languages
Nicobarese Languages
BT Languages
NT Vietnamese

Austronesian Languages
DC 06650
HN Formerly (1973-1991) DC au10.
BT Languages
NT Malayo Polynesian Languages
Oceanic Languages

Authentic Documents
Use Authentic Texts

Authentic Texts
DC 06700
HN Added, 1992.
UF Authentic Documents
BT Language Teaching Materials
RT Language Textbooks

Authorship
DC 06750
HN Added, 1992.
RT Creativity (Psychology)
Drama
Literature
Poetry
Statistical Analysis of Style
Textual Criticism
Writing

Autism
DC 06800
HN Formerly (1973-1991) DC au11.
BT Psychosis
RT Behavior Disorders
Emotional Disturbances
Interpersonal Behavior
Language Pathology
Language Therapy
Schizophrenia

Autochthonous Languages
Use Indigenous Languages

Autoinstructional Methods
Use Programmed Instruction

Autolexical Grammar
DC 06850
HN Added, 1992.
BT Grammar Theories
RT Grammatical Analysis
Morphology
Syntax

Automatic Data Processing
Use Data Processing

Automatic Translation (Machine)
Use Machine Translation

Autosegmental Phonology
DC 06900
SN Any synthesis of elements of various theories of autosegmental phonology. Most syntheses include a linear skeleton representing successive phonological units onto which various segmental or prosodic features are mapped from positions in tiers extending away from the skeleton in different dimensions.
HN Formerly (1973-1991) DC au11c.
BT Phonology
RT Generative Phonology
Metrical Phonology
Suprasegmentals

Auxiliary Verbs
DC 06950
HN Formerly (1973-1991) DC au12, Auxiliary Verb.
UF Helping Verbs
BT Verbs
RT Aspect
Conjugation
Modal Verbs
Mood (Grammatical)
Person
Tense
Voice (Grammatical)

Avestan
Use Iranian Languages

Awareness
Use Perception

Azerbaijan
DC 06990
HN Added, 1992.
BT Commonwealth of Independent States
RT Union of Soviet Socialist Republics

Azerbaijani
DC 07100
HN Added, 1992.
BT Turkic Languages

Azores
DC 07150
HN Added, 1992.
BT Western Europe

Aztec
Use Uto Aztecan Languages

Baby Talk
DC 07200
HN Added, 1992.
BT Speech
RT Adult Child Interaction
Infants
Child Language
Children
Infant Vocalization
Infants
Language Acquisition
Linguistic Accommodation
Maternal Speech
Natural Phonology
Parent Child Interaction
Registers (Sociolinguistics)

Backward Masking
Use Masking

Baga
Use West Atlantic Languages

Bahrain
DC 07250
HN Added, 1992.
BT Arab Countries
Middle East

Balkan Romance
Use Romanian

Balkan States
DC 07300
HN Added, 1992.
BT Europe
NT Albania
Bosnia Herzegovina
Bulgaria
Croatia
Greece
Macedonia
Montenegro
Romania
Serbia
Slovenia
Turkey
Yugoslavia
RT Eastern Europe

Baltic Languages
DC 07350
HN Formerly (1983-1991) DC az1a.
BT Indo European Languages
NT Lettish
Lithuanian

Baltic States
DC 07400
HN Added, 1992.
BT Western Europe
NT Estonia
   Finland
   Latvia

Balto Finnic Languages
Use Finno Ugric Languages

Bambara
Use Mande Languages

Bangla Bhasa
Use Bengali

Bangladesh
DC 07450
HN Added, 1992.
BT South Asia

Bantoid Languages
DC 07500
HN Added, 1992.
UF Bantu Languages
   Bemba
   Kikuyu
   Kirundi
   Kituba
   Kongo
   Lingala
   Luganda
   Makua
   Rwanda (Language)
   Shona
BT Benue Congo Phylum
NT Swahili
RT Click Languages

Bantu Languages
Use Bantoid Languages

Bar Hillel, Yehoshua
DC 07550
SN Born 1915 - Died 1975.
HN Formerly (1973-1991) DC ba1, Bar
   Hillel.

Basal Reading
DC 07600
HN Added, 1992.
BT Reading
   Reading Instruction
RT Beginning Reading
   Phonics
   Reading Materials

Base Forms
Use Roots (Morphology)

Basic English (1973-1991)
Use English as an International Language

Basic Writing
DC 07750
HN Added, 1992.
UF Remedial Writing
BT Writing
RT Adult Literacy
   Literacy Programs
   Remedial Reading
   Written Language Instruction

Basque
DC 07800
HN Formerly (1985-1991) DC ba2a.
BT Language Isolates

Baule
Use Akan

Bavarian
Use German

Beginning Reading
DC 07850
HN Added, 1992.
BT Reading
RT Basal Reading
   Childrens Literature
   Decoding (Reading)
   Early Literacy
   Initial Teaching Alphabet
   Language Experience Approach
   Phonics
   Reading Readiness

Behavior Disorders
DC 07900
HN Formerly (1973-1991) DC be1a, Be-
   havioral Disturbances.
UF Behavioral Disturbances (1973-1991)
BT Disorders
RT Alcoholism
   Attention Deficit Disorders
   Autism
   Drug Effects
   Emotional Disturbances
   Nervous System Disorders
   Psychoanalysis
   Special Education (Handicapped)

Behavioral Disturbances (1973-1991)
HN DC be1a.
Use Behavior Disorders

Behavioral Therapy
Use Psychotherapy

Behavioristic Linguistic Theory
DC 07950
HN Formerly (1973-1991) DC be2.
BT Linguistic Theories
RT Applied Linguistics
   Learning Theories
   Mediation Theory
   Psycholinguistics

Belarus
DC 08160
HN Added, 1992.
BT Commonwealth of Independent
   States
RT Union of Soviet Socialist Republics

Belgium
DC 07990
HN Added, 1992.
BT Western Europe
NT Flanders

Beliefs
DC 08100
HN Formerly (1973-1991) DC be3, Be-
   lief.
NT Presuppositions
RT Attitudes
   Credibility
   Culture
   Linguistic Relativity
   Persuasion
   Religions
   Stereotypes
   Truth

Believability
Use Credibility

Belize
DC 08150
HN Added, 1992.
UF British Honduras
BT Central America

Belorussian
DC 08170
HN Added, 1992.
UF Bielorussian
   Byelorussian
   White Russian
BT Slavic Languages

Bemba
Use Bantoid Languages

Bender Gestalt Test
Use Projective Techniques

Bengali
DC 08200
HN Added, 1992.
UF Bangla Bhasa
BT Indic Languages

Benin
DC 08230
HN Added, 1992.
UF Dahomey
BT Sub Saharan Africa

Benue Chad Languages
Use Chadic Languages

Benue Congo Phylum
DC 08250
HN Added, 1992.
BT Niger Congo Languages
NT Bantoid Languages
   Efik

Benveniste, Emil
DC 08350
SN Born 1902 - Died 1976.
HN Formerly (1973-1991) DC be4, Ben-
   veniste.

Berber Languages
DC 08400
HN Formerly (1977-1982) DC be5, Ber-
   ber Languages. Reinstated, 1992.
UF Kabyle
   Riff
   Shluh
   Tamashek
BT Afroasiatic Languages

Bermuda
DC 08450
HN Added, 1992.
BT North America

Bernstein, Basil
DC 08500
SN Born 1924 - .
HN Added, 1992.

Berta
Use Chari Nile Languages

Bhutan
DC 08550
HN Added, 1992.
BT Himalayan States
   South Asia

Bible
DC   08600
HN   Added, 1992.
BT   Religious Literature
RT   Literature
      Religions

Bielorussian
Use   Belorussian

Bilingual Dictionaries
DC   08700
HN   Added, 1992.
UF   Translation Dictionaries
BT   Dictionaries
RT   Bilingual Teaching Materials
      Second Language Learning
      Translation

Bilingual Education
DC   08750
HN   Added, 1992.
BT   Education
RT   Bilingual Teaching Materials
      Bilingualism
      FLES
      Immersion Programs
      Language Maintenance
      Language of Instruction
      Language Planning
      Language Policy
      Language Rights
      Limited English Proficiency
      Multilingualism
      Native Language Instruction
      Native Speakers
      Official Languages
      Preschool Children
      Second Language Instruction
      Second Language Learning

Bilingual Teaching Materials
DC   08800
HN   Added, 1992.
BT   Teaching Materials
RT   Bilingual Dictionaries
      Bilingual Education
      Bilingualism
      Language Maintenance
      Language of Instruction
      Language Teaching Materials
      Second Language Instruction

Bilingualism
DC   08850
HN   Formerly (1973-1991) DC bi1.
RT   Bilingual Education
      Bilingual Teaching Materials
      Child Language
      Code Switching
      Cross Cultural Communication
      Diglossia
      Immersion Programs
      Indigenous Languages
      Language Contact
      Language Diversity
      Language Maintenance
      Language Planning
      Language Policy
      Language Rights
      Language Shift
      Language Use
      Languages
      Limited English Proficiency
      Linguistic Interference
      Minority Groups
      Monolingualism
      Multilingualism

Bilingualism (cont'd)
RT   Native Language
      Native Speakers
      Psycholinguistics
      Second Dialect Learning
      Second Language Learning
      Second Languages
      Social Factors
      Sociolinguistics
      Translation

Binaural Stimulation
DC   08900
HN   Formerly (1973-1991) DC bi2.
UF   Dichotic Stimulation
BT   Auditory Stimulation
RT   Ear Preference
      Monaural Stimulation

Bini
Use   Kwa Languages

Biological, Physical, Physiological
(1973-1991)
HN   DC bi3, deleted 1992. See now Anatomical Systems or Biology.

Biology
DC   08950
HN   Added, 1992. Prior to 1992, see DC bi3, Biological, Physical, Physiological.
RT   Anatomical Systems
      Disorders
      Drug Effects
      Genetics
      Medicine

Black Americans
DC   09100
HN   Formerly (1973-1991) DC am4, American Negro.
UF   African Americans
      American Blacks
BT   North American Cultural Groups
RT   Anglo Americans
      Asian Americans
      Black English
      Hispanic Americans
      Jewish Americans

Black English
DC   09150
HN   Formerly (1973-1991) DC bl1.
BT   American English
RT   Black Americans
      Nonstandard Dialects
      Regional Dialects

Blindness
Use   Vision Disorders

Bloomfield, Leonard
DC   09200
SN   Born 1887 - Died 1949.
HN   Formerly (1982-1991) DC bl3, Bloomfield.

Body Language
Use   Kinesics

Bolivia
DC   09250
HN   Added, 1992.
BT   South America

Bone Conduction (1973-1991)
HN   DC bo1.
Use   Auditory System

Bororo Languages
Use   Ge Pano Carib Languages

Borrowing
DC   09300
SN   The adoption of words or other language elements from one language into another language, characteristically with adaptation to the phonology, morphology, and syntax of the adopting language, and frequently with alterations in meaning.
HN   Formerly (1973-1991) DC bo2.
UF   Calquing
      Contamination (Lexical)
      Lexical Borrowing
      Linguistic Borrowing
      Loan (1975-1982)
      Loanword Borrowing
      Phonological Borrowing
      Syntactic Borrowing
      Word Borrowing
RT   Code Switching
      Cognates
      Creoles
      Diachronic Linguistics
      Indigenous Languages
      Language Change
      Language Contact
      Language Patterns
      Language Usage
      Lexicology
      Lexicon
      Morphology
      Phonology
      Pidgins
      Sociolinguistics
      Trade Languages

Bosnia Herzegovina
DC   09310
HN   Added, 1992.
BT   Balkan States
      Eastern Europe
RT   Yugoslavia

Botswana
DC   09320
HN   Added, 1992.
BT   Sub Saharan Africa

Bound Morphemes
Use   Affixes

Bracketing
Use   Word Structure

Braille
Use   Reading Aids for the Blind

Brain
DC   09350
HN   Formerly (1973-1991) DC br1, Brain Anatomy.
UF   Brocas Area
      Motor Cortex
      Occipital Lobe
      Parietal Lobe
      Wernickes Area
BT   Anatomical Systems
RT   Brain Damage
      Brocas Aphasia
      Cerebral Dominance
      Cognitive Processes
      Evoked Responses

Brain (cont'd)
- **RT** Language Thought Relationship
- Memory
- Memory Disorders
- Mental Disorders
- Motor Theory of Speech Perception
- Nervous System Disorders
- Neurolinguistics
- Wernickes Aphasia

Brain Damage
- **DC** 09400
- **HN** Added, 1992.
- **UF** Brain Injuries
- **BT** Nervous System Disorders
- **RT** Aphasia
- Brain
- Memory Disorders
- Mental Retardation
- Neurolinguistics

Brain Disease
- **Use** Nervous System Disorders

Brain Injuries
- **Use** Brain Damage

Brazil
- **DC** 09450
- **HN** Added, 1992.
- **BT** South America

Brazilian Portuguese
- **DC** 09550
- **HN** Added, 1992.
- **BT** Portuguese

Breton
- **DC** 09600
- **HN** Added, 1992.
- **BT** Celtic Languages

British Columbia
- **DC** 09650
- **HN** Added, 1992.
- **BT** Canada

British English
- **DC** 09700
- **HN** Added, 1992.
- **BT** English

British Guiana
- **Use** Guyana

British Honduras
- **Use** Belize

Brocas Aphasia
- **DC** 09750
- **HN** Added, 1992.
- **BT** Aphasia
- **RT** Brain
- Wernickes Aphasia

Brocas Area
- **Use** Brain

Brothers
- **Use** Siblings

Bruder Grimm
- **Use** Grimm, Jacob and Wilhelm

Brunei Darussalam
- **DC** 09790
- **HN** Added, 1992.
- **BT** Southeast Asia

Bulgaria
- **DC** 09800
- **HN** Added, 1992.
- **BT** Balkan States
- Eastern Europe

Bulgarian
- **DC** 09900
- **HN** Added, 1992.
- **BT** Slavic Languages

Burkina Faso
- **DC** 09930
- **HN** Added, 1992.
- **UF** Upper Volta
- **BT** Sub Saharan Africa

Burma
- **Use** Myanmar

Burmese
- **Use** Tibeto Burman Languages

Burundi
- **DC** 09960
- **HN** Added, 1992.
- **BT** Sub Saharan Africa

Burushaski
- **DC** 09970
- **HN** Added, 1992.
- **BT** Language Isolates
- **RT** India

Bushman Languages
- **Use** Khoisan Languages

Business
- **DC** 10100
- **HN** Added, 1992.
- **UF** Commerce
- Industry
- Manufacturing
- **RT** Business English
- Economic Factors
- Merchants
- Occupations
- Registers (Sociolinguistics)
- Scientific Technical Lanuguage
- Trade Languages

Business English
- **DC** 10120
- **HN** Added, 1992.
- **BT** English for Special Purposes
- **RT** Business
- Scientific Technical Language
- Trade Languages

Byelorussia
- **Use** Belarus

Byelorussian
- **Use** Belorussian

Cahuapan Languages
- **Use** Andean Equatorial Phylum

CAI
- **Use** Computer Assisted Instruction

California
- **DC** 10200
- **HN** Added, 1992.
- **BT** United States of America
- Western States

Calques
- **Use** Borrowing

Cambodia
- **DC** 10220
- **HN** Added, 1992.
- **UF** Kampuchea
- Khmer Republic
- **BT** Southeast Asia

Cambodian
- **Use** Austro Asiatic Languages

Cameroon
- **DC** 10230
- **HN** Added, 1992.
- **BT** Sub Saharan Africa

Camuni
- **Use** Italic Languages

Canada
- **DC** 10250
- **HN** Added, 1992.
- **BT** North America
- **NT** Alberta
- British Columbia
- Manitoba
- New Brunswick
- Newfoundland
- Northwest Territories
- Nova Scotia
- Ontario
- Prince Edward Island
- Quebec
- Saskatchewan
- Yukon

Canadian English
- **Use** American English

Canadian French
- **DC** 10350
- **HN** Added, 1992.
- **UF** Quebec French
- **BT** French

Canary Islands
- **DC** 10400
- **HN** Added, 1992.
- **BT** Western Europe
- **RT** North Africa

Cantonese
- **DC** 10450
- **HN** Added, 1992.
- **BT** Chinese

Cape Dutch
- **Use** Afrikaans

Cape Verde Islands
- **DC** 10470
- **HN** Added, 1992.
- **BT** Sub Saharan Africa

Careers
- **Use** Occupations

Carib Languages
- **Use** Ge Pano Carib Languages

Caribbean
- **DC** 10500
- **HN** Added, 1992.
- **UF** West Indies
- **BT** Latin America
- **NT** Cuba
- Puerto Rico
- **RT** Caribbean Cultural Groups
- Central America

Caribbean Amerindian Languages (1973-1982)
HN DC ca1. Prior to 1992, users were instructed to see Central Amerindian Languages.
Use South Amerindian Languages

Caribbean Cultural Groups
DC 10600
HN Added, 1992.
BT Latin American Cultural Groups
RT Caribbean
North American Cultural Groups

Carnap, Rudolf
DC 10650
SN Born 1891 - Died 1970.
HN Formerly (1973-1991) DC ca2, Carnap.

Case
DC 10700
SN Defined variously, according to school of linguistics; in syntactic terms, a category of grammatical relations expressing the role of clause constituent, other than the verb, with respect to the verb or the clause as a whole. Also used for the corresponding semantic elements within a proposition or predication; semantic case relations may also be described as thematic roles. (In traditional grammars, cases are categories of noun/pronoun inflection that often express case relations; for this meaning, use the descriptor Case Marking.)
HN Formerly (1973-1991) DC ca3.
UF Ablative Case
Accusative Case
Dative Case
Genitive Case
Vocative Case
BT Grammatical Categories
RT Adjectives
Case Grammar
Case Marking
Form Classes
Functional Grammar
Government Binding Theory
Government (Grammatical)
Inflection (Morphology)
Language Universals
Morphology
Nouns
Pronouns
Reflexivity
Syntax
Thematic Roles
Valence

Case Grammar
DC 10800
SN A language-universal approach to sentence semantics, focusing on the semantic roles played by verbs and other elements of sentence structure; it describes sentences in terms of modality, predicate, and labeled arguments.
HN Formerly (1973-1991) DC ca4.
BT Generative Grammar
RT Agent Patient Relationship (Grammatical)
Case
Case Marking
Deep Structure
Semantic Analysis
Semantics
Syntax

Case Marking
DC 10810
SN The overt expression of case (a category of grammatical relations or semantic relations, according to linguistic model) by noun inflection, verb inflection (voice), prepositions, word order, or other means.
HN Added, 1992.
UF Exceptional Case Marking
RT Case
Case Grammar
Deep Structure
Government (Grammatical)
Grammatical Analysis
Grammatical Relations
Inflection (Morphology)
Semantic Features
Verbs
Word Order

Case Studies
DC 10820
HN Added, 1992.
RT Longitudinal Studies
Research Design

Catalan
DC 10850
HN Added, 1992.
BT Romance Languages

Catalonia, Spain
DC 10900
SN A region in northeastern Spain extending along the Mediterranean Sea from the French border.
HN Added, 1992.
BT Spain

Categorial Grammar
DC 11100
SN A set of generative phrase structure grammars, developed originally by Polish logicians to be adequate for the description of logical and mathematical languages; related to logical type theory and combinatorial logic. A categorial grammar consists only of a starting point, vocabulary, syntactic categories, and rules of derivation and category assignment; categories are defined to have combinatorial properties.
HN Formerly (1988-1991) DC ca4b.
BT Grammar Theories
RT Computational Linguistics
Computer Generated Language Analysis
Grammatical Analysis
Montague Grammar
Syntax

Categories (Semantic)
Use Semantic Categories

Caucasian Languages
DC 11200
HN Formerly (1977-1991) DC ca5.
UF Georgian
Kartvelian Languages
BT Languages

Caucasians
Use Whites

Causative Voice
Use Voice (Grammatical)

Celtic Languages
DC 11250
HN Formerly (1979-1991) DC ce1.
UF Cornish
Gaulish
Keltic Languages
Manx
BT Indo European Languages
NT Breton
Irish Gaelic
Scottish Gaelic
Welsh

Central African Republic
DC 11290
HN Added, 1992.
BT Sub Saharan Africa

Central America
DC 11300
HN Added, 1992.
BT Latin America
NT Belize
Costa Rica
El Salvador
Guatemala
Honduras
Nicaragua
Panama
RT Caribbean
Mexico

Central Amerindian Languages
DC 11400
HN Formerly (1982-1991) DC ce1a.
BT Amerindian Languages
NT Mexican Amerindian Languages
RT North Amerindian Languages
South Amerindian Languages

Central Sudanic Languages
Use Chari Nile Languages

Cerebral Dominance
DC 11500
HN Formerly (1973-1991) DC ce2.
UF Hemispheric Dominance
Lateral Dominance
Laterality
Left Brain Dominance
Right Brain Dominance
RT Brain
Cognitive Processes
Ear Preference
Handedness
Perception

Cerebral Palsy
Use Nervous System Disorders

Ceylon
Use Sri Lanka

Chad
DC 11590
HN Added, 1992.
BT Sub Saharan Africa

Chad Languages
Use Chadic Languages

Chadic Languages
DC 11600
HN Formerly (1977-1982) DC cd4, Chad. Reinstated, 1992.
UF Benue Chad Languages
Chad Languages
Niger Chad Languages
BT Afroasiatic Languages
NT Hausa

Chaldean
  Use Aramaic

Channel Islands
  DC 11650
  HN Added, 1992.
  BT Western Europe

Chanting
  Use Singing

Chapacura Wanhaman Languages
  Use Andean Equatorial Phylum

Character
  Use Personality

Character Recognition
  Use Letter Recognition

Characters (Written Language)
  Use Ideographs

Chari Nile Languages
  DC 11750
  HN Added, 1992.
  UF Berta
      Central Sudanic Languages
      Eastern Sudanic Languages
      Kunama
      Macro Sudanic Languages
  BT Nilo Saharan Languages

Cheremis
  Use Finno Ugric Languages

Chibchan Languages
  Use Macro Chibchan Phylum

Chicanos
  Use Mexican Americans

Child Adult Interaction
  Use Adult Child Interaction

Child Language
  DC 11800
  HN Formerly (1973-1991) DC ch1.
  BT Language
  RT Adolescent Language
      Adult Language
      Age Differences
      Baby Talk
      Bilingualism
      Children
      Cognitive Development
      Delayed Language Acquisition
      Imitation
      Immersion Programs
      Infant Vocalization
      Infants
      Language Acquisition
      Language Experience Approach
      Language Patterns
      Maternal Speech
      Mean Length of Utterance
      Monolingualism
      Natural Phonology
      Oral Language
      Principles and Parameters Approach
      Pronunciation
      Psycholinguistics

Child Parent Interaction
  Use Parent Child Interaction

Children
  DC 11850
  HN Added, 1992.
  NT Infants

Children (cont'd)
  NT Preschool Children
  RT Adolescents
      Adult Child Interaction
      Baby Talk
      Child Language
      Childrens Literature
      Elementary School Students
      Infant Vocalization
      Language Acquisition
      Maternal Speech
      Parent Child Interaction
      Siblings

Childrens Literature
  DC 11900
  HN Added, 1992.
  UF Juvenile Literature
  BT Literature
  RT Beginning Reading
      Children
      Early Literacy
      Reading Materials

Chile
  DC 11950
  HN Added, 1992.
  BT South America

Chinese
  DC 12100
  HN Formerly (1973-1991) DC ch2.
  BT Sino Tibetan Languages
  NT Cantonese
      Mandarin

Choctaw
  Use Muskogean Languages

Chomsky, Avram Noam
  DC 12200
  SN Born 1928 - .
  HN Formerly (1973-1991) DC ch3, Chomsky.

Chukchee Kamchatkan Languages
  DC 12230
  HN Added, 1992.
  UF Chukot Kamchat Languages
      Kamchadal
      Luoravetlan
  BT Languages
  RT Eskimo Aleut Languages

Chukot Kamchat Languages
  Use Chukchee Kamchatkan Languages

Church Slavonic
  Use Old Church Slavic

Cinema
  Use Films

Cineradiography
  Use Radiography

Classical Conditioning
  Use Conditioning

Classical Greek
  Use Ancient Greek

Classification of Languages
  Use Language Classification

Classroom Activities
  Use Educational Activities

Classroom Communication
  DC 12250
  HN Added, 1992.
  UF Student Teacher Communication
      Teacher Student Communication
  BT Communication
  RT Classroom Observation
      Group Communication
      Student Teacher Relationship
      Students
      Teachers
      Teaching Methods

Classroom Observation
  DC 12260
  HN Added, 1992.
  RT Classroom Communication
      Educational Activities
      Instruction
      Measures (Instruments)
      Student Teacher Relationship
      Students
      Teachers
      Teaching Methods

Clauses
  DC 12350
  HN Formerly (1973-1991) DC cl1, Clause.
  BT Linguistic Units
  NT Conditional Clauses
      Relative Clauses
  RT Coordination (Grammatical)
      Embedded Construction
      Grammatical Analysis
      Passive Voice
      Phrases
      Predicate
      Sentence Structure
      Sentences
      Subordination (Grammatical)
      Syntactic Structures
      Syntax
      Word Order

Cleft Lip
  Use Cleft Palate

Cleft Palate
  DC 12400
  HN Formerly (1973-1991) DC cl2, Cleft Lip and Palate.
  UF Cleft Lip
      Hare Lip
  BT Disorders
  RT Articulation Disorders
      Oral Cavity
      Prosthetic Devices
      Speech Pathology
      Speech Therapy
      Voice Disorders

Click Languages
  DC 12450
  HN Formerly (1981-1991) DC cl2a.
  BT Language
  RT Bantoid Languages
      Khoisan Languages

Clitics
  DC 12500
  SN Linguistic units that have the syntactic status of independent words, but cannot function independently in an utterance, eg, pronouns, particles, or auxiliary verbs.
  HN Formerly (1973-1991) DC cl2b, Clitic.
  BT Lexicon
  RT Linguistic Units
      Pronouns
      Syntax
      Words

Cloze Procedure
- **DC** 12600
- **SN** Technique used in reading instruction and reading comprehension testing, in which the reader uses context to guess the words that have been omitted from a text.
- **HN** Formerly (1973-1991) DC cl3, Clozes.
- **RT** Context Clues
  Language Tests
  Readability
  Reading
  Reading Comprehension
  Reading Tests

Cochlear Implants
- **Use** Hearing Aids

Code Switching
- **DC** 12650
- **HN** Formerly (1987-1991) DC cm3.
- **UF** Switching (Language)
- **RT** Bilingualism
  Borrowing
  Diglossia
  Indigenous Languages
  Language Contact
  Language Patterns
  Language Usage
  Language Use
  Lexicon
  Linguistic Interference
  Morphology
  Multilingualism
  Sociolinguistics

Code, Coding (1982-1991)
- **HN** DC cm1, deleted 1992. See now Code Switching, Decoding (Cognitive Process), or Encoding (Cognitive Process).

Codification (of Language)
- **Use** Language Standardization

Cognates
- **DC** 12800
- **SN** Words in related languages that developed from the same word in the parent language by the processes of language change.
- **HN** Formerly (1973-1991) DC co1, Cognate.
- **BT** Lexicon
- **RT** Borrowing
  Comparative Linguistics
  Diachronic Linguistics
  Etymology

Cognition
- **Use** Cognitive Processes

Cognition Language Relationship
- **Use** Language Thought Relationship

Cognitive Development
- **DC** 12850
- **HN** Added, 1992.
- **UF** Intellectual Development
  Mental Development
- **NT** Language Acquisition
- **RT** Child Language
  Cognitive Processes
  Cognitive Style
  Concept Formation
  Conservation (Concept)
  Judgment
  Language Thought Relationship
  Learning

Cognitive Function of Language
- **Use** Cognitive Processes

Cognitive Imagery
- **Use** Imagery

Cognitive Mediation
- **Use** Mediation Theory

Cognitive Processes
- **DC** 12950
- **HN** Formerly (1973-1991) DC co1b.
- **UF** Cognition
  Cognitive Function of Language
  Human Information Processing
  Reasoning
  Thinking
  Thought
- **NT** Associative Processes
  Decoding (Cognitive Process)
  Encoding (Cognitive Process)
  Information Processing
  Judgment
  Language Processing
  Learning Processes
  Memory
  Metacognition
  Perception
  Problem Solving
  Reading Processes
  Semantic Processing
- **RT** Artificial Intelligence
  Attention
  Brain
  Cerebral Dominance
  Cognitive Development
  Cognitive Style
  Comprehension
  Conservation (Concept)
  Gestalt Theory
  Imagery
  Inner Speech
  Intelligence
  Learning Disabilities
  Learning Theories
  Logic
  Mediation Theory
  Metalanguage
  Neural Networks
  Psycholinguistics
  Psychometric Analysis
  Repair
  Signal Detection
  Slips of the Tongue
  Syntactic Processing

Cognitive Style
- **DC** 13100
- **HN** Added, 1992.
- **UF** Learning Style
  Perceptual Style
- **RT** Cognitive Development
  Cognitive Processes
  Encoding (Cognitive Process)
  Language Thought Relationship
  Learning Processes
  Personality

Cohesion
- **DC** 13200
- **HN** Added, 1992.
- **RT** Comprehension
  Discourse Analysis
  Language Usage
  Sentence Structure
  Story Grammar
  Stylistics
  Syntax

Cohesion (cont'd)
- **RT** Text Analysis
  Text Structure
  Writing

College Graduate Education
- **Use** Graduate Education

College Students
- **DC** 13250
- **HN** Added, 1992.
- **UF** University Students
- **BT** Students
- **RT** Graduate Education
  Higher Education
  Undergraduate Education
  Young Adults

College Undergraduate Education
- **Use** Undergraduate Education

Colloquial Language
- **DC** 13300
- **HN** Added, 1992.
- **BT** Language
- **RT** Dialectology
  Diglossia
  Idioms
  Language Attitudes
  Language Diversity
  Language Styles
  Language Usage
  Literary Language
  Nonstandard Dialects
  Oral Language
  Phraseologisms
  Registers (Sociolinguistics)
  Slang
  Social Factors
  Sociolinguistics
  Speech
  Spoken Written Language Relationship
  Standard Dialects
  Written Language

Colombia
- **DC** 13350
- **HN** Added, 1992.
- **BT** South America

Color
- **DC** 13450
- **HN** Formerly (1973-1991) DC co2.
- **UF** Hue
- **RT** Art
  Stroop Color Word Test
  Vision
  Visual Perception
  Visual Stimulation

Colorado
- **DC** 13500
- **HN** Added, 1992.
- **BT** United States of America
  Western States

Coman Languages
- **Use** Nilo Saharan Languages

Commands
- **Use** Imperative Sentences

Commerce
- **Use** Business

Commercial Dialects
　Use　Trade Languages

Commercials
　Use　Advertisements

Commonwealth of Independent States
　DC　13560
　HN　Added, 1992.
　BT　Eastern Europe
　NT　Armenia
　　　Azerbaijan
　　　Belarus
　　　Estonia
　　　Georgia (Republic)
　　　Kazakhstan
　　　Kyrgyzstan
　　　Latvia
　　　Lithuania
　　　Moldova
　　　Russia
　　　Siberia
　　　Tajikistan
　　　Turkmenistan
　　　Ukraine
　　　Uzbekistan
　RT　Asian Cultural Groups
　　　Commonwealth of Independent
　　　　States Cultural Groups
　　　Slavic Cultural Groups
　　　Union of Soviet Socialist Republics

Commonwealth of Independent States Cultural Groups
　DC　13570
　HN　Added, 1992.
　BT　Cultural Groups
　RT　Asian Cultural Groups
　　　Commonwealth of Independent
　　　　States
　　　Slavic Cultural Groups
　　　Union of Soviet Socialist Republics

Communication
　DC　13600
　HN　Added, 1992.
　UF　Communication Theory (1973-1991)
　NT　Animal Communication
　　　Classroom Communication
　　　Cross Cultural Communication
　　　Group Communication
　　　Human Computer Communication
　　　Interpersonal Communication
　　　Interspecies Communication
　　　Nonverbal Communication
　　　Persuasion
　RT　Ambiguity
　　　Communicative Competence
　　　Communicative Function of Lan-
　　　　guage
　　　Content Analysis
　　　Credibility
　　　Cybernetics
　　　Discourse Analysis
　　　Feedback
　　　Information Processing
　　　Intelligibility
　　　Language
　　　Language Arts
　　　Mass Media
　　　Receptive Language
　　　Spoken Written Language Relation-
　　　　ship
　　　Symbolism
　　　Translation
　　　Writing

Communication in Groups (1973-1991)
　HN　DC co3.
　Use　Group Communication

Communication Theory (1973-1991)
　HN　DC co4.
　Use　Communication

Communications Media
　Use　Mass Media

Communicative Approach
　Use　Communicative Language Teaching

Communicative Competence
　DC　13650
　HN　Added, 1992.
　UF　Communicative Efficiency
　RT　Communication
　　　Communicative Function of Lan-
　　　　guage
　　　Communicative Language Teaching
　　　Conversation Courses
　　　Fluency
　　　Intelligibility
　　　Interpersonal Communication
　　　Language Acquisition
　　　Language Tests
　　　Limited English Proficiency
　　　Linguistic Competence
　　　Nonverbal Communication
　　　Oral Language Instruction
　　　Second Language Learning
　　　Written Language Instruction

Communicative Efficiency
　Use　Communicative Competence

Communicative Function of Art
　Use　Art

Communicative Function of Language
　DC　13700
　HN　Formerly (1973-1991) DC co5.
　RT　Communication
　　　Communicative Competence
　　　Functional Linguistics
　　　Graffiti
　　　Linguistic Theories
　　　Pragmatics
　　　Speech Acts
　　　Systemic Linguistics

Communicative Interference
　Use　Linguistic Interference

Communicative Language Teaching
　DC　13750
　HN　Added, 1992.
　UF　Communicative Approach
　BT　Language Teaching Methods
　RT　Audiolingual Language Teaching
　　　Communicative Competence
　　　Direct Method of Language Teaching
　　　Second Language Instruction

Comoro Islands
　DC　13830
　HN　Added, 1992.
　BT　Sub Saharan Africa

Comparative Forms
　Use　Comparison

Comparative Linguistics
　DC　13850
　HN　Formerly (1973-1991) DC co6.
　UF　Contrastive Analysis of Linguistic Ma-
　　　　terial
　　　Contrastive Linguistics
　　　Linguistic Comparison
　BT　Linguistics
　RT　Areal Linguistics
　　　Cognates
　　　Descriptive Linguistics
　　　Diachronic Linguistics
　　　Dialectology
　　　Grammatical Analysis
　　　Language Classification
　　　Language Diversity
　　　Language Typology
　　　Lexicology
　　　Linguistic Interference
　　　Linguistic Theories
　　　Neogrammarians
　　　Nostratic Theory
　　　Phonemes
　　　Phonemics
　　　Phonological Analysis
　　　Phonology
　　　Semantic Analysis
　　　Semantics
　　　Structuralist Linguistics
　　　Syntax

Comparison
　DC　13900
　HN　Added, 1992.
　UF　Comparative Forms
　　　Superlative Forms
　RT　Adjectives
　　　Adverbs
　　　Semantics
　　　Syntax

Competence (Linguistic)
　Use　Linguistic Competence

Competence and Performance (1973-1991)
　HN　DC co7, deleted 1992. See now sep-
　　　arate terms Linguistic Competence
　　　and Linguistic Performance.

Componential Analysis
　DC　13930
　SN　The semantic analysis of sets of
　　　words into components of meaning
　　　on the analogy of distinctive feature
　　　analysis in phonology.
　HN　Added, 1992.
　RT　Anthropological Linguistics
　　　Distinctive Features
　　　Lexicology
　　　Linguistic Theories
　　　Meaning
　　　Phonology
　　　Research Design
　　　Semantic Analysis
　　　Semantic Features
　　　Semantics
　　　Sound Spectrographs
　　　Structuralist Linguistics

Composing Processes (Writing)
　Use　Writing Processes

Composition Instruction
　Use　Written Language Instruction

Compound Words
DC 13940
HN Added, 1992.
BT Words
RT Lexicon
    Morphemes
    Neologisms
    Word Formation
    Word Structure

Comprehension
DC 13950
SN Knowledge or understanding of the meaning, significance, or principles of an object, situation, event, or printed or spoken language.
HN Added, 1992.
NT Listening Comprehension
    Reading Comprehension
RT Cognitive Processes
    Cohesion
    Concept Formation
    Context Clues
    Decoding (Cognitive Process)
    Encoding (Cognitive Process)
    Familiarity
    Intelligence
    Language Processing
    Language Thought Relationship
    Meaning
    Metacognition
    Repair

Comprehensive Schools (British)
Use Secondary Education

Computational Linguistics
DC 14100
SN Branch of linguistics that applies mathematical techniques, often with the aid of a computer, to linguistic, phonetic, and literary research.
HN Formerly (1973-1991) DC co7b.
BT Linguistics
NT Natural Language Processing
RT Categorial Grammar
    Computer Applications
    Computer Generated Language Analysis
    Computer Software
    Databases
    Language Processing
    Linguistic Theories
    Machine Translation
    Markov Models
    Mathematical Linguistics
    Mathematics
    Neural Networks
    Parallel Distributed Processing Models
    Parsing
    Phonetics
    Semantic Analysis
    Semantics
    Set Theory
    Speech Synthesis
    Statistical Analysis
    Statistical Analysis of Style
    Voice Recognition
    Word Frequency

Computer Aided Text Analysis
Use Computer Generated Language Analysis

Computer Applications
DC 14150
HN Added, 1992.
RT Artificial Intelligence

Computer Applications (cont'd)
RT Computational Linguistics
    Computer Assisted Instruction
    Computer Generated Language Analysis
    Computer Languages
    Computer Software
    Cybernetics
    Data Processing
    Databases
    Human Computer Communication
    Machine Translation
    Natural Language Processing
    Speech Synthesis
    Statistical Analysis
    Textual Criticism
    Voice Recognition
    Word Processing

Computer Assisted Instruction
DC 14200
HN Formerly (1973-1991) DC co8.
UF CAI
    Teaching Machines (1973-1991)
BT Programmed Instruction
RT Audiovisual Language Teaching
    Computer Applications
    Computer Software
    Educational Activities
    Feedback
    Human Computer Communication
    Interactive Video
    Language Laboratories
    Teaching Materials

Computer Assisted Translation
Use Machine Translation

Computer Generated Language Analysis
DC 14300
SN The analysis of a language, text, phonetic system, etc, produced using a computer program or system.
HN Formerly (1983-1991) DC co7aa.
UF Computer Aided Text Analysis
RT Categorial Grammar
    Computational Linguistics
    Computer Applications
    Computer Software
    Cybernetics
    Data Processing
    Databases
    Descriptive Linguistics
    Discourse Analysis
    Grammatical Analysis
    Machine Translation
    Markov Models
    Natural Language
    Natural Language Processing
    Neural Networks
    Phonological Analysis
    Statistical Analysis
    Statistical Analysis of Style
    Word Frequency

Computer Human Communication
Use Human Computer Communication

Computer Languages
DC 14350
HN Formerly (1979-1991) DC co8b.
UF Programming Languages
BT Artificial Languages
RT Computer Applications
    Computer Software
    Data Processing
    Human Computer Communication

Computer Software
DC 14360
SN A logical sequence of actions or instructions that a computer can execute, and accompanying documentation.
HN Added, 1992.
RT Computational Linguistics
    Computer Applications
    Computer Assisted Instruction
    Computer Generated Language Analysis
    Computer Languages
    Data Processing
    Interactive Video
    Language Laboratories
    Machine Translation
    Natural Language Processing
    Statistical Analysis
    Word Processing

Concept Formation
DC 14450
HN Formerly (1973-1991) co9, Concept Formation and Identification.
UF Concept Identification
    Conceptualization
BT Learning Processes
RT Cognitive Development
    Comprehension
    Conservation (Concept)
    Creativity (Psychology)
    Decoding (Cognitive Process)
    Discrimination Learning
    Encoding (Cognitive Process)
    Generalization
    Learning

Concept Identification
Use Concept Formation

Conceptualization
Use Concept Formation

Concord
Use Agreement

Conditional Clauses
DC 14460
HN Added, 1992.
UF If Clauses
BT Clauses
RT Conjunctions
    Modal Verbs
    Mood (Grammatical)
    Tense

Conditioning
DC 14500
HN Formerly (1973-1991) DC co11.
UF Classical Conditioning
    Operant Conditioning
    Psychological Conditioning
    Respondent Conditioning
    Verbal Conditioning
NT Discrimination Learning
RT Evoked Responses
    Familiarity
    Feedback
    Learning
    Learning Processes
    Learning Theories
    Memory
    Reinforcement
    Stimulation

Congo
DC 14540
HN Added, 1992.
BT Sub Saharan Africa

Congo Kordofanian Languages
DC 14550
HN Formerly (1973-1991) DC col2.
UF Kordofanian Languages
BT African Languages
NT Niger Congo Languages

Conjugation
DC 14570
SN In traditional grammar, the inflectional system of a verb, especially in languages where verbs are classified by their inflectional paradigm (eg, Latin), the set of conjugations in such a language consisting of systems of allomorphs of the same inflectional morphemes.
HN Added, 1992.
UF Verbal Paradigm
RT Affixes
    Agreement
    Auxiliary Verbs
    Inflection (Morphology)
    Mood (Grammatical)
    Morphology
    Number (Grammatical)
    Person
    Syntax
    Tense
    Verbs
    Word Formation

Conjunctions
DC 14650
HN Formerly (1973-1991) DC col3, Conjunction.
UF Connectives
BT Form Classes
RT Conditional Clauses
    Coordination (Grammatical)
    Function Words
    Subordination (Grammatical)

Connacht
Use Irish Gaelic

Connecticut
DC 14700
HN Added, 1992.
BT Northern States
    United States of America

Connectionist Models
Use Parallel Distributed Processing Models

Connectives
Use Conjunctions

Connotation
DC 14800
HN Added, 1992.
UF Affective Meaning
    Connotative Meaning
    Emotive Meaning
    Subjective Meaning
BT Meaning
RT Associative Processes
    Emotions
    Semantic Analysis
    Semantics
    Word Meaning

Connotative Meaning
Use Connotation

Conservation (Concept)
DC 14850
HN Added, 1992.
RT Cognitive Development
    Cognitive Processes
    Concept Formation
    Learning Processes

Consonance
Use Phonological Stylistics

Consonant Identification
Use Sound Identification

Consonants
DC 14900
HN Formerly (1973-1991) DC col4, Consonant.
UF Obstruents
    Resonants
BT Phonemes
NT Fricatives
    Stops
RT Articulation
    Distinctive Features
    Length (Phonological)
    Nasalization
    Orthographic Symbols
    Palatalization
    Phonetics
    Phonology
    Syllables
    Voicing
    Vowels

Constructed Languages
Use Artificial Languages

Constructions (Syntax)
Use Syntactic Structures

Contamination (Lexical)
Use Borrowing

Content Analysis
DC 15150
HN Formerly (1973-1991) DC col5.
RT Communication
    Discourse Analysis
    Literary Criticism
    Literature
    Mass Media
    Readability
    Text Analysis

Content and Expression (1973-1991)
HN DC col6.
Use Sign Theory

Content Area Reading
DC 15200
HN Added, 1992.
UF Content Reading
    Reading in Content Areas
BT Reading
    Reading Instruction
RT Readability
    Reading Comprehension

Content Reading
Use Content Area Reading

Context
DC 15250
HN Added, 1992.
RT Context Clues
    Context Free Grammar

Context (cont'd)
RT Context Sensitive Grammar
    Discourse Analysis
    Text Analysis
    Word Frequency

Context Clues
DC 15300
HN Added, 1992. Prior to 1992 see DC col7, Context Effects in Perception.
RT Ambiguity
    Associative Processes
    Comprehension
    Context
    Context Effects (Perception)
    Cloze Procedure
    Decoding (Reading)
    Meaning
    Miscue Analysis
    Reading
    Reading Comprehension
    Word Meaning
    Word Recognition

Context Effects (Perception)
DC 15350
HN Formerly (1973-1991) DC col7, Context Effects in Perception.
UF Context Effects in Perception (1973-1990)
    Contextual Associations
    Figure Ground Phenomena (1976-1986)
    Situational Determinants
RT Associative Processes
    Context Clues
    Decoding (Reading)
    Learning Theories
    Perception
    Psycholinguistics
    Reading Processes
    Word Recognition

Context Effects in Perception (1973-1991)
HN DC col7.
Use Context Effects (Perception)

Context Free Grammar
DC 15450
HN Formerly (1973-1991) DC col8.
BT Grammar Theories
RT Context
    Context Sensitive Grammar
    Phrase Structure Grammar
    Structuralist Linguistics
    Syntax

Context Sensitive Grammar
DC 15550
HN Formerly (1973-1991) DC col9.
BT Grammar Theories
RT Context
    Context Free Grammar
    Phrase Structure Grammar
    Structuralist Linguistics
    Syntax

Contextual Associations
Use Context Effects (Perception)

Contrastive Analysis of Linguistic Material
Use Comparative Linguistics

Contrastive Linguistics
Use Comparative Linguistics

Control Subjects
Use Research Subjects

Conversation
DC 15600
HN Added, 1992.
BT Interpersonal Communication
RT Discourse Analysis
Dyadic Interaction
Group Communication
Implicature
Pragmatics
Registers (Sociolinguistics)
Repair
Topics
Turn Taking

Conversation Courses
DC 15610
HN Added, 1992.
UF Conversational Language Courses
Foreign Language Conversation
Courses
Second Language Conversation
Courses
RT Audiolingual Language Teaching
Communicative Competence
Direct Method of Language Teaching
Fluency
Oral Language Instruction
Second Language Instruction
Second Language Learning

Conversational Implicature
Use Implicature

Conversational Language Courses
Use Conversation Courses

Conversational Turns
Use Turn Taking

Coordinate Clauses
Use Coordination (Grammatical)

Coordination (Grammatical)
DC 15650
SN A syntactic relation between two or
more sentences or sentence ele-
ments such that the set has the
same status/function as each of its
elements.
HN Added, 1992.
UF Coordinate Clauses
RT Clauses
Conjunctions
Linguistic Units
Sentences
Subordination (Grammatical)
Syntax

Coptic
Use Egyptian Coptic

Cornish
Use Celtic Languages

Corsica
DC 15700
HN Added, 1992.
BT France

Costa Rica
DC 15750
HN Added, 1992.
BT Central America

Courtesy
Use Politeness

Creative Ability
Use Creativity (Psychology)

Creative Aspect of Language Use
(1973-1991)
HN DC cr1.
Use Creativity (Linguistics)

Creative Spelling
Use Spelling Errors

Creative Writing
DC 15850
HN Added, 1992.
BT Writing
RT Creativity (Psychology)
Poetics
Poetry
Prose
Rhetorical Figures
Written Language Instruction

Creativity (Linguistics)
DC 15900
SN The capacity of native speakers to
generate new linguistic forms within
their language system. Also the prop-
erty of language that permits an infi-
nite number of sentences to be cre-
ated from a finite set of sounds and
syntactic structures.
HN Formerly (1973-1991) DC cr1, Cre-
ative Aspect of Language Use.
UF Creative Aspect of Language Use
(1973-1991)
Language Creativity
Lexical Creativity
Linguistic Creativity
Productivity (Linguistics)
RT Generalization
Grammaticality
Language Patterns
Language Processing
Language Usage
Neologisms
Psycholinguistics

Creativity (Psychology)
DC 15950
HN Added, 1992.
UF Creative Ability
Innovativeness
Originality
RT Art
Authorship
Concept Formation
Creative Writing
Intelligence
Poetics
Problem Solving

Credibility
DC 16100
HN Formerly (1973-1991) DC cr2.
UF Believability
Source Credibility
Trustworthiness
RT Beliefs
Communication
Interpersonal Communication
Judgment
Perception
Persuasion
Social Perception
Truth

Cree
Use Algonquian Languages

Creoles
DC 16150
SN Languages that developed from pid-
gins by expanding their vocabularies
and developing more complex gram-
matical systems, and that have be-
come the native languages of their
speech communities.
HN Formerly (1973-1991) DC cr3.
UF Creolized Languages
BT Languages
RT Borrowing
Cross Cultural Communication
Diglossia
Indigenous Languages
Language Contact
Language Diversity
Language Use
Native Speakers
Pidgins
Trade Languages

Creolized Languages
Use Creoles

Croatia
DC 16250
HN Added, 1992.
BT Balkan States
Eastern Europe
RT Yugoslavia

Croatian
Use Serbo Croatian

Cross Cultural Communication
DC 16300
SN Verbal and nonverbal communication
between people of different cultures.
HN Added, 1992.
UF Intercultural Communication
BT Communication
NT Native Nonnative Speaker Communi-
cation
RT Acculturation
Artificial Languages
Bilingualism
Creoles
Cultural Background
Cultural Change
Cultural Differences
Cultural Factors
Cultural Groups
Culture
Immigrants
Indigenous Populations
International Languages
Language Culture Relationship
Linguistic Accommodation
Minority Groups
Multilingualism
Pidgins
Social Factors
Sociolinguistics
Trade Languages
Translation

Cross Modality Matching
Use Perception

Crossword Puzzles
Use Word Games

Crow
Use Macro Siouan Phylum

Crying (Infant)
Use Infant Vocalization

Cuba
DC 16320
HN Added, 1992.
BT Caribbean

Cued Recall
Use Aided Recall

Cultural Background
DC 16350
HN Formerly (1973-1991) DC cul.
UF Cultural Heritage
Ethnic Heritage
BT Cultural Factors
RT Acculturation
Cross Cultural Communication
Cultural Change
Cultural Differences
Cultural Groups
Culture
Immigrants
Language Culture Relationship

Cultural Change
DC 16360
HN Added, 1992.
UF Cultural Evolution
RT Acculturation
Cross Cultural Communication
Cultural Background
Cultural Differences
Cultural Factors
Cultural Groups
Culture
Indigenous Populations
Language Change
Language Culture Relationship
Language Death
Language Modernization
Language Shift

Cultural Differences
DC 16400
HN Added, 1992.
UF Cultural Diversity
BT Cultural Factors
RT Acculturation
Cross Cultural Communication
Cultural Background
Cultural Change
Cultural Groups
Culture
Indigenous Populations
Language Culture Relationship
Minority Groups

Cultural Diversity
Use Cultural Differences

Cultural Evolution
Use Cultural Change

Cultural Factors
DC 16500
HN Added, 1992.
UF Cultural Influences
NT Cultural Background
Cultural Differences
RT Acculturation
Address Forms
Anthropological Linguistics
Cross Cultural Communication
Cultural Change

Cultural Factors (cont'd)
RT Cultural Groups
Culture
Language Culture Relationship
Language Status
Politeness
Social Factors
Socialization
Sociolinguistics
Turn Taking

Cultural Groups
DC 16550
HN Added, 1992.
NT African Cultural Groups
Arab Cultural Groups
Asian Cultural Groups
Australasian Cultural Groups
Commonwealth of Independent
States Cultural Groups
European Cultural Groups
Latin American Cultural Groups
Middle Eastern Cultural Groups
North American Cultural Groups
Oceanic Cultural Groups
Slavic Cultural Groups
RT Acculturation
Cross Cultural Communication
Cultural Background
Cultural Change
Cultural Differences
Cultural Factors
Culture
Ethnographic Linguistics
Ethnolinguistics
Language Culture Relationship
Minority Groups
Religions

Cultural Heritage
Use Cultural Background

Cultural Influences
Use Cultural Factors

Culture
DC 16700
HN Added, 1992.
RT Acculturation
Beliefs
Cross Cultural Communication
Cultural Background
Cultural Change
Cultural Differences
Cultural Factors
Cultural Groups
Folklore
Language Culture Relationship
Religions
Secret Languages

Culture Language Relationship
Use Language Culture Relationship

Cuneiform
Use Writing Systems

Cursive Writing
Use Handwriting

Cushitic Languages
DC 16800
HN Formerly (1973-1982) DC cula,
Cushitic. Reinstated, 1992.
UF Galla
Kushitic Languages
Omotic Languages
Somali (Language)
BT Afroasiatic Languages

Cutaneous Sense
Use Tactual Perception

CVC Trigrams
Use Nonsense Syllables

Cybernetics
DC 16900
HN Added, 1992.
RT Artifical Intelligence
Communication
Computer Applications
Computer Generated Language Analysis
Feedback
Human Computer Communication
Information Processing

Cymraeg
Use Welsh

Cyprus
DC 16950
HN Added, 1992.
BT Mediterranean Countries
Middle East
Western Europe

Czech
DC 17100
HN Added, 1992.
BT Slavic Languages

Czechoslovakia
DC 17200
HN Added, 1992.
BT Eastern Europe

D Structure
Use Deep Structure

Dahomey
Use Benin

Daic Languages
Use Kam Tai Languages

Dakota
Use Macro Siouan Phylum

Danish
DC 17250
HN Added, 1992.
BT Germanic Languages
Scandinavian Languages

Dano Norwegian
Use Norwegian

Dardic Languages
Use Indic Languages

Data Collection
DC 17300
HN Added, 1992.
BT Information Processing
RT Data Processing
Databases
Fieldwork
Interviews
Longitudinal Studies
Research Design
Surveys

Data Processing
DC 17350
HN Formerly (1973-1991) DC dal, Data
Processing and Retrieval.
UF Automatic Data Processing
Electronic Data Processing
RT Computer Applications
Computer Generated Language Analysis

Data Processing (cont'd)
- **RT** Computer Languages
  Computer Software
  Data Collection
  Databases
  Information Processing
  Research Design
  Statistical Analysis
  Word Processing

Databanks
- **Use** Databases

Databases
- **DC** 17400
- **HN** Added, 1992.
- **UF** Databanks
- **RT** Computational Linguistics
  Computer Applications
  Computer Generated Language Analysis
  Data Collection
  Data Processing
  Research Design
  Statistical Analysis

Dative Case
- **Use** Case

Dead Languages
- **Use** Language Death

Deafness
- **Use** Hearing Disorders

Declarative Sentences
- **DC** 17450
- **HN** Formerly (1973-1991) DC de2, Declarative Statement.
- **BT** Sentences
- **RT** Grammatical Analysis
  Imperative Sentences
  Interrogative Sentences
  Mood (Grammatical)

Declension
- **Use** Inflection (Morphology)

Decoding (Cognitive Process)
- **DC** 17500
- **HN** Added, 1992.
- **BT** Cognitive Processes
- **NT** Decoding (Reading)
- **RT** Auditory Stimulation
  Comprehension
  Concept Formation
  Encoding (Cognitive Process)
  Information Processing
  Language Processing
  Language Thought Relationship
  Listening Comprehension
  Phonological Processing
  Receptive Language
  Semantic Analysis
  Semantic Processing
  Semantics
  Syntactic Processing

Decoding (Reading)
- **DC** 17600
- **HN** Added, 1992.
- **BT** Decoding (Cognitive Process)
  Reading Processes
- **RT** Beginning Reading
  Context Clues
  Context Effects (Perception)
  Grapheme Phoneme Correspondence
  Letter Recognition

Decoding (Reading) (cont'd)
- **RT** Miscue Analysis
  Oral Reading
  Phonics
  Reading
  Reading Ability
  Reading Comprehension
  Word Recognition

Deductive Logic
- **Use** Logic

Deep Dyslexia
- **Use** Dyslexia

Deep Grammar
- **Use** Deep Structure

Deep Structure
- **DC** 17650
- **SN** A concept in transformational-generative grammar that describes and accounts for sentence structure; it is the base component of generative grammar, encoding the lexical properties of sentence constituents and representing the basic grammatical relations in a sentence.
- **HN** Added, 1992. Prior to 1992, see DC de3, Deep Structure and Surface Structure.
- **UF** D Structure
  Deep Grammar
  Underlying Structure
- **RT** Case Grammar
  Case Marking
  Extended Standard Theory
  Form (Language Structure)
  Grammar Theories
  Grammatical Analysis
  Phrase Structure Grammar
  Semantic Analysis
  Semantics
  Sentence Structure
  Sentences
  Surface Structure
  Syntax
  Thematic Roles
  Transformation Rules
  Transformational Generative Grammar

Deep Structure and Surface Structure (1973-1991)
- **HN** DC de3, deleted 1992. See now separate terms Deep Structure and Surface Structure.

Defense Mechanisms
- **DC** 17700
- **HN** Formerly (1973-1991) DC de4.
- **UF** Displacement (Defense Mechanism)
  Perceptual Defense
- **RT** Emotions
  Mental Disorders
  Personality
  Self Concept

Definite Articles
- **Use** Articles

Deictic Reference
- **Use** Deixis

Deixis
- **DC** 17750
- **SN** The semantic function of deictics, a class of words and phrases whose referents vary depending on the personal, temporal, and spatial context of the speech event in which they occur.

Deixis (cont'd)
- **HN** Added, 1992.
- **UF** Deictic Reference
  Indexical Expressions
- **RT** Anaphora
  Demonstratives
  Meaning
  Morphology
  Person
  Pronouns
  Reference (Grammatical)
  Semantics
  Space
  Time

Delaware
- **DC** 17800
- **HN** Added, 1992.
- **BT** Northern States
  United States of America

Delayed Auditory Feedback
- **DC** 17900
- **HN** Formerly (1973-1991) DC de5.
- **UF** Auditory Feedback (Delayed)
- **BT** Feedback
- **RT** Auditory Perception
  Auditory Stimulation
  Hearing

Delayed Language Acquisition
- **DC** 17950
- **HN** Formerly (1973-1991) DC de6.
- **UF** Retarded Speech Development
- **BT** Language Acquisition
- **RT** Child Language
  Language Pathology
  Language Therapy
  Speech Therapy

Delayed Recall
- **Use** Long Term Memory

Demonstrative Pronouns
- **Use** Demonstratives

Demonstratives
- **DC** 18100
- **HN** Formerly (1973-1991) DC de7, Demonstrative.
- **UF** Demonstrative Pronouns
- **BT** Form Classes
- **RT** Deixis
  Determiners
  Pronouns

Denmark
- **DC** 18150
- **HN** Added, 1992.
- **BT** Scandinavia
- **NT** Faeroe Islands

Denotation
- **Use** Meaning

Dependency Grammar
- **DC** 18250
- **SN** A model of grammar developed by Lucien Tesniere and others during the 1950s which explains grammatical relations in terms of the dependencies and governing relations between the components of a clause, phrase, or other structure.
- **HN** Added, 1992.
- **BT** Grammar Theories
- **RT** Government (Grammatical)
  Grammatical Relations
  Syntax
  Valence

Dependent Clauses
  Use Subordination (Syntax)

Depth Perception
  Use Visual Perception

Derivation (Diachronic Linguistics)
  Use Etymology

Derivation (Morphology)
  DC 18300
  SN The formation of words by adding af-
       fixes or other morphological entities
       to simpler words.
  HN Added, 1992.
  BT Word Formation
  RT Affixes
       Form Classes
       Inflection (Morphology)
       Morphology
       Roots (Morphology)
       Syntax

Descriptive Linguistics
  DC 18350
  SN Objective, systematic linguistic ap-
       proach concerned with the observa-
       tion and analysis of the sound sys-
       tem, grammar, and vocabulary of a
       language at a particular point in
       time.
  HN Formerly (1973-1991) DC de8.
  BT Linguistics
  RT Comparative Linguistics
       Computer Generated Language Anal-
       ysis
       Indigenous Languages
       Language Contact
       Language Status
       Language Typology
       Language Usage
       Linguistic Theories
       Onomastics
       Phonemics
       Phonology
       Semantic Analysis
       Semantics
       Synchronic Linguistics
       Syntax

Determinant (1973-1991)
  HN DC de9.
  Use Determiners

Determiners
  DC 18400
  HN Added, 1992. Prior to 1992, see DC
       de9, Determinant.
  UF Determinant (1973-1991)
  BT Form Classes
  RT Adjectives
       Articles
       Demonstratives
       Numerals
       Quantifiers

Developmental Differences
  Use Age Differences

Developmental Dyslexia
  Use Dyslexia

Deviant Sentences
  Use Anomalous Strings

Diachronic Linguistics
  DC 18500
  SN Branch of linguistics concerned with
       the historical changes in a language
       over time.
  HN Formerly (1973-1991) DC di1.

Diachronic Linguistics (cont'd)
  UF Glottochronology
       Historical Linguistics
       History of Language
       Language History
  BT Linguistics
  RT Analogy (Language Change)
       Anthropological Linguistics
       Archaeological Evidence
       Assimilation (Language Change)
       Borrowing
       Cognates
       Comparative Linguistics
       Etymology
       Grammatical Change
       Indigenous Languages
       Language Change
       Language Classification
       Language Contact
       Language Modernization
       Language Patterns
       Language Planning
       Language Shift
       Language Status
       Language Universals
       Language Use
       Lexicology
       Linguistic Theories
       Manuscripts
       Morphological Change
       Neogrammarians
       Nostratic Theory
       Onomastics
       Origin of Language
       Paleography
       Paleolinguistics
       Phonemics
       Phonological Change
       Proto Indo European
       Semantic Change
       Sociolinguistics
       Sound Change
       Synchronic Linguistics
       Toponymy
       Unknown Languages

Diacritical Marks
  Use Orthographic Symbols

Diacritics
  Use Orthographic Symbols

Diagnostic Tests
  DC 18550
  SN Tests used to identify the nature and
       origin of an individual's disabilities,
       disorders, or learning difficulties.
  HN Formerly (1973-1991) DC di2, Diag-
       nostic Testing.
  BT Tests
  RT Disorders
       Learning Disabilities
       Personality Measures
       Phonetically Balanced Lists
       Prognostic Tests
       Projective Techniques

Dialect Death
  Use Language Death

**Dialectical Materialistic Linguistic
Theory**
  DC 18600
  HN Formerly (1984-1991) DC di2a.
  BT Linguistic Theories
  RT Economic Factors
       Linguistics
       Marxist Analysis
       Social Factors
       Sociolinguistics

Dialectology
  DC 18650
  HN Formerly (1973-1991) DC di3.
  BT Linguistics
  RT Areal Linguistics
       Colloquial Language
       Comparative Linguistics
       Dialects
       Diglossia
       Etymology
       Language Classification
       Language Diversity
       Language Patterns
       Language Standardization
       Language Use
       Languages
       Nonstandard Dialects
       Regional Dialects
       Second Dialect Learning
       Sociolinguistics
       Standard Dialects

Dialects
  DC 18750
  SN Distinctive language varieties shared
       by speakers within socially or geo-
       graphically defined groups.
  HN Added, 1992.
  UF Koines (Dialects)
  BT Languages
  NT Nonstandard Dialects
       Regional Dialects
       Standard Dialects
  RT Dialectology
       Diglossia
       Idioms
       Intelligibility
       Language
       Language Classification
       Language Death
       Language Diversity
       Language Standardization
       Language Use
       Native Language
       Native Speakers
       Oral Language
       Second Dialect Learning
       Social Factors
       Sociolinguistics
       Speech Communities

Dialogue
  Use Dyadic Interaction

Dichotic Listening
  Use Ear Preference

Dichotic Stimulation
  Use Binaural Stimulation

Dictionaries
  DC 18800
  HN Formerly (1973-1991) DC di4, Dictio-
       nary.
  UF Glossaries
  NT Bilingual Dictionaries
  RT Etymology
       Language Teaching Materials
       Lexicography
       Lexicology
       Lexicon
       Orthography
       Semantics
       Words

Digits (Numbers)
  Use Numerals

Diglossia
  DC 18850
  SN Use of two languages or dialects for different functions or at different social levels within a single speech community.
  HN Formerly (1973-1991) DC di4aa, Diglossia.
  BT Language Use
  RT Bilingualism
      Code Switching
      Colloquial Language
      Creoles
      Dialectology
      Dialects
      Indigenous Languages
      Intelligibility
      Language Classification
      Language Contact
      Language Diversity
      Language Shift
      Language Standardization
      Multilingualism
      Nonstandard Dialects
      Registers (Sociolinguistics)
      Sociolinguistics

Diphthongs
  DC 18950
  HN Formerly (1973-1991) DC di4b, Diphthong.
  BT Phonemes
  RT Phonology
      Vowels

Direct Method of Language Teaching
  DC 19150
  SN Approach to language instruction that stresses oral techniques such as question and answer, and conversation in the foreign language.
  HN Formerly (1973-1991) DC di5.
  BT Language Teaching Methods
  RT Audiolingual Language Teaching
      Communicative Language Teaching
      Conversation Courses
      Oral Language Instruction
      Second Language Instruction
      Second Language Learning

Disabilities
  Use Disorders

Disabled
  Use Handicapped

Discourse Analysis
  DC 19200
  SN Study of cohesion and other relationships between sentences in larger units of spoken or written language, such as paragraphs or conversations.
  HN Formerly (1973-1991) DC di6.
  NT Political Discourse
  RT Cohesion
      Communication
      Computer Generated Language Analysis
      Content Analysis
      Context
      Conversation
      Ellipsis
      Focus
      Foregrounding
      Functional Sentence Perspective

Discourse Analysis (cont'd)
  RT Grammatical Analysis
      Language
      Language Patterns
      Language Usage
      Literary Criticism
      Mean Length of Utterance
      Meaning
      Narrative Structure
      Natural Language Processing
      Oral Language
      Paragraphs
      Pauses
      Performative Utterances
      Pragmatics
      Repair
      Rheme
      Semantic Analysis
      Semantics
      Sentences
      Speech
      Speech Acts
      Story Grammar
      Stylistics
      Syntax
      Tagmemics
      Text Analysis
      Turn Taking
      Written Language

Discrimination Learning
  DC 19300
  HN Formerly (1973-1991) DC di7.
  UF Discriminative Learning
  BT Conditioning
      Learning
  RT Auditory Perception
      Concept Formation
      Generalization
      Letter Recognition
      Paired Associate Learning
      Verbal Learning
      Visual Perception

Discriminative Learning
  Use Discrimination Learning

Diseases
  Use Disorders

Disorders
  DC 19450
  HN Added, 1992.
  UF Disabilities
      Diseases
      Dysfunctions
      Pathologies
  NT Alcoholism
      Articulation Disorders
      Attention Deficit Disorders
      Behavior Disorders
      Cleft Palate
      Hearing Disorders
      Learning Disabilities
      Memory Disorders
      Mental Disorders
      Muscular Disorders
      Nervous System Disorders
      Phonation Disorders
      Reading Deficiencies
      Stuttering
      Vision Disorders
      Voice Disorders
      Writing Disorders
  RT Anatomical Systems
      Biology
      Diagnostic Tests
      Genetics
      Medicine
      Patients
      Therapy

Displacement (Defense Mechanism)
  Use Defense Mechanisms

Disposition (Personality)
  Use Personality

Distinctive Features
  DC 19550
  SN Linguistic features that function as contrastive elements of language composing larger linguistic units (phonemes, words, etc., according to the model of language used).
  HN Formerly (1973-1991) DC di8, Distinctive Feature Theory.
  RT Acoustic Phonetics
      Articulatory Phonetics
      Componential Analysis
      Consonants
      Generative Phonology
      Language Universals
      Linguistic Theories
      Markedness
      Phonemes
      Phonetics
      Phonology
      Redundancy
      Voicing

Distortion of Speech Signal
  DC 19650
  HN Formerly (1973-1991) DC di9.
  UF Signal Distortion (Speech)
      Speech Signal Distortion
  RT Acoustic Phonetics
      Acoustics
      Audiometry
      Auditory Perception
      Signal Detection

Djibouti
  DC 19670
  HN Added, 1992.
  UF Somaliland
  BT Sub Saharan Africa

Doctors (Medical)
  Use Physicians

Downs Syndrome
  DC 19700
  HN Added, 1992.
  UF Mongolism
  BT Mental Retardation
  RT Genetics
      Special Education (Handicapped)

Drama
  DC 19750
  HN Added, 1992.
  UF Plays (Theatrical)
  BT Literature
  RT Art
      Authorship
      Fiction
      Films
      Folklore
      Literary Genres
      Poetry
      Prose

Dravidian Languages
  DC 19800
  HN Formerly (1973-1991) DC dr1.
  UF Kannada
      Malayalam
      Telugu
  BT Languages
  NT Tamil

Drills (Language Patterns)
Use Pattern Drills

Drug Effects
DC 19900
HN Formerly (1973-1990) DC dr2.
UF Side Effects (Drugs)
RT Alcoholism
Behavior Disorders
Biology
Medicine
Muscular Disorders
Therapy

Drum Languages
Use Nonverbal Languages

Duration of Speech
Use Speech Duration

Dutch
DC 20100
HN Added, 1992.
UF Netherlandic
BT Germanic Languages
RT Afrikaans
Flemish

Dyadic Interaction
DC 20150
HN Formerly (1973-1991) DC dy1.
UF Dialogue
BT Interpersonal Behavior
RT Adult Child Interaction
Conversation
Interviews
Parent Child Interaction
Turn Taking

Dying Languages
Use Language Death

Dysacusis
Use Hearing Disorders

Dysarthria
Use Articulation Disorders

Dysfunctions
Use Disorders

Dysgraphia
Use Writing Disorders

Dyslexia
DC 20250
HN Added, 1992.
UF Acquired Dyslexia
Deep Dyslexia
Developmental Dyslexia
Word Blindness
BT Learning Disabilities
Reading Deficiencies
RT Letter Recognition
Remedial Reading
Visual Perception
Writing Disorders

Dysphasia
Use Aphasia

Dysphonia
Use Voice Disorders

Dyula
Use Mande Languages

Ear
Use Auditory System

Ear Preference
DC 20350
HN Formerly (1981-1991) DC ea2.
UF Dichotic Listening
RT Audiometry
Auditory Perception
Auditory System
Binaural Stimulation
Cerebral Dominance
Hearing
Listening
Monaural Stimulation
Speech Perception

Early Literacy
DC 20400
HN Added, 1992.
UF Early Reading
Preschool Literacy
BT Literacy
RT Beginning Reading
Childrens Literature
Preschool Children
Preschool Education
Reading Readiness

Early Reading
Use Early Literacy

Early Second Language Learning
DC 20450
HN Added, 1992.
BT Second Language Learning
RT Elementary Education
FLES
Immersion Programs
Language of Instruction

East Germany
Use Germany

East Pakistan
Use Bangladesh

Eastern Austronesian Languages
Use Oceanic Languages

Eastern Europe
DC 20500
HN Added, 1992.
BT Europe
NT Albania
Bosnia Herzegovina
Bulgaria
Commonwealth of Independent
States
Croatia
Czechoslovakia
Hungary
Macedonia
Montenegro
Poland
Romania
Serbia
Slovenia
Union of Soviet Socialist Republics
Yugoslavia
RT Slavic Cultural Groups
Western Europe

Eastern Sudanic Languages
Use Chari Nile Languages

Economic Factors
DC 20600
HN Added, 1992.
UF Economic Influences
RT Business
Dialectical Materialistic Linguistic
Theory
Low Income Groups
Marxist Analysis
Occupations
Social Class
Social Factors
Socioeconomic Status
Sociolinguistics

Economic Influences
Use Economic Factors

Ecuador
DC 20800
HN Added, 1992.
BT South America

Education
DC 20900
HN Added, 1992.
UF Schools
NT Bilingual Education
Elementary Education
Higher Education
Preschool Education
Secondary Education
Special Education (Handicapped)
RT Academic Achievement
Educational Activities
Instruction
Learning
Literacy Programs
Socialization
Socioeconomic Status
Students
Teachers
Teaching Materials
Teaching Methods
Tests

Educational Activities
DC 20910
HN Added, 1992.
UF Classroom Activities
Learning Activities
RT Academic Achievement
Classroom Observation
Computer Assisted Instruction
Education
Educational Television
Grammar Instruction
Instruction
Learning
Linguistics Instruction
Literacy Programs
Native Language Instruction
Oral Language Instruction
Programmed Instruction
Reading Instruction
Reinforcement
Second Language Instruction
Special Education (Handicapped)
Spelling Instruction
Students
Teachers
Teaching Materials
Teaching Methods
Translation Instruction
Vocabulary Instruction
Written Language Instruction

Educational Attainment
Use Academic Achievement

Educational Materials
Use Teaching Materials

Educational Television
DC 20950
HN Formerly (1973-1991) DC te3, Television and Teaching.
UF Televised Instruction
Television and Teaching (1973-1991)
BT Television
RT Audiovisual Language Teaching
Educational Activities
Teaching Methods

Efik
DC 21150
HN Added, 1992.
BT Benue Congo Phylum

Ego
Use Self Concept

Egypt
DC 21200
HN Added, 1992.
UF United Arab Republic
BT Arab Countries
Mediterranean Countries
North Africa

Egyptian Coptic
DC 21250
HN Formerly (1973-1982) DC eg1, Egyptian-Coptic. Reinstated, 1992.
UF Ancient Egyptian
Coptic
BT Afroasiatic Languages

El Salvador
DC 21300
HN Added, 1992.
BT Central America

Elderly
DC 21350
HN Added, 1992.
UF Aged
Older Adults
Senior Citizens
BT Adults
RT Age Differences

Electronic Data Processing
Use Data Processing

Elementary Education
DC 21500
HN Formerly (1973-1991) DC el1, Elementary School.
UF Primary School Education
BT Education
RT Early Second Language Learning
Elementary School Students
FLES
Kindergarten

Elementary School Students
DC 21520
HN Added, 1992.
UF Grade School Students
Primary School Students
BT Students
RT Children
Elementary Education

Ellipsis
DC 21540
SN The absence in a syntactic structure of a constituent that, if present, would render the expression more explicit without altering its meaning; in processal models of syntax, the omission of a constituent in the output or surface structure representation.
HN Added, 1992.
UF Reduced Constructions
RT Discourse Analysis
Grammatical Analysis
Language Usage
Sentence Structure
Syntax

Embedded Construction
DC 21550
SN In several models of generative grammar, a construction consisting of a sentence that has been incorporated into another sentence by a specified process that, in many instances, alters the form of the embedded sentences.
HN Formerly (1973-1991) DC em1.
RT Clauses
Grammatical Analysis
Sentences
Subordination (Grammatical)
Syntax
Transformational Generative Grammar

Emotional Disturbances
DC 21570
HN Formerly (1973-1991) DC em3.
UF Psychosomatic Disorders
BT Mental Disorders
RT Anxiety
Attention Deficit Disorders
Autism
Behavior Disorders
Emotions
Learning Disabilities
Neurosis
Psychosis
Psychoanalysis
Psychotherapy
Schizophrenia

Emotions
DC 21600
HN Formerly (1973-1991) DC em2, Emotion.
UF Affect
Feelings
RT Anxiety
Attitudes
Connotation
Defense Mechanisms
Emotional Disturbances
Expressive Function of Language
Personality

Emotive Meaning
Use Connotation

Encephalitis (1976-1982)
HN DC en1.
Use Nervous System Disorders

Encoding (Cognitive Process)
DC 21750
HN Added, 1992.
BT Cognitive Processes
RT Aided Recall
Cognitive Style

Encoding (Cognitive Process)
(cont'd)
RT Comprehension
Concept Formation
Decoding (Cognitive Process)
Information Processing
Language Processing
Language Thought Relationship
Learning Processes
Memory
Perception
Phonological Processing
Recall (Memory)
Recognition
Retention (Memory)
Unaided Recall

England
DC 21800
HN Added, 1992.
BT Great Britain

English
DC 21900
HN Formerly (1973-1991) DC en2.
BT Germanic Languages
NT American English
Australian English
British English
English as a Second Language
English as an International Language
English for Special Purposes
Middle English
Old English

English as a Second Language
DC 22100
HN Added, 1992.
UF ESL
BT English
Second Languages
RT English as an International Language
English for Special Purposes
Limited English Proficiency
TESOL

English as a Second Language Tests
DC 22150
HN Added, 1992.
UF ESL Tests
BT Second Language Tests

English as an International Language
DC 22200
HN Added, 1992.
UF Basic English (1973-1991)
World English
BT English
International Languages
RT English as a Second Language

English for Special Purposes
DC 22300
SN English language skills, including vocabulary & usage, required for effective communication in specific occupations and fields of expertise; typically used to designate a specialized form of English as a second language instruction.
HN Added, 1992.
BT English
Language for Special Purposes
NT Business English
RT English as a Second Language
Limited English Proficiency
Second Language Instruction
Terminology

Entailment
DC 22350
SN A logical relation between two propositions such that the truth value of one must follow from the truth value of the other, but not necessarily vice versa.
HN Formerly (1973-1991) DC en3.
RT Logic of Language
Natural Language
Presuppositions
Semantics
Sentences
Truth

Environmental Noise (1977-1991)
HN DC en4.
Use Noise

Epigraphy
Use Paleography

Epilepsy
Use Nervous System Disorders

Equatorial Guinea
DC 22390
HN Added, 1992.
BT Sub Saharan Africa

Equitorial Languages
Use Andean Equatorial Phylum

ERP
Use Evoked Responses

Error Analysis (Language)
DC 22400
HN Formerly (1973-1991) DC er1.
RT Anomalous Strings
Grammaticality
Interlanguage
Language Patterns
Language Tests
Language Usage
Linguistic Interference
Repair
Second Language Instruction
Second Language Learning
Semantic Analysis
Semantics
Slips of the Tongue
Spelling Errors

Error Repair
Use Repair

Erythraic Languages
Use Afroasiatic Languages

Eskimo Aleut Languages
DC 22500
HN Formerly (1973-1991) DC es1, Eskimo/Aleut.
UF Aleut
Greenlandic
Inuit
Inupiak
Yupik
BT North Amerindian Languages
RT Chukchee Kamchatkan Languages

ESL
Use English as a Second Language

ESL Tests
Use English as a Second Language Tests

Esophageal Speech
DC 22600
HN Formerly (1982-1991) DC es1a.
UF Oesphageal Speech
BT Speech
RT Laryngectomy
Prosthetic Devices
Speech Pathology
Speech Therapy
Surgery

Esperanto
DC 22650
HN Added, 1992.
BT Artificial Languages
International Languages

Estonia
DC 22700
HN Added, 1992.
BT Baltic States
Commonwealth of Independent States
RT Union of Soviet Socialist Republics

Estonian
DC 22800
HN Added, 1992.
BT Finno Ugric Languages

Ethiopia
DC 22830
HN Added, 1992.
BT Sub Saharan Africa

Ethnic Heritage
Use Cultural Background

Ethnic Minorities
Use Minority Groups

Ethnographic Linguistics
DC 22850
SN Application of the techniques and tools of ethnography to the study of the place of language in culture and society.
HN Formerly (1973-1991) DC et1.
BT Linguistics
RT Anthropological Linguistics
Cultural Groups
Ethnolinguistics
Fieldwork
Indigenous Languages
Language Contact
Language Culture Relationship
Language Usage
Linguistic Theories
Social Factors
Sociolinguistics

Ethnolinguistics
DC 22950
SN Study of language in relation to ethnic groups and cultural behavior.
HN Formerly (1979-1991) DC et2.
BT Linguistics
RT Anthropological Linguistics
Cultural Groups
Ethnographic Linguistics
Folklore
Kinship Terminology
Language Culture Relationship
Linguistic Theories
Minority Groups
Religions
Social Factors
Sociolinguistics

Etruscan
DC 23150
HN Added, 1992.
BT Language Isolates

Etymology
DC 23250
SN The study of the origins and history of words; a set of statements about the origin and changes in form and meaning of a morpheme, word, or syntactic structure.
HN Added, 1992.
UF Derivation (Diachronic Linguistics)
Roots (Diachronic Linguistics)
RT Cognates
Diachronic Linguistics
Dialectology
Dictionaries
Grammatical Change
Language Change
Language Classification
Language Typology
Lexicography
Lexicology
Lexicon
Morphological Change
Onomastics
Phonological Change
Polysemy
Semantic Change
Semantics
Sound Change
Toponymy
Words

Europe
DC 23340
HN Added, 1992.
NT Balkan States
Eastern Europe
Western Europe
RT European Cultural Groups
Mediterranean Countries

European Cultural Groups
DC 23350
HN Added, 1992.
BT Cultural Groups
NT Gypsies
Slavic Cultural Groups
RT Europe
Jewish Cultural Groups

European Linguistic Theory (1973-1991)
HN DC eu1, deleted 1992. See now specific linguistic theories and theoreticians, or History of Linguistics.

Evaluative Thinking
Use Judgment

Event Related Potentials
Use Evoked Responses

Evoked Potentials
Use Evoked Responses

Evoked Responses
DC 23450
HN Formerly (1973-1991) DC ev1, Evoked Response.
UF Auditory Evoked Responses
ERP
Event Related Potentials
Evoked Potentials
RT Brain
Conditioning
Semantic Processing
Stimulation

Ewe
  Use Kwa Languages

Exceptional Case Marking
  Use Case Marking

Exotic Languages (1973-1991)
  HN DC ex1.
  Use Non Western Languages

Experimental Data Handling (1973-1991)
  HN DC ex2.
  Use Statistical Analysis

Experimental Design
  Use Research Design

Experimental Subjects
  Use Research Subjects

Expert Systems
  Use Artificial Intelligence

Expository Writing Instruction
  Use Written Language Instruction

Expressive Aphasia
  Use Aphasia

Expressive Function of Language
  DC 23500
  HN Formerly (1973-1991) DC ex3.
  RT Attitudes
       Emotions
       Graffiti
       Intonation
       Language
       Linguistic Theories
       Oral Language
       Phonological Stylistics

Extended Standard Theory
  DC 23550
  SN A model of transformational-generative grammar developed by Noam Chomsky and others during the 1970s, distinguished from its 1960s predecessor (standard theory) by X-bar theory and other constraints on transformations, and by increasing specification of interactions among syntax, lexicon, and semantic interpretation. This model evolved into government and binding theory in the 1980s.
  HN Added, 1992.
  BT Grammar Theories
  RT Deep Structure
       Focus
       Government Binding Theory
       Semantics
       Surface Structure
       Syntax
       Transformational Generative Grammar
       X Bar Theory

Eye Fixations
  Use Eye Movements

Eye Movements
  DC 23600
  HN Formerly (1973-1991) DC ey1, Eye Movement.
  UF Eye Fixations
       Oculomotor Responses
       Rapid Eye Movements
  RT Anatomical Systems
       Facial Expressions

Eye Movements (cont'd)
  RT Nonverbal Communication
       Reading Processes
       Sleep
       Tachistoscopes
       Vision
       Vision Disorders
       Visual Perception

Eyesight
  Use Vision

Facial Expressions
  DC 23700
  HN Added, 1992.
  UF Grimaces
       Smiles
  BT Nonverbal Communication
  RT Eye Movements
       Gestures
       Kinesics
       Nonverbal Languages

Faeroe Islands
  DC 23750
  HN Added, 1992.
  BT Denmark

Fairy Tales
  Use Folklore

Faliscan
  Use Italic Languages

Familiarity
  DC 23800
  HN Formerly (1973-1991) DC fa1.
  RT Comprehension
       Conditioning
       Identification
       Language Processing
       Perception
       Rating Scales
       Recall (Memory)
       Recognition
       Retention (Memory)
       Word Recognition

Far East
  DC 23850
  HN Added, 1992.
  BT Asia
  NT Hong Kong
       Japan
       Macao
       Mongolia
       North Korea
       Peoples Republic of China
       South Korea
       Taiwan

Farsi
  Use Persian

Fathers
  Use Parents

Federal Republic of Germany
  Use Germany

Feedback
  DC 23950
  HN Formerly (1973-1991) DC fe1.
  UF Negative Feedback
       Positive Feedback
  NT Delayed Auditory Feedback
  RT Communication
       Computer Assisted Instruction
       Conditioning

Feedback (cont'd)
  RT Cybernetics
       Interference (Learning)
       Learning
       Programmed Instruction
       Reinforcement
       Stimulation

Feelings
  Use Emotions

Females
  DC 24000
  HN Added, 1992.
  UF Women
  RT Males
       Maternal Speech
       Sex Differences

Feminism
  DC 24100
  HN Added, 1992.
  RT Language Usage
       Sexism

Fiction
  DC 24120
  HN Added, 1992.
  BT Prose
  NT Novels
  RT Drama
       Humor
       Literary Genres
       Literature
       Nonfiction
       Poetry

Field Research
  Use Fieldwork

Fieldwork
  DC 24140
  SN Empirical research involving the direct observation of subjects in their natural environment, rather than under laboratory or classroom conditions.
  HN Added, 1992.
  UF Field Research
  RT Data Collection
       Ethnographic Linguistics
       Interviews
       Research Design
       Surveys

Figurative Language
  Use Rhetorical Figures

Figure Ground Phenomena (1976-1986)
  HN DC fi1.
  Use Context Effects (Perception)

Figures of Speech
  Use Rhetorical Figures

Fiji Islands
  DC 24150
  HN Added, 1992.
  BT Melanesia

Filled Pauses
  Use Pauses

Fillmore, Charles
  DC 24250
  SN Born 1929 - .
  HN Prior to 1992, users were instructed to see Case Grammar.

Films
- **DC** 24300
- **HN** Added, 1992.
- **UF** Cinema
  Motion Pictures
  Movies
- **BT** Mass Media
- **RT** Art
  Drama
  Videotape Recordings
  Visual Media

Fine Arts
- **Use** Art

Finland
- **DC** 24400
- **HN** Added, 1992.
- **BT** Baltic States
  Scandinavia

Finnic Languages
- **Use** Finno Ugric Languages

Finnish
- **DC** 24450
- **HN** Added, 1992.
- **BT** Finno Ugric Languages
  Scandinavian Languages

Finno Ugric Languages
- **DC** 24550
- **HN** Added, 1992.
- **UF** Balto Finnic Languages
  Cheremis
  Finnic Languages
  Lappic Languages
  Permic Languages
  Volgaic Languages
- **BT** Uralic Languages
- **NT** Estonian
  Finnish
  Ugric Languages
- **RT** Scandinavian Languages

First Language
- **Use** Native Language

Firth, John Rupert
- **DC** 24600
- **SN** Born 1890 - Died 1960.
- **HN** Formerly (1973-1991) DC fi3, Firth.

Flanders
- **DC** 24700
- **HN** Added, 1992.
- **BT** Belgium

Flection
- **Use** Inflection (Morphology)

Flemish
- **DC** 24800
- **HN** Added, 1992.
- **BT** Germanic Languages
- **RT** Dutch

FLES
- **DC** 24850
- **HN** Formerly (1973-1991) DC fl1.
- **UF** Foreign Languages in Elementary School
- **RT** Bilingual Education
  Early Second Language Learning
  Elementary Education
  Immersion Programs
  Language of Instruction
  Second Language Instruction
  Second Language Learning

Florida
- **DC** 24900
- **HN** Added, 1992.
- **BT** Southern States
  United States of America

Fluency
- **DC** 24910
- **HN** Added, 1992.
- **UF** Language Fluency
- **RT** Communicative Competence
  Conversation Courses
  Grammaticality
  Language Acquisition
  Languages
  Linguistic Performance
  Second Language Learning
  Threshold Level (Language)
  Well Formedness

Focus
- **DC** 24920
- **HN** Added, 1992.
- **RT** Discourse Analysis
  Extended Standard Theory
  Foregrounding
  Functional Sentence Perspective
  Grammatical Analysis
  Prague School
  Rheme
  Semantic Analysis
  Semantics
  Sentences
  Subject (Grammatical)
  Syntax
  Topic and Comment

Folklore
- **DC** 24950
- **HN** Formerly (1973-1991) DC fl2.
- **UF** Fairy Tales
  Folktales
- **RT** Art
  Culture
  Drama
  Ethnolinguistics
  Literature
  Music
  Mythology
  Phraseologisms
  Poetry
  Religions
  Sociolinguistics
  Story Telling

Folktales
- **Use** Folklore

Follow Up Studies
- **Use** Longitudinal Studies

Fonts
- **Use** Printed Materials

Foregrounding
- **DC** 25000
- **HN** Added, 1992.
- **RT** Discourse Analysis
  Focus
  Poetics
  Pragmatics
  Rheme
  Stylistics

Foreign Accent
- **DC** 25100
- **HN** Formerly (1973-1991) fo1.
- **UF** Accent (Second Language)
- **RT** Intelligibility
  Linguistic Interference

Foreign Accent (cont'd)
- **RT** Oral Language
  Phonology
  Pronunciation
  Pronunciation Accuracy
  Second Languages
  Speech

Foreign Language Conversation Courses
- **Use** Conversation Courses

Foreign Language for Special Purposes
- **Use** Language for Special Purposes

Foreign Language Instruction
- **Use** Second Language Instruction

Foreign Language Learning
- **Use** Second Language Learning

Foreign Language Reading Instruction
- **Use** Second Language Reading Instruction

Foreign Language Tests
- **Use** Second Language Tests

Foreign Language Textbooks
- **Use** Language Textbooks

Foreign Languages
- **Use** Second Languages

Foreign Languages in Elementary School
- **Use** FLES

Foreigner Talk
- **Use** Native Nonnative Speaker Communication

Foreigners
- **DC** 25120
- **HN** Added, 1992.
- **UF** Aliens
- **RT** Immigrants
  Indigenous Populations
  Minority Groups
  Refugees

Forgetting (1973-1991)
- **HN** DC fo2.
- **Use** Memory

Form (Language Structure)
- **DC** 25200
- **HN** Added, 1992.
- **NT** Logical Form
- **RT** Deep Structure
  Form Classes
  Language Universals
  Linguistic Units
  Meaning
  Morphology
  Structural Linguistics
  Stylistics
  Surface Structure
  Syntax
  Well Formedness

Form and Substance (1973-1991)
- **HN** DC fo3, deleted 1992. See now Form (Language Structure) coordinated with appropriate terms.

Form Classes
- **DC** 25250
- **HN** Added, 1992.
- **UF** Parts of Speech
  Word Classes
- **NT** Adjectives
  Adverbs
  Articles
  Conjunctions
  Demonstratives
  Derivation (Morphology)
  Determiners
  Function Words
  Nouns
  Prepositions
  Pronouns
  Quantifiers
  Verbs
- **RT** Affixes
  Case
  Form (Language Structure)
  Functional Linguistics
  Grammatical Analysis
  Grammatical Categories
  Language Patterns
  Lexical Functional Grammar
  Lexicon
  Linguistic Units
  Morphology
  Number (Grammatical)
  Phrase Structure Grammar
  Tagmemics
  Taxonomic Approaches
  Tense
  Word Formation
  Words

Formal Logic
- **Use** Logic

Formant Frequency (1973-1991)
- **HN** DC fo4.
- **Use** Formants

Formants
- **DC** 25300
- **HN** Formerly (1973-1991) DC fo4, Formant Frequency.
- **UF** Formant Frequency (1973-1991)
- **BT** Frequency (Acoustics)
- **RT** Acoustic Phonetics
  Acoustics
  Sound Spectrographs
  Vowels

Forms of Address
- **Use** Address Forms

Forward Masking
- **Use** Masking

Français Fondamental
- **Use** International Languages

France
- **DC** 25500
- **HN** Added, 1992.
- **BT** Mediterranean Countries
  Western Europe
- **NT** Corsica

Free Association
- **DC** 25600
- **HN** Formerly (1973-1991) DC fr1.
- **BT** Associative Processes
- **RT** Word and Letter Association

Free Recall
- **Use** Unaided Recall

Free Translation
- **Use** Translation

Frege, Friedrich Ludwig Gottlob
- **DC** 25700
- **SN** Born 1848 - Died 1925.
- **HN** Formerly (1981-1991) DC fr16, Frege, G.

French
- **DC** 25750
- **HN** Formerly (1973-1991) DC fr2.
- **BT** Romance Languages
- **NT** Canadian French
  French as a Second Language
- **RT** Provencal

French as a Second Language
- **DC** 25800
- **HN** Added, 1992.
- **BT** French
  Second Languages

French Guiana
- **DC** 25900
- **HN** Added, 1992.
- **BT** South America

French Polynesia
- **DC** 25950
- **HN** Added, 1992.
- **BT** Polynesia

Frequency (Acoustics)
- **DC** 26100
- **HN** Formerly (1973-1991) DC fr3, Frequency of Vibration.
- **UF** Pitch (Acoustics)
- **NT** Formants
  Fundamental Frequency
- **RT** Acoustic Phonetics
  Acoustics
  Auditory Stimulation
  Radio
  Sound Spectrographs

Frequency of Voice
- **Use** Fundamental Frequency

Freud, Sigmund
- **DC** 26150
- **SN** Born 1856 - Died 1939.
- **HN** Formerly (1973-1991) DC fr4, Freud.

Fricatives
- **DC** 26200
- **SN** Sounds produced by forcing air through a sufficiently narrow opening in the speech tract that the friction results in a steady, easily audible noise (eg, [f, s, h]).
- **HN** Added, 1992.
- **UF** Sibilants
  Spirants
- **BT** Consonants
- **RT** Pharyngeal Structures

Fries, Charles Carpenter
- **DC** 26250
- **SN** Born 1887 - Died ????.
- **HN** Formerly (1973-1991) DC fr5, Fries.

Friesian
- **Use** Frisian

Frisian
- **DC** 26300
- **HN** Added, 1992.
- **UF** Friesian
- **BT** Germanic Languages

Ful
- **Use** West Atlantic Languages

Fulani
- **Use** West Atlantic Languages

Function Words
- **DC** 26400
- **HN** Formerly (1973-1991) DC fu1, Function Word.
- **UF** Functors
- **BT** Form Classes
- **RT** Articles
  Conjunctions
  Prepositions
  Sentence Structure
  Surface Structure

Functional Grammar
- **DC** 26440
- **SN** A social-interaction model of language introduced in 1978 by Simon C. Dik. It includes a lexicon and syntactic, semantic, and pragmatic levels; predications are constructed from predicate frames in the lexicon and mapped onto linguistic expressions by expression rules. Do not confuse with Lexical Functional Grammar.
- **HN** Added, 1992.
- **BT** Grammar Theories
- **RT** Agreement
  Case
  Functional Linguistics
  Generative Grammar
  Grammatical Analysis
  Intonation
  Lexical Functional Grammar
  Lexicon
  Pragmatics
  Syntax
  Systemic Linguistics
  Thematic Roles

Functional Illiteracy
- **Use** Functional Literacy

Functional Linguistics
- **DC** 26450
- **SN** A perspective that regards language as an instrument of social interaction and requires linguistic forms to be described, at least partially, in terms of the communicative function of language.
- **HN** Formerly (1979-1991) DC fu1a.
- **BT** Linguistics
- **RT** Communicative Function of Language
  Form Classes
  Functional Grammar
  Functional Sentence Perspective
  Interpersonal Communication
  Linguistic Theories
  Pragmatics
  Prague School
  Sociolinguistics
  Structuralist Linguistics

Functional Literacy
DC 26500
HN Added, 1992.
UF Functional Illiteracy
BT Literacy
RT Adult Literacy
    Literacy Programs
    Reading Ability

Functional Sentence Perspective
DC 26550
SN An approach to language developed chiefly by the Prague School, which relates sentences to discourse by analyzing the distribution in sentences of old and new discourse information (theme and rheme, respectively).
HN Formerly (1990-1991) DC fu1b.
BT Linguistic Theories
RT Discourse Analysis
    Focus
    Functional Linguistics
    Grammatical Analysis
    Prague School
    Rheme
    Sentences
    Word Order

Functors
Use Function Words

Fundamental Frequency
DC 26600
HN Formerly (1973-1991) DC fu2.
UF Frequency of Voice
    Voice Frequency
BT Frequency (Acoustics)
RT Acoustic Phonetics
    Acoustics
    Pitch (Phonology)
    Speech

Fur (Language)
Use Nilo Saharan Languages

Ga
DC 26750
HN Added, 1992.
UF Incran
BT Kwa Languages

Gabon
DC 26760
HN Added, 1992.
BT Sub Saharan Africa

Gaelic (Irish)
Use Irish Gaelic

Gaelic (Scottish)
Use Scottish Gaelic

Galician
Use Portuguese

Galla
Use Cushitic Languages

Gambia
DC 26780
HN Added, 1992.
BT Sub Saharan Africa

Gaulish
Use Celtic Languages

Gbaya
Use Adamawa Eastern Phylum

Ge Pano Carib Languages
DC 26900
HN Added, 1992.
UF Bororo Languages
    Carib Languages
    Macro Carib Phylum
    Macro Ge Bororo Phylum
    Macro Panoan Phylum
    Pano Languages
    Tacana Languages
BT South Amerindian Languages

Gemination
Use Length (Phonological)

Gender (Grammatical)
DC 27100
SN A type of noun class that determines the form of syntactically related words (eg, adjectives, pronouns); often involves such contrasts as masculine/feminine/neuter or animate/inanimate.
HN Formerly (1973-1991) DC ge1, Gender.
BT Grammatical Categories
RT Adjectives
    Agreement
    Inflection (Morphology)
    Morphology
    Nouns
    Number (Grammatical)
    Person
    Pronouns
    Syntax
    Verbs

General Linguistics (1973-1991)
HN DC ge1a.
Use Linguistics

General Medicine
Use Medicine

Generalization
DC 27200
HN Formerly (1973-1990) DC ge2.
UF Overgeneralization
BT Learning Processes
RT Associative Processes
    Concept Formation
    Creativity (Linguistics)
    Discrimination Learning
    Interference (Learning)
    Interlanguage
    Learning Theories
    Logic
    Mediation Theory
    Transfer (Learning)

Generalized Phrase Structure Grammar
DC 27250
SN A type of generative grammar developed in the 1980s that rejects the deep structure, transformation rules, and coindexing devices of transformational-generative grammar and government and binding theory. Although this type of grammar is context-free, syntactic categories have internal structure; rules are defined by a metagrammar.
HN Added, 1992.
BT Phrase Structure Grammar
RT Agreement
    Grammar Theories
    Grammatical Analysis
    Natural Language Processing
    Phrases
    Principles and Parameters Approach
    Syntax

Generative Grammar
DC 27350
SN Models of grammar that use ordered rules or other processes capable of generating all the well-formed sentences of a language, thereby accounting for the grammaticality or ungrammaticality of individual sentences.
HN Added, 1992. Prior to 1992, see DC tr4, Transformational and Generative Grammar.
UF Network Grammar
    Realistic Grammar
BT Grammar Theories
NT Case Grammar
    Lexical Functional Grammar
    Montague Grammar
    Phrase Structure Grammar
    Relational Grammar
    Transformational Generative Grammar
RT Functional Grammar
    Generative Phonology
    Generative Semantics
    Government Binding Theory
    Government (Grammatical)
    Lexical Phonology
    Linguistic Competence
    Linguistic Performance
    Markedness
    Movement (Grammatical)
    Parsing
    Principles and Parameters Approach
    Pro Drop Parameter
    Psycholinguistics
    Reflexivity
    Sentence Structure
    Syntax
    Trace Theory
    X Bar Theory

Generative Phonology
DC 27550
SN An approach to the phonetic realization of syntactic structures developed by Morris Halle and others during the 1950s and 1960s; it has been associated with transformational-generative grammar, its successors, and its variants.
HN Formerly (1973-1991) DC ge3.
UF Natural Generative Phonology
BT Phonology
RT Autosegmental Phonology
    Distinctive Features
    Generative Grammar
    Linguistic Competence
    Markedness
    Mora
    Natural Phonology
    Opacity
    Phonemics
    Phonetics
    Phonological Change
    Surface Structure
    Transformational Generative Grammar

Generative Semantics
DC 27580
HN Added, 1992.
BT Semantics
RT Generative Grammar
    Semantic Analysis
    Sentence Structure
    Transformational Generative Grammar

Generative Transformational Gram-mar
Use Transformational Generative Grammar

Genetics
DC 27600
HN Added, 1992. Prior to 1992, see DC he5, Heredity.
UF Heredity (1973-1991)
RT Biology
Disorders
Downs Syndrome
Medicine

Genitive Case
Use Case

Geographical Dialects
Use Regional Dialects

Geographical Linguistics
Use Areal Linguistics

Georgia (Republic)
DC 27640
HN Added, 1992.
BT Commonwealth of Independent States
RT Union of Soviet Socialist Republics

Georgia (USA)
DC 27650
HN Added, 1992.
BT Southern States
United States of America
RT Appalachia

Georgian
Use Caucasian Languages

German
DC 27700
HN Formerly (1973-1991) DC ge4.
UF Bavarian
Middle High German
Old High German
Plattdeutsch
Silesian
BT Germanic Languages
NT German as a Second Language
RT Yiddish

German as a Second Language
DC 27750
HN Added, 1992.
BT German
Second Languages

German Democratic Republic
Use Germany

Germanic Languages
DC 27800
HN Formerly (1973-1991) DC ge5.
BT Indo European Languages
NT Afrikaans
Danish
Dutch
English
Flemish
Frisian
German
Gothic
Icelandic
Norwegian
Swedish
Yiddish
RT Scandinavian Languages

Germany
DC 27820
HN Added, 1992.
UF East Germany
Federal Republic of Germany
German Democratic Republic
West Germany
BT Western Europe

Gestalt Theory
DC 27850
HN Formerly (1973-1991) DC ge6.
RT Cognitive Processes
Linguistic Theories
Perception
Psycholinguistics

Gestalt Therapy
Use Psychotherapy

Gestures
DC 27950
HN Formerly (1973-1991) DC ge8.
BT Nonverbal Communication
RT Facial Expressions
Kinesics
Nonverbal Languages
Paralinguistics
Sign Language
Speech

Ghana
DC 28000
HN Added, 1992.
BT Sub Saharan Africa

Gheg
Use Albanian

Gibraltar
DC 28050
HN Added, 1992.
BT Western Europe

Gift of Tongues
Use Glossolalia

Glossaries
Use Dictionaries

Glossolalia
DC 28150
SN Spontaneous, generally unintelligible speech occuring during episodes of extreme religious fervor, hypnotic or mediumistic trances, or psychopathic states.
HN Formerly (1973-1991) DC gl1.
UF Gift of Tongues
Speaking in Tongues
RT Artificial Languages
Mental Disorders
Religions

Glottochronology
Use Diachronic Linguistics

Glottodidactics
Use Second Language Instruction

Goal Agent Relationship (Grammati-cal)
Use Agent Patient Relationship (Gram-matical)

Goor Languages
Use Gur Languages

Gothic
DC 28200
HN Added, 1992.
BT Germanic Languages

Government (Grammatical)
DC 28300
SN A traditional concept in grammar that has gained renewed currency in government and binding theory; a grammatical relation between two sentence constituents such that the presence of one determines the form or other properties of the other.
HN Added, 1992.
UF Syntactic Government
RT Agreement
Case
Case Marking
Dependency Grammar
Generative Grammar
Government Binding Theory
Grammatical Analysis
Grammatical Relations
Inflection (Morphology)
Morphology
Syntax

Government Binding Theory
DC 28350
SN A model of grammar distinguished by having two levels of syntactic representation called D-structure and S-structure, logical form, and phonetic form, all related by movement and constraints on movement. It is used as a collective designation for theories of government, binding, bounding, and control, the projection principle, theta criterion, and empty category principle.
HN Formerly (1987-1991) DC go1, Government & Binding Theory.
BT Grammar Theories
RT Agent Patient Relationship (Gram-matical)
Agreement
Anaphora
Case
Extended Standard Theory
Generalized Phrase Structure Gram-mar
Generative Grammar
Government (Grammatical)
Grammatical Analysis
Incorporation (Grammatical)
Logical Form
Movement (Grammatical)
Principles and Parameters Approach
Pro Drop Parameter
Reference (Grammatical)
Reflexivity
Syntax
Thematic Roles
Trace Theory
Well Formedness
Wh Phrases
X Bar Theory

Grabar
Use Armenian

Grade School Students
Use Elementary School Students

Graduate Education
DC 28400
HN Formerly (1973-1991) included in DC gr1, Graduate and Professional Schools.

Graduate Education (cont'd)
- **UF** College Graduate Education
  University Graduate Education
- **BT** Higher Education
- **RT** College Students
  Professional Education

Graffiti
- **DC** 28450
- **HN** Added, 1992.
- **RT** Communicative Function of Language
  Expressive Function of Language
  Sociolinguistics
  Written Language

Grammaire générale et raisonnée
- **Use** Port Royal School

Grammar Instruction
- **DC** 28550
- **HN** Added, 1992.
- **BT** Instruction
- **RT** Agrammatism
  Educational Activities
  Grammar Translation Method of Language Teaching
  Grammatical Categories
  Grammatical Relations
  Grammaticality
  Language Arts
  Native Language Instruction
  Second Language Instruction
  Syntax

Grammar Theories
- **DC** 28600
- **HN** Added, 1992.
- **BT** Linguistic Theories
- **NT** Autolexical Grammar
  Categorial Grammar
  Context Free Grammar
  Context Sensitive Grammar
  Dependency Grammar
  Extended Standard Theory
  Functional Grammar
  Generalized Phrase Structure Grammar
  Generative Grammar
  Government Binding Theory
  Prescriptive Grammar
  Principles and Parameters Approach
  Stratificational Grammar
  Universal Grammar
  X Bar Theory
- **RT** Deep Structure
  Grammatical Analysis
  Grammatical Relations
  Incorporation (Grammatical)
  Movement (Grammatical)
  Surface Structure
  Syntagmatic Relations
  Syntax
  Systemic Linguistics
  Tagmemics
  Taxonomic Approaches
  Transformation Rules
  Well Formedness

Grammar Translation Method of Language Teaching
- **DC** 28650
- **HN** Added, 1992.
- **BT** Language Teaching Methods
- **RT** Grammar Instruction
  Second Language Instruction
  Translation

Grammatical Acceptability
- **Use** Grammaticality

Grammatical Ambiguity
- **Use** Ambiguity

Grammatical Analysis
- **DC** 28700
- **HN** Formerly (1973-1991) DC gr2.
- **UF** Syntactic Analysis
- **NT** Parsing
- **RT** Agent Patient Relationship (Grammatical)
  Agreement
  Autolexical Grammar
  Case Marking
  Categorial Grammar
  Clauses
  Comparative Linguistics
  Computer Generated Language Analysis
  Declarative Sentences
  Deep Structure
  Discourse Analysis
  Ellipsis
  Embedded Construction
  Focus
  Form Classes
  Functional Grammar
  Functional Sentence Perspective
  Generalized Phrase Structure Grammar
  Government (Grammatical)
  Government Binding Theory
  Grammar Theories
  Grammatical Categories
  Grammatical Change
  Grammatical Relations
  Grammaticality
  Idioms
  Imperative Sentences
  Interrogative Sentences
  Linguistic Units
  Logical Form
  Montague Grammar
  Morphology
  Movement (Grammatical)
  Phrase Structure Grammar
  Phrases
  Port Royal School
  Principles and Parameters Approach
  Redundancy
  Reference (Grammatical)
  Reflexivity
  Semantic Analysis
  Semantics
  Sentence Structure
  Sentences
  Statistical Analysis
  Stratificational Grammar
  Structuralist Linguistics
  Surface Structure
  Syntactic Structures
  Syntax
  Tagmemics
  Word Order

Grammatical Categories
- **DC** 28750
- **HN** Added, 1992.
- **NT** Aspect
  Case
  Gender (Grammatical)
  Mood (Grammatical)
  Number (Grammatical)
  Person
  Tense
  Voice (Grammatical)
- **RT** Form Classes
  Grammar Instruction

Grammatical Categories (cont'd)
- **RT** Grammatical Analysis
  Morphology
  Parsing
  Predicate
  Prepositions
  Semantic Fields
  Syntax

Grammatical Change
- **DC** 28950
- **SN** Change over time in the syntax and/or morphology of a language.
- **HN** Formerly (1973-1991) DC gr3.
- **UF** Syntactic Change
- **BT** Language Change
- **RT** Analogy (Language Change)
  Diachronic Linguistics
  Etymology
  Grammatical Analysis
  Morphological Change
  Syntax

Grammatical Person
- **Use** Person

Grammatical Relations
- **DC** 29150
- **SN** Relations posited to exist between linguistic units (morphemes, words, phrases, etc.) within the domain of word and sentence structure.
- **HN** Formerly (1988-1991) DC re9c, Relation (Grammatical).
- **UF** Paradigmatic Relations
  Relations (Grammatical) (1973-1991)
  Syntactic Relations
- **NT** Agent Patient Relationship (Grammatical)
  Syntagmatic Relations
- **RT** Agreement
  Case Marking
  Dependency Grammar
  Government (Grammatical)
  Grammar Instruction
  Grammar Theories
  Grammatical Analysis
  Linguistic Units
  Logical Form
  Parsing
  Predicate
  Reference (Grammatical)
  Relational Grammar
  Subject (Grammatical)
  Syntax
  Word Order

Grammaticality
- **DC** 29200
- **SN** A consensus of native speaker judgments that a given sentence or other linguistic construct conforms to the system of their language.
- **HN** Added, 1992.
- **UF** Grammatical Acceptability
  Ungrammaticality
- **RT** Anomalous Strings
  Creativity (Linguistics)
  Error Analysis
  Fluency
  Grammar Instruction
  Grammatical Analysis
  Idioms
  Language Acquisition
  Language Attitudes
  Language Processing
  Language Usage
  Linguistic Competence
  Native Speakers

Grammaticality (cont'd)
- RT Prescriptive Grammar
-     Psycholinguistics
-     Second Language Learning
-     Social Factors
-     Sociolinguistics
-     Spoken Written Language Relationship
-     Syntactic Processing
-     Syntax
-     Well Formedness

Grapheme Phoneme Correspondence
- DC 29250
- HN Formerly (1973-1991) DC gr4.
- UF Letter Sound Correspondence
-     Phoneme Grapheme Correspondence
- RT Decoding (Reading)
-     Graphemics
-     Language Patterns
-     Miscue Analysis
-     Orthographic Symbols
-     Orthography
-     Phonemic Transcription
-     Phonemes
-     Phonemics
-     Phonics
-     Phonology
-     Reading
-     Spelling Instruction
-     Spoken Written Language Relationship
-     Written Language

Graphemic Analysis
- Use Graphemics

Graphemics
- DC 29350
- HN Formerly (1973-1991) DC gr5.
- UF Graphemic Analysis
- RT Grapheme Phoneme Correspondence
-     Orthographic Symbols
-     Orthography
-     Phonemes
-     Phonemics
-     Punctuation
-     Written Language
-     Writing Systems

Great Britain
- DC 29400
- SN England, Scotland, and Wales.
- HN Added, 1992.
- BT United Kingdom
- NT England
-     Scotland
-     Wales

Greece
- DC 29550
- HN Added, 1992.
- BT Balkan States
-     Mediterranean Countries
-     Western Europe

Greek
- DC 29600
- HN Formerly (1973-1991) DC gr6, Greek, Ancient & Modern.
- UF Hellenic
- BT Indo European Languages
- NT Ancient Greek

Greenland
- DC 29650
- HN Added, 1992.
- BT North America
-     Scandinavia
- RT Arctic Regions

Greenlandic
- Use Eskimo Aleut Languages

Grice, H. Paul
- DC 29720
- SN Born 1912 - Died 1988.
- HN Added, 1992.

Grimaces
- Use Facial Expressions

Grimm, Jacob and Wilhelm
- DC 29730
- SN Jacob: Born 1785 - Died 1863; Wilhelm: Born 1786 - Died 1863.
- HN Added, 1992.
- UF Bruder Grimm

Group Communication
- DC 29750
- HN Formerly (1973-1991) DC co3, Communication in Groups.
- UF Communication in Groups (1973-1991)
- BT Communication
- RT Classroom Communication
-     Conversation
-     Interpersonal Communication
-     Secret Languages
-     Turn Taking

Guahibo Pamigua Languages
- Use Andean Equatorial Phylum

Guang
- Use Akan

Guatemala
- DC 29800
- HN Added, 1992.
- BT Central America

Guillaume, Gustave
- DC 29900
- SN Born 1883 - Died 1960.
- HN Formerly (1973-1991) DC gu1, Guillaume.

Guinea
- DC 29910
- HN Added, 1992.
- BT Sub Saharan Africa

Guinea Bissau
- DC 29930
- HN Added, 1992.
- BT Sub Saharan Africa

Gujarati
- Use Indic Languages

Gur Languages
- DC 29950
- HN Added, 1992.
- UF Goor Languages
-     Lele
-     Mossi
-     Senufo
-     Voltaic Languages
- BT Niger Congo Languages

Guyana
- DC 30200
- HN Added, 1992.
- UF British Guiana
- BT South America

Gymnasium (German)
- Use Secondary Education

Gypsies
- DC 30220
- HN Added, 1992.
- UF Romani (People)
- BT European Cultural Groups
- RT Migrants
-     Romany (Language)

Gypsy (Language)
- Use Romany (Language)

Hadza
- Use Khoisan Languages

Halle, Morris
- DC 30380
- SN Born 1923 -.
- HN Formerly (1973-1991) DC ha1.

Halliday, Michael Alexander Kirkwood
- DC 30400
- SN Born 1925 - .
- HN Formerly (1973-1991) DC ha1a, Halliday.

Hamito-Semitic Languages
- Use Afroasiatic Languages

Handedness
- DC 30450
- HN Formerly (1973-1991) DC ha2.
- UF Ambidexterity
-     Left Handedness
-     Right Handedness
- RT Cerebral Dominance
-     Handwriting

Handicapped
- DC 30550
- HN Formerly (1973-1991) DC ha2a, Handicap.
- UF Disabled
- RT Articulation Disorders
-     Hearing Disorders
-     Learning Disabilities
-     Mental Retardation
-     Muscular Disorders
-     Nervous System Disorders
-     Phonation Disorders
-     Special Education (Handicapped)
-     Therapy
-     Vision Disorders
-     Voice Disorders

Handwriting
- DC 30600
- HN Formerly (1973-1991) DC ha3.
- UF Cursive Writing
-     Printscript (Handwriting)
- BT Language Arts
- RT Handedness
-     Writing
-     Writing Disorders
-     Written Language
-     Written Language Instruction

Haptic Perception
Use Tactual Perception

Hard of Hearing
Use Hearing Disorders

Hare Lip
Use Cleft Palate

Harris, Zellig Sabbettai
DC 30650
SN Born 1909 - Died 1992.
HN Formerly (1973-1991) DC ha4, Harris.

Hatsa
Use Khoisan Languages

Hausa
DC 30850
HN Added, 1992.
BT Chadic Languages

Hawaii
DC 30900
HN Added, 1992.
BT Polynesia
     United States of America

Hawaiian
Use Polynesian Languages

Hearing
DC 31150
HN Added, 1992.
UF Audition
BT Sensory Systems
RT Acoustics
     Audiology
     Audiometry
     Auditory Localization
     Auditory Masking
     Auditory Perception
     Auditory Stimulation
     Auditory System
     Auditory Thresholds
     Delayed Auditory Feedback
     Ear Preference
     Hearing Disorders
     Listening
     Noise
     Psychoacoustics
     Speech Perception

Hearing Aids
DC 31250
HN Formerly (1973-1991) DC he1.
UF Cochlear Implants
BT Prosthetic Devices
RT Audiology
     Auditory System
     Hearing Disorders
     Hearing Improvement

Hearing Conservation
DC 31350
HN Formerly (1973-1991) included in DC he2, Hearing Conservation and Improvement.
RT Audiology
     Hearing Disorders
     Noise

Hearing Conservation and Improvement (1973-1991)
DC 31360
HN DC he2, deleted 1992. See now Hearing Conservation or Hearing Improvement.

Hearing Disorders
DC 31450
HN Formerly (1973-1991) DC he3a.
UF Auditory Disorders
     Aural Disorders
     Deafness
     Dysacusis
     Hard of Hearing
     Hearing Loss
     Hypoacusis
     Presbyacusis
BT Disorders
NT Menieres Disease
RT Audiology
     Audiometry
     Auditory Perception
     Auditory System
     Auditory Thresholds
     Handicapped
     Hearing
     Hearing Aids
     Hearing Conservation
     Hearing Improvement
     Lipreading
     Phonetically Balanced Lists
     Proprioception
     Sign Language
     Special Education (Handicapped)
     Speech Pathology
     Speech Therapy

Hearing Improvement
DC 31550
HN Formerly (1973-1991) included in DC he2, Hearing Conservation and Improvement.
RT Hearing Disorders
     Hearing Aids
     Surgery
     Therapy

Hearing Loss
Use Hearing Disorders

Hearing Measurement
Use Audiometry

Hearing Structures
Use Auditory System

Hearing Testing
Use Audiometry

Hearing Thresholds
Use Auditory Thresholds

Hebrew
DC 31650
HN Added, 1992.
BT Semitic Languages

Hellenic
Use Greek

Helping Verbs
Use Auxiliary Verbs

Hemispheric Dominance
Use Cerebral Dominance

Heredity (1973-1991)
HN DC he5.
Use Genetics

Hidden Markov Models
Use Markov Models

Hieroglyphics
Use Writing Systems

High School Education
Use Secondary Education

High School Students
DC 31700
HN Added, 1992.
BT Secondary School Students
RT Adolescents
     Junior High School Students
     Secondary Education

Higher Education
DC 31750
HN Added, 1992.
UF Postsecondary Education
     Tertiary Education
BT Education
NT Graduate Education
     Professional Education
     Undergraduate Education
RT College Students

Himalayan States
DC 31850
HN Added, 1992.
BT South Asia
NT Bhutan
     Nepal

Hindi
DC 31950
HN Added, 1992.
UF Urdu
BT Indic Languages

Hispanic Americans
DC 32100
HN Added, 1992.
UF Spanish Americans
BT North American Cultural Groups
NT Mexican Americans
RT Anglo Americans
     Asian Americans
     Black Americans
     Jewish Americans

Historical Linguistics
Use Diachronic Linguistics

History of Language
Use Diachronic Linguistics

History of Linguistics
DC 32150
HN Formerly (1973-1991) DC hi1.
RT Linguistic Theories
     Linguistics
     Linguistics Instruction
     Linguists
     London School
     Neogrammarians
     Port Royal School
     Prague School
     Stratificational Grammar
     Theoretical Linguistics

Hitchiti
Use Muskogean Languages

Hittite
Use Anatolian Languages

Hjelmslev, Louis
DC 32200
SN Born 1899 - Died 1965.
HN Formerly (1973-1991) DC hj1, Hjelmslev.

Hmong
Use Sino Tibetan Languages

Hoarseness
Use Voice Disorders

Hokan Phylum
Use North Amerindian Languages

Holland
Use Netherlands

Homographs
DC 32350
SN Words identical in spelling, but different on phonological, morphological, syntactic, or semantic grounds.
HN Formerly (1977-1991) DC hm1, Homograph.
BT Lexicon
RT Ambiguity
Meaning
Orthography
Semantics
Word Meaning

Homonyms
DC 32450
SN Words identical in form, but different on morphological, syntactic, or semantic grounds.
HN Formerly (1973-1991) DC ho1, Homonym.
BT Lexicon
RT Ambiguity
Homophones
Meaning
Polysemy
Semantics
Word Meaning

Homophones
DC 32550
SN Words identical in phonemic shape (pronunciation), but different on orthographic, morphological, syntactic, or semantic grounds.
HN Formerly (1973-1991) DC ho2, Homophone.
BT Lexicon
RT Ambiguity
Homonyms
Meaning
Semantics
Word Meaning

Honduras
DC 32650
HN Added, 1992.
BT Central America

Hong Kong
DC 32750
HN Added, 1992.
BT Far East
RT Peoples Republic of China

Hottentot Languages
Use Khoisan Languages

Hue
Use Color

Human Animal Communication
Use Interspecies Communication

Human Computer Communication
DC 32790
HN Added, 1992.
UF Computer Human Communication
BT Communication
RT Artificial Intelligence
Computer Applications
Computer Assisted Instruction
Computer Languages
Cybernetics

Human Information Processing
Use Cognitive Processes

Human Subjects (Research)
Use Research Subjects

Humboldt, Karl Wilhelm von
DC 32800
SN Born 1767 - Died 1835.
HN Added, 1992.

Humor
DC 32950
HN Formerly (1973-1991) DC hu3a.
UF Jokes
RT Fiction
Literary Genres
Literature
Word Play

Hungarian
DC 33150
HN Added, 1992.
BT Ugric Languages

Hungary
DC 33200
HN Added, 1992.
BT Eastern Europe

Husbands
Use Spouses

Hyperbole
Use Rhetorical Figures

Hypoacusis
Use Hearing Disorders

Iberian
DC 33300
HN Added, 1992.
BT Language Isolates

Ibo
DC 33350
HN Added, 1992.
UF Igbo
BT Kwa Languages

Iceland
DC 33550
HN Added, 1992.
BT Scandinavia

Icelandic
DC 33600
HN Added, 1992.
BT Germanic Languages
Scandinavian Languages

Idaho
DC 33650
HN Added, 1992.
BT United States of America
Western States

Identification
DC 33700
HN Formerly (1973-1991)DC id1.
NT Sound Identification
RT Familiarity
Perception
Recognition

Identity (Personal)
Use Self Concept

Ideograph Recognition
Use Letter Recognition

Ideographs
DC 33800
SN Conventional graphic representations, forming part of a writing system and corresponding to semantic units or constructs, words, morphemes, or other units of language, but usually not corresponding consistently to phonological units as such.
HN Added, 1992.
UF Characters (Written Language)
BT Writing Systems
RT Alphabets
Orthographic Symbols

Idiomatic Expressions
Use Idioms

Idiomatic Speech (1973-1991)
HN DC id2.
Use Idioms

Idioms
DC 34150
HN Added, 1992.
UF Idiomatic Expressions
Idiomatic Speech (1973-1991)
BT Lexicon
RT Colloquial Language
Dialects
Grammatical Analysis
Grammaticality
Language Patterns
Language Styles
Languages
Meaning
Phraseologisms
Phraseology
Regional Dialects
Semantics
Slang
Syntagmatic Relations
Syntax

If Clauses
Use Conditional Clauses

Igbo
Use Ibo

Ijo
Use Kwa Languages

Illinois
DC 34250
HN Added, 1992.
BT Midwestern States
United States of America

Illinois Test of Psycholinguistic Abilities
DC 34350
SN Formal standardized test designed to assess children's auditory and visual reception, association, sequential memory, and closure, as well as verbal and manual expression, grammatical closure, and sound blending.
HN Formerly (1973-1991) DC il1.
BT Tests
RT Intelligence Tests
Language Tests

Illiteracy
Use Literacy

Illiterate Adults
Use Adult Literacy

Illocutionary Acts
Use Speech Acts

Imagery
DC 34400
HN Formerly (1973-1991) DC im1.
UF Cognitive Imagery
Visual Imagery
RT Cognitive Processes
Language Thought Relationship
Literature
Metaphors
Rhetorical Figures
Symbolism
Visual Media

Imitation
DC 34600
HN Formerly (1973-1991) DC im2.
UF Modeling
RT Child Language
Language Acquisition
Learning Processes
Pronunciation
Second Language Learning
Socialization

Immediate Recall
Use Short Term Memory

Immersion Programs
DC 34650
HN Added, 1992.
RT Bilingual Education
Bilingualism
Child Language
Early Second Language Learning
FLES
Language of Instruction
Language Planning
Native Speakers
Second Language Instruction
Second Language Learning
Second Languages

Immigrants
DC 34670
HN Added, 1992.
RT Acculturation
Cross Cultural Communication
Cultural Background
Foreigners
Migrants
Minority Groups
Refugees
Second Language Learning

Imperative Sentences
DC 34700
HN Added, 1992.
UF Commands
BT Sentences
RT Declarative Sentences
Grammatical Analysis
Interrogative Sentences
Mood (Grammatical)
Subjunctive
Verbs

Implicature
DC 34800
SN The use of unwritten cooperative rules of conversation to communicate unexpressed meanings; also, any interpretation of a speaker's intended meaning based on such rules.
HN Formerly (1981-1991) DC im3a.
UF Conversational Implicature
BT Meaning
RT Conversation
Pragmatics
Semantic Analysis
Semantics
Word Meaning

Implosives
Use Stops

Inanimate Nouns
Use Animacy and Inanimacy

Incorporation (Grammatical)
DC 35000
HN Added, 1992.
RT Affixes
Government Binding Theory
Grammar Theories
Inflection (Morphology)
Morphology
Movement (Grammatical)
Nouns
Pro Drop Parameter
Thematic Roles
Verbs
X Bar Theory

Incran
Use Ga

Indefinite Articles
Use Articles

Indexical Expressions
Use Deixis

India
DC 35100
HN Added, 1992.
BT South Asia
RT Burushaski

Indiana
DC 35200
HN Added, 1992.
BT Midwestern States
United States of America

Indians (American)
Use American Indians

Indic Languages
DC 35300
HN Formerly (1973-1991) DC in1.
UF Dardic Languages
Gujarati
Indo Aryan Languages
Marathi
Nepalese
Panjabi
Punjabi
Rajasthani
Sindhi
Sinhalese
BT Indo European Languages
NT Bengali
Hindi
Romany (Language)
Sanskrit
RT Iranian Languages

Indigenous Languages
DC 35320
HN Added, 1992.
UF Autochthonous Languages
BT Languages
RT Areal Linguistics
Bilingualism
Borrowing
Code Switching
Creoles
Cross Cultural Communication
Descriptive Linguistics
Diachronic Linguistics
Diglossia
Ethnographic Linguistics
Indigenous Populations
Language Change
Language Contact
Language Death
Language Diversity
Language Maintenance
Language Rights
Language Shifts
Language Status
Language Use
Minority Languages
Multilingualism
Pidgins
Sociolinguistics
Trade Languages
Unknown Languages

Indigenous Populations
DC 35350
HN Added, 1992.
RT Aboriginal Australians
Acculturation
American Indians
Cross Cultural Communication
Cultural Change
Cultural Differences
Foreigners
Indigenous Languages
Language Contact
Minority Groups

Indo Aryan Languages
Use Indic Languages

Indo European Languages
DC 35400
HN Formerly (1979-1991) DC in1a, Indo-European Languages.
BT Languages
NT Albanian
Anatolian Languages
Armenian
Baltic Languages
Celtic Languages
Germanic Languages
Greek
Indic Languages
Iranian Languages
Italic Languages
Proto Indo European
Romance Languages
Slavic Languages

Indo Pacific Languages
DC 35450
HN Formerly (1984-1991) DC in2aa, Indo-Pacific Languages.
UF Papuan Languages
Melanesian Languages
New Guinea Non Austronesian Languages
BT Languages

Indo-Iranian Languages (1973-1991)
- HN DC in2, deleted 1992. See now Indic Languages or Iranian Languages.

Indonesia
- DC 35500
- HN Added, 1992.
- BT Southeast Asia

Inductive Logic
- Use Logic

Industry
- Use Business

Infant Vocalization
- DC 35650
- HN Formerly (1973-1991) DC in3.
- UF Crying (Infant)
       Infantile Vocalization
- BT Phonation
- RT Baby Talk
       Child Language
       Children
       Infants
       Language Acquisition
       Nonverbal Communication

Infantile Vocalization
- Use Infant Vocalization

Infants
- DC 35660
- SN Persons aged 0 to 24 months.
- HN Added, 1992.
- BT Children
- RT Baby Talk
       Child Language
       Infant Vocalization
       Language Acquisition
       Maternal Speech
       Nonverbal Communication
       Parent Child Interaction

Infinitives
- DC 35700
- HN Added, 1992.
- BT Verbs
- RT Tense

Infixes
- Use Affixes

Inflection (1973-1991)
- HN DC in4, deleted 1991. See now Inflection (Morphology) or Intonation.

Inflection (Morphology)
- DC 35850
- SN The process or result of adding an affix to a word to signal certain grammatical relationships (eg, case, possessives, tense).
- HN Added, 1992. Prior to 1992, see Inflection.
- UF Declension
       Flection
- BT Word Formation
- RT Affixes
       Agreement
       Case
       Case Marking
       Conjugation
       Derivation (Morphology)
       Gender (Grammatical)
       Government (Grammatical)
       Incorporation (Grammatical)
       Morphology
       Number (Grammatical)

Inflection (Morphology) (cont'd)
- RT Person
       Roots (Morphology)
       Syntax
       Tense
       Word Order

Inflection (Phonology)
- Use Intonation

Inflectional Endings
- Use Suffixes

Informants
- Use Respondents

Information Processing
- DC 35900
- HN Added, 1992.
- BT Cognitive Processes
- NT Data Collection
- RT Associative Processes
       Communication
       Cybernetics
       Data Processing
       Decoding (Cognitive Process)
       Encoding (Cognitive Process)
       Language Thought Relationship
       Learning Processes
       Learning Theories
       Memory
       Semantic Processing

Ingressive Air Flow
- Use Air Flow

Initial Teaching Alphabet
- DC 36200
- HN Formerly (1973-1991) DC in5.
- UF ITA
- BT Alphabets
- RT Beginning Reading
       Phonics
       Reading
       Reading Instruction
       Remedial Reading

Inner Ear (1973-1991)
- HN DC in6.
- Use Auditory System

Inner Speech
- DC 36300
- HN Added, 1992.
- UF Subliminal Speech
       Subvocal Response (1973-1991)
       Subvocalization
- BT Speech
- RT Cognitive Processes
       Language Thought Relationship
       Private Language
       Silent Reading
       Spontaneous Speech
       Whispering

Innovativeness
- Use Creativity (Psychology)

Insanity
- Use Psychosis

Instruction
- DC 36350
- HN Added, 1992.
- UF Pedagogy
       Teaching (Process)
- NT Grammar Instruction
       Linguistics Instruction
       Native Language Instruction

Instruction (cont'd)
- NT Oral Language Instruction
       Programmed Instruction
       Reading Instruction
       Second Language Instruction
       Spelling Instruction
       Translation Instruction
       Vocabulary Instruction
       Written Language Instruction
- RT Classroom Observation
       Education
       Educational Activities
       Language of Instruction
       Learning
       Student Teacher Relationship
       Teachers
       Teaching Materials
       Teaching Methods

Instructional Language
- Use Language of Instruction

Instructional Materials
- Use Teaching Materials

Instructional Methods
- Use Teaching Methods

Instructor Attitudes
- Use Teacher Attitudes

Instructors
- Use Teachers

Insults
- Use Verbal Aggression

Intellectual Development
- Use Cognitive Development

Intelligence
- DC 36450
- HN Formerly (1973-1991) DC in8.
- UF Intelligence Quotient
       IQ
- RT Artificial Intelligence
       Cognitive Processes
       Comprehension
       Creativity (Psychology)
       Intelligence Tests
       Language Thought Relationship
       Mental Retardation
       Problem Solving

Intelligence Quotient
- Use Intelligence

Intelligence Tests
- DC 36550
- HN Formerly (1973-1991) DC in9, Intelligence Testing.
- UF Stanford Binet Test
       Wechsler Intelligence Tests
- BT Tests
- NT Peabody Picture Vocabulary Test
- RT Aptitude Tests
       Illinois Test of Psycholinguistic Abilities
       Intelligence
       Psychometric Analysis

Intelligibility
- DC 36600
- HN Formerly (1973-1990) in11.
- UF Speech Intelligibility
- RT Communication
       Communicative Competence
       Dialects
       Diglossia

Intelligibility (cont'd)
- RT Foreign Accent
  Languages
  Linguistic Accommodation
  Native Nonnative Speaker Communication
  Oral Language
  Pronunciation
  Pronunciation Accuracy
  Speech
  Speech Rate

Intensity (Acoustics)
- DC 36650
- HN Formerly (1973-1991) DC in12, Intensity of Vibration.
- UF Loudness
  Volume (Acoustics)
- RT Accentuation
  Acoustic Phonetics
  Acoustics
  Auditory Stimulation
  Noise

Inter Andine Languages
- Use Macro Chibchan Phylum

Interactive Video
- DC 36750
- HN Added, 1992.
- RT Computer Assisted Instruction
  Computer Software
  Teaching Materials

Intercultural Communication
- Use Cross Cultural Communication

Interference (Learning)
- DC 37150
- SN Negative effects on learning caused by competing memories, thoughts, or behavior patterns.
- HN Added, 1992.
- NT Linguistic Interference
- RT Feedback
  Generalization
  Learning
  Learning Processes
  Memory
  Retention (Memory)
  Stroop Color Word Test
  Transfer (Learning)

Interlanguage
- DC 37250
- SN Unique and evolving language system created and used by an individual in the process of learning a second language; represents a transition from the native language to the target language.
- HN Added, 1992.
- BT Language
- RT Error Analysis (Language)
  Generalization
  Learning Processes
  Linguistic Competence
  Linguistic Interference
  Linguistic Performance
  Psycholinguistics
  Second Language Learning
  Second Languages
  Transfer (Learning)

Interlingua
- Use International Languages

Internal Juncture
- Use Juncture

International Languages
- DC 37350
- HN Formerly (1973-1991) DC in14.
- UF Francais Fondamental
  Interlingua
- BT Languages
- NT English as an International Language
  Esperanto
- RT Artificial Languages
  Cross Cultural Communication
  Language Status
  Trade Languages

International Phonetic Alphabet
- DC 37450
- HN Added, 1992.
- UF IPA
- BT Alphabets
- RT Phonetic Transcription
  Place of Articulation
  Pronunciation

Interpersonal Behavior
- DC 37550
- HN Formerly (1973-1991) DC in15.
- NT Adult Child Interaction
  Dyadic Interaction
- RT Address Forms
  Autism
  Interpersonal Communication
  Politeness
  Silence
  Social Perception
  Socialization
  Speech Communities
  Stereotypes
  Student Teacher Relationship
  Verbal Aggression

Interpersonal Communication
- DC 37700
- HN Added, 1992. Prior to 1992 see Interpersonal Behavior.
- BT Communication
- NT Conversation
  Native Nonnative Speaker Communication
  Verbal Aggression
- RT Address Forms
  Adult Child Interaction
  Communicative Competence
  Credibility
  Functional Linguistics
  Group Communication
  Interpersonal Behavior
  Interviews
  Nonverbal Communication
  Oral Language
  Parent Child Interaction
  Persuasion
  Practitioner Patient Relationship
  Pragmatics
  Secret Languages
  Social Perception
  Speech
  Speech Communities
  Spontaneous Speech
  Student Teacher Relationship
  Turn Taking

Interpersonal Perception
- Use Social Perception

Interpretation
- Use Translation

Interpreters
- Use Translators

Interpreting
- Use Translation

Interrogative Sentences
- DC 37800
- HN Formerly (1973-1991) DC in16, Interrogative Statement.
- UF Questions
- BT Sentences
- RT Declarative Sentences
  Grammatical Analysis
  Imperative Sentences
  Mood (Grammatical)
  Negation
  Wh Phrases

Interspecies Communication
- DC 37900
- HN Formerly (1973-1991) DC in13, Inter- and Intraspecies Communication.
- UF Animal Human Communication
  Human Animal Communication
- BT Communication
- RT Animal Communication
  Primates

Interviewees
- Use Respondents

Interviews
- DC 37950
- HN Added, 1992.
- RT Data Collection
  Dyadic Interaction
  Fieldwork
  Interpersonal Communication
  Measures (Instruments)
  Research Design
  Respondents
  Surveys
  Verbal Accounts

Intonation
- DC 38100
- SN Meaningful, discrete, and contrastive patterns of pitch, stress, and/or juncture occurring over the full extent of utterances or utterance fragments.
- HN Formerly (1973-1991) DC in17.
- UF Inflection (Phonology)
- BT Suprasegmentals
- RT Accentuation
  Expressive Function of Language
  Functional Grammar
  Morphology
  Paralinguistics
  Phonemes
  Phonology
  Pitch (Phonology)
  Sentences
  Stress
  Syllables
  Tone

Intra Oral Air Pressure (1973-1991)
- HN DC in18.
- Use Air Flow

Inuit
- Use Eskimo Aleut Languages

Inupiak
  Use Eskimo Aleut Languages

Invented Spelling
  Use Spelling Errors

Inventories (Measures)
  Use Measures (Instruments)

Iowa
  DC 38200
  HN Added, 1992.
  BT Midwestern States
       United States of America

IPA
  Use International Phonetic Alphabet

IQ
  Use Intelligence

Iran
  DC 38300
  HN Added, 1992.
  UF Persia
  BT Middle East

Iranian Languages
  DC 38400
  HN Added, 1992.
  UF Avestan
       Kurdish
       Ossetic
       Pashto
  BT Indo European Languages
  NT Persian
  RT Indic Languages

Iraq
  DC 38500
  HN Added, 1992.
  BT Arab Countries
       Middle East

Ireland
  DC 38600
  HN Added, 1992.
  BT Western Europe
  RT Northern Ireland

Irish Gaelic
  DC 38700
  HN Added, 1992.
  UF Connacht
       Gaelic (Irish)
       Leinster
       Munster
  BT Celtic Languages

Iroquois
  Use Macro Siouan Phylum

Israel
  DC 38800
  HN Added, 1992.
  BT Mediterranean Countries
       Middle East
  RT Palestine

ITA
  Use Initial Teaching Alphabet

Italian
  DC 38950
  HN Formerly (1973-1991) DC it1.
  BT Romance Languages

Italic Languages
  DC 38960
  HN Added, 1992.
  UF Camuni
       Faliscan
       Oscan
       Paelignian
       Sabellian
       Umbrian
  BT Indo European Languages
  NT Latin
  RT Romance Languages

Italy
  DC 39100
  HN Added, 1992.
  BT Mediterranean Countries
       Western Europe
  NT Sardinia
       Sicily
  RT San Marino

Ivory Coast
  DC 39180
  HN Added, 1992.
  BT Sub Saharan Africa

Jakobson, Roman
  DC 39200
  SN Born 1896 - Died 1982.
  HN Formerly (1973-1991) DC ja1, Jakobson.

James, William
  DC 39300
  SN Born 1842 - Died 1910.
  HN Formerly (1973-1991) DC ja1a.

Japan
  DC 39400
  HN Added, 1992.
  BT Far East

Japanese
  DC 39500
  HN Formerly (1973-1991) DC ja2.
  BT Altaic Languages

Jargon
  Use Terminology

Jesperson, Jens Otto Harry
  DC 39600
  SN Born 1860 - Died 1943.
  HN Added, 1992.

Jewish Americans
  DC 39650
  HN Added, 1992.
  BT North American Cultural Groups
  RT Anglo Americans
       Asian Americans
       Black Americans
       Hispanic Americans
       Jewish Cultural Groups

Jewish Cultural Groups
  DC 39700
  HN Added, 1992.
  RT European Cultural Groups
       Jewish Americans
       North American Cultural Groups

Jivaroan Languages
  Use Andean Equatorial Phylum

Jobs
  Use Occupations

Jokes
  Use Humor

Jordan
  DC 39800
  HN Added, 1992.
  BT Arab Countries
       Middle East
  RT Palestine

Judgment
  DC 39900
  HN Formerly (1973-1991) DC jd1, Judgment Tasks.
  UF Evaluative Thinking
  BT Cognitive Processes
  RT Attitudes
       Cognitive Development
       Credibility
       Language Processing
       Learning Processes
       Problem Solving
       Rating Scales
       Verbal Tasks

Judicial Language
  Use Legal Language

Juncture
  DC 40150
  SN In phonology, a boundary marked by distinctive phonetic characteristics; or, a suprasegmental phoneme realized by the phonetic transition from one segmental phoneme to another.
  HN Formerly (1973-1991) DC ju1.
  UF Internal Juncture
       Open Juncture
       Terminal Juncture
  BT Suprasegmentals
  RT Metrical Phonology
       Morphology
       Phonemes
       Stress
       Tone

Junggrammatiker
  Use Neogrammarians

Junior High School Education
  DC 40200
  HN Formerly (1973-1991) DC ju2, Junior High, Middle School.
  UF Middle School Education
  BT Secondary Education
  RT Secondary School Students

Junior High School Students
  DC 40210
  HN Added, 1992.
  BT Secondary School Students
  RT Adolescents
       High School Students
       Secondary Education

Juvenile Literature
  Use Childrens Literature

Kabyle
  Use Berber Languages

Kam Tai Languages
  DC 40250
  HN Formerly (1973-1991) DC th1, Thai Languages.
  UF Daic Languages
       Tai Languages

Kam Tai Languages (cont'd)
 UF Thai Languages (1973-1991)
 BT Sino Tibetan Languages
 RT Vietnamese

Kamchadal
 Use Chukchee Kamchatkan Languages

Kampuchea
 Use Cambodia

Kannada
 Use Dravidian Languages

Kansas
 DC 40450
 HN Added, 1992.
 BT Midwestern States
     United States of America

Kardutjara
 Use Australian Macro Phylum

Kartvelian Languages
 Use Caucasian Languages

Kazakh
 Use Turkic Languages

Kazakhstan
 DC 40480
 HN Added, 1992.
 BT Commonwealth of Independent
     States
 RT Union of Soviet Socialist Republics

Kechua
 Use Quechua

Keltic Languages
 Use Celtic Languages

Kentucky
 DC 40550
 HN Added, 1992.
 BT Southern States
     United States of America
 RT Appalachia

Kenya
 DC 40600
 HN Added, 1992.
 BT Sub Saharan Africa

Khmer
 Use Austro Asiatic Languages

Khmer Republic
 Use Cambodia

Khoisan Languages
 DC 40650
 HN Formerly (1980-1991) DC ko1a,
     Khoi-San Languages.
 UF Bushman Languages
     Hadza
     Hatsa
     Hottentot Languages
     Sandawe
 BT African Languages
 RT Click Languages

Kikuyu
 Use Bantoid Languages

Kindergarten
 DC 40750
 HN Formerly (1973-1991) DC ki1.
 RT Elementary Education
     Preschool Children

Kindergarten (cont'd)
 RT Preschool Education

Kinesics
 DC 40850
 SN The study of the communicative use
     of body movement and stance; the
     analysis of meaningful components
     of body movement and stance.
 HN Formerly (1979-1991) DC ki1a.
 UF Body Language
 RT Facial Expressions
     Gestures
     Nonverbal Communication
     Paralinguistics

Kinship Terminology
 DC 40900
 SN The set of classificatory words and
     phrases used within a cultural group
     to refer to or address different cate-
     gories of relatives (by blood or mar-
     riage).
 HN Added, 1992.
 BT Terminology
 RT Address Forms
     Anthropological Linguistics
     Ethnolinguistics
     Sociolinguistics

Kirghiz
 Use Turkic Languages

Kirghizia
 Use Kyrgyzstan

Kirgizstan
 Use Kyrgyzstan

Kirundi
 Use Bantoid Languages

Kiswahili
 Use Swahili

Kituba
 Use Bantoid Languages

Koasiti
 Use Muskogean Languages

Koines (Dialects)
 Use Dialects

Koman Languages
 Use Nilo Saharan Languages

Komoro
 Use Swahili

Kongo
 Use Bantoid Languages

Koran
 Use Religious Literature

Kordofanian Languages
 Use Congo Kordofanian Languages

Korean
 DC 40950
 HN Formerly (1982-1991) DC ko2.
 BT Altaic Languages

Kuder Preference Record
 Use Personality Measures

Kunama
 Use Chari Nile Languages

Kurdish
 Use Iranian Languages

Kurzweil Reading Machine
 Use Reading Aids for the Blind

Kushitic Languages
 Use Cushitic Languages

Kuwait
 DC 41100
 HN Added, 1992.
 BT Arab Countries
     Middle East

Kwa Languages
 DC 41250
 HN Added, 1992.
 UF Bini
     Ewe
     Ijo
     Nupe
 BT Niger Congo Languages
 NT Akan
     Ga
     Ibo
     Yoruba

Kyrgyzstan
 DC 41260
 HN Added, 1992.
 UF Kirghizia
     Kirgizstan
 BT Commonwealth of Independent
     States
 RT Union of Soviet Socialist Republics

Labov, William A.
 DC 41300
 SN Born 1927 - .
 HN Formerly (1973-1991) DC kv1, La-
     bov, William.

Lamb, Sydney MacDonald
 DC 41400
 SN Born 1929 - .
 HN Formerly (1973-1991) DC la1, Lamb.

Language
 DC 41500
 HN Added, 1992.
 NT Adolescent Language
     Adult Language
     Child Language
     Colloquial Language
     Interlanguage
     Language for Special Purposes
     Language of Instruction
     Literary Language
     Native Language
     Natural Language
     Official Languages
     Oral Language
     Private Language
     Second Languages
     Written Language
 RT Communication
     Dialects
     Discourse Analysis
     Expressive Function of Language
     Language Acquisition
     Language Arts
     Language Attitudes
     Language Change
     Language Classification
     Language Contact
     Language Culture Relationship
     Language Death

Language (cont'd)
- **RT** Language Diversity
- Language Maintenance
- Language Modernization
- Language Pathology
- Language Patterns
- Language Planning
- Language Policy
- Language Processing
- Language Rights
- Language Shift
- Language Standardization
- Language Tests
- Language Therapy
- Language Usage
- Language Universals
- Languages
- Langue and Parole
- Lexicon
- Linguistics
- Logic of Language
- Metalanguage
- Morphology
- Onamastics
- Origin of Language
- Philosophy of Language
- Receptive Language
- Registers (Sociolinguistics)
- Semantic Analysis
- Semantics
- Semiotics
- Speech
- Syntax
- Word Frequency

Language Acquisition
- **DC** 41600
- **HN** Added, 1992.
- **UF** Language Development
- **BT** Cognitive Development
- **NT** Delayed Language Acquisition
- **RT** Baby Talk
- Child Language
- Children
- Communicative Competence
- Fluency
- Grammaticality
- Imitation
- Infant Vocalization
- Infants
- Language
- Language Arts
- Language Pathology
- Language Processing
- Language Universals
- Linguistic Competence
- Linguistic Performance
- Longitudinal Studies
- Maternal Speech
- Mean Length of Utterance
- Native Language
- Native Language Instruction
- Natural Phonology
- Oral Language
- Phonological Processing
- Principles and Parameters Approach
- Psycholinguistics
- Receptive Language
- Secret Languages
- Socialization
- Verbal Learning
- Written Language

Language and Culture (1973-1991)
- **HN** DC la2, deleted 1992. See now Cross Cultural Communication, Cultural Differences, Cultural Factors, Culture, or Language Culture Relationship.

Language Arts
- **DC** 41700
- **HN** Added, 1992.
- **NT** Handwriting
- Listening
- Public Speaking
- Reading
- Rhetoric
- Story Telling
- Writing
- **RT** Communication
- Grammar Instruction
- Language
- Language Acquisition
- Language Teaching Methods
- Lexicology
- Literature
- Native Language Instruction
- Orthography
- Reading Writing Relationship
- Verbal Learning
- Whole Language Approach

Language Attitudes
- **DC** 41800
- **SN** Beliefs about the characteristics of one's own language or another language, such as linguistic complexity or ease of learning. Also value-laden attitudes toward the use of particular languages, dialects, accents, or language or speech patterns.
- **HN** Added, 1992.
- **UF** Linguistic Attitudes
- **BT** Attitudes
- **RT** Colloquial Language
- Grammaticality
- Language
- Language Diversity
- Language Planning
- Language Rights
- Language Status
- Minority Languages
- Social Factors
- Socialization
- Sociolinguistics
- Stereotypes

Language Change
- **DC** 41850
- **SN** All forms of change occurring in a language over any period of time.
- **HN** Added, 1992.
- **UF** Linguistic Change
- **NT** Grammatical Change
- Language Modernization
- Language Standardization
- Morphological Change
- Phonological Change
- Semantic Change
- Sound Change
- **RT** Borrowing
- Cultural Change
- Diachronic Linguistics
- Etymology
- Indigenous Languages
- Language
- Language Contact
- Language Death
- Language Planning
- Sociolinguistics

Language Classification
- **DC** 41900
- **SN** The grouping and subgrouping of languages according to hypotheses of relationship.
- **HN** Added, 1992.

Language Classification (cont'd)
- **UF** Classification of Languages
- **NT** Language Typology
- **RT** Comparative Linguistics
- Diachronic Linguistics
- Dialectology
- Dialects
- Diglossia
- Etymology
- Language
- Language Patterns
- Languages
- Taxonomic Approaches

Language Contact
- **DC** 42100
- **SN** Interaction between two languages, mediated by individuals who speak both, and the effects over time of such interaction on the phonology, morphology, syntax, semantics, and lexicon of each language.
- **HN** Formerly (1973-1991) DC la8a, Languages in Contact.
- **RT** Acculturation
- Areal Linguistics
- Bilingualism
- Borrowing
- Code Switching
- Creoles
- Descriptive Linguistics
- Diachronic Linguistics
- Diglossia
- Ethnographic Linguistics
- Indigenous Languages
- Indigenous Populations
- Language
- Language Change
- Language Death
- Language Diversity
- Language Maintenance
- Language Rights
- Language Shift
- Linguistic Interference
- Minority Languages
- Multilingualism
- Pidgins
- Social Factors
- Sociolinguistics
- Trade Languages

Language Creativity
- **Use** Creativity (Linguistics)

Language Culture Relationship
- **DC** 42150
- **HN** Added, 1992.
- **UF** Culture Language Relationship
- **RT** Acculturation
- Anthropological Linguistics
- Archaeological Evidence
- Cross Cultural Communication
- Cultural Background
- Cultural Change
- Cultural Differences
- Cultural Factors
- Cultural Groups
- Culture
- Ethnographic Linguistics
- Ethnolinguistics
- Language
- Language Death
- Language Diversity
- Language Maintenance
- Language Modernization
- Language Rights
- Language Status
- Literature
- Marxist Analysis
- Social Factors
- Sociolinguistics

Language Death
DC 42200
SN Processes by which a language loses all living native speakers who use it; includes dead and dying languages.
HN Added, 1992.
UF Dead Languages
Dialect Death
Dying Languages
Language Decay
Language Obsolescence
RT Cultural Change
Dialects
Indigenous Languages
Language
Language Change
Language Contact
Language Culture Relationship
Language Maintenance
Language Planning
Language Policy
Language Shift
Language Status
Language Use
Languages
Minority Languages
Native Speakers
Social Factors
Sociolinguistics
Unknown Languages

Language Decay
Use Language Death

Language Development
Use Language Acquisition

Language Disorders
Use Language Pathology

Language Diversity
DC 42350
SN The extent and nature of variations in the form of a language, with reference to social and geographic context and implications for successful communication, social cohesion, and political unity.
HN Formerly (1973-1991) DC la2bb.
RT Bilingualism
Colloquial Language
Comparative Linguistics
Creoles
Dialectology
Dialects
Diglossia
Indigenous Languages
Language
Language Attitudes
Language Contact
Language Culture Relationship
Language for Special Purposes
Language Policy
Language Rights
Language Standardization
Language Styles
Language Use
Languages
Minority Languages
Multilingualism
National Languages
Nonstandard Dialects
Official Languages
Pidgins
Social Factors
Sociolinguistics
Standard Dialects

Language Experience Approach
DC 42450
HN Added, 1992.
BT Language Teaching Methods
RT Beginning Reading
Child Language
Reading Comprehension
Reading Instruction
Whole Language Approach

Language Fluency
Use Fluency

Language for Special Purposes
DC 42550
SN Language skills, including vocabulary and usage, required for effective communication in specific occupations and fields of expertise; typically used to designate a specialized form of second-language instruction.
HN Added, 1992.
UF Foreign Language for Special Purposes
Second Languages for Special Purposes
Special Languages (1973-1991)
BT Language
NT English for Special Purposes
Legal Language
Literary Language
Medical Language
Scientific Technical Language
Trade Languages
RT Language Diversity
Language Styles
Language Usage
Occupations
Political Discourse
Pragmatics
Registers (Sociolinguistics)
Second Language Instruction
Second Language Learning
Second Languages
Slang
Terminology

Language Games
Use Word Games

Language History
Use Diachronic Linguistics

Language Isolates
DC 42750
HN Formerly (1979-1991) DC la8aa, Languages without Classification.
UF Languages without Classification (1979-1991)
BT Languages
NT Basque
Burushaski
Etruscan
Iberian
Sumerian

Language Laboratories
DC 42850
HN Formerly (1973-1991) DC la3, Language Laboratory.
RT Audiolingual Methods
Audiovisual Language Teaching
Computer Assisted Instruction
Computer Software
Language Teaching Methods
Languages
Programmed Instruction
Second Language Instruction

Language Learning (Foreign)
Use Second Language Learning

Language Maintenance
DC 42950
SN The continued use of a language in contexts and situations where another language is available; includes factors and practices that forestall language death and prevent diminished use of a language.
HN Added, 1992.
RT Bilingual Education
Bilingual Teaching Materials
Bilingualism
Indigenous Languages
Language
Language Contact
Language Culture Relationship
Language Death
Language of Instruction
Language Planning
Language Policy
Language Rights
Language Shift
Language Status
Language Usage
Language Use
Languages
Minority Languages
Multilingualism
National Languages
Native Speakers
Nonstandard Dialects
Official Languages
Social Factors
Sociolinguistics

Language Minorities
Use Minority Languages

Language Modernization
DC 43150
HN Added, 1992.
BT Language Change
RT Cultural Change
Diachronic Linguistics
Language
Language Culture Relationship
Language Planning
Language Policy
Language Standardization
Language Status
Languages
Orthography Reform

Language Obsolescence
Use Language Death

Language of Instruction
DC 43180
HN Added, 1992.
UF Instructional Language
Medium of Instruction (Language)
Teaching Language
BT Language
RT Bilingual Education
Bilingual Teaching Materials
Early Second Language Learning
FLES
Immersion Programs
Instruction
Language Maintenance
Language Planning
Language Policy
Language Rights
Language Shift
Language Use
Languages

Language of Instruction (cont'd)
- RT Native Speakers
  Official Languages
  Second Language Instruction
  Second Language Learning
  Second Languages
  Sociolinguistics

Language of Law
- Use Legal Language

Language of Medicine
- Use Medical Language

Language of Politics
- Use Political Discourse

Language of Science
- Use Scientific Technical Language

Language Origin
- Use Origin of Language

Language Pathology
- DC 43250
- SN Study of central nervous system disorders affecting the reception, processing, or expression of language. Use speech pathology for disorders of the physiological mechanisms required for the production of speech.
- HN Formerly (1973-1991) DC la4.
- UF Language Disorders
- BT Medicine
- RT Agrammatism
  Aphasia
  Autism
  Delayed Language Acquisition
  Language
  Language Acquisition
  Learning Disabilities
  Nervous System Disorders
  Neurolinguistics
  Phonation Disorders
  Reading Deficiencies
  Receptive Language
  Speech Pathology
  Writing Disorders

Language Patterns
- DC 43300
- HN Formerly (1977-1991) DC pa4b, Patterns (Language).
- UF Linguistic Patterns
  Patterns (Language) (1977-1991)
- NT Linguistic Accommodation
- RT Borrowing
  Child Language
  Code Switching
  Creativity (Linguistics)
  Diachronic Linguistics
  Dialectology
  Discourse Analysis
  Error Analysis (Language)
  Form Classes
  Grapheme Phoneme Correspondence
  Idioms
  Language
  Language Classification
  Language Styles
  Language Universals
  Language Usage
  Language Use
  Languages
  Linguistics
  Morphology
  Native Nonnative Speaker Communication
  Native Speakers

Language Patterns (cont'd)
- RT Oral Language
  Phonemes
  Phonemics
  Pragmatics
  Registers (Sociolinguistics)
  Repair
  Semantic Analysis
  Semantics
  Semiotics
  Speech
  Speech Acts
  Stylistics
  Syntax
  Tagmemics
  Turn Taking
  Word Order
  Written Language

Language Planning
- DC 43400
- SN The formulation of goals, usually at a governmental level, for the adoption of an official language, promotion of the use of a language, planned language change, or the solution of communication problems; includes procedures to achieve these goals.
- HN Formerly (1979-1991) DC la4a.
- NT Language Standardization
- RT Applied Linguistics
  Bilingual Education
  Bilingualism
  Diachronic Linguistics
  Immersion Programs
  Language
  Language Attitudes
  Language Change
  Language Death
  Language Maintenance
  Language Modernization
  Language of Instruction
  Language Policy
  Language Rights
  Language Shift
  Language Status
  Language Use
  Languages
  Multilingualism
  National Languages
  Official Languages
  Orthography Reform
  Second Languages
  Social Factors
  Sociolinguistics
  Terminology

Language Policy
- DC 43450
- SN Stated or de facto policies of governments and other organizations that affect the use or form of a language.
- HN Formerly (1974-1991) DC la5.
- UF Linguistic Policy
- RT Bilingual Education
  Bilingualism
  Language
  Language Death
  Language Diversity
  Language Maintenance
  Language Modernization
  Language of Instruction
  Language Planning
  Language Rights
  Language Shift
  Language Standardization
  Language Status
  Language Use

Language Policy (cont'd)
- RT Languages
  Minority Languages
  Multilingualism
  National Languages
  Official Languages
  Social Factors
  Sociolinguistics

Language Processing
- DC 43550
- HN Added, 1992.
- BT Cognitive Processes
- NT Phonological Processing
  Receptive Language
  Syntactic Processing
  Translation
- RT Anomalous Strings
  Applied Linguistics
  Auditory Perception
  Comprehension
  Computational Linguistics
  Creativity (Linguistics)
  Decoding (Cognitive Process)
  Encoding (Cognitive Process)
  Familiarity
  Grammaticality
  Judgment
  Language
  Language Acquisition
  Language Thought Relationship
  Language Usage
  Learning Processes
  Linguistic Interference
  Linguistic Performance
  Linguistics
  Listening
  Listening Comprehension
  Natural Language
  Neurolinguistics
  Parallel Distributed Processing Models
  Psycholinguistics
  Reading
  Reading Processes
  Semantic Processing
  Sound Identification
  Speech Perception
  Stroop Color Word Test
  Verbal Tasks
  Visual Perception
  Writing
  Writing Processes

Language Rights
- DC 43650
- HN Added, 1992.
- UF Linguistic Rights
- RT Bilingual Education
  Bilingualism
  Indigenous Languages
  Language
  Language Attitudes
  Language Contact
  Language Culture Relationship
  Language Diversity
  Language Maintenance
  Language of Instruction
  Language Planning
  Language Policy
  Language Standardization
  Language Status
  Language Usage
  Language Use
  Minority Languages
  Multilingualism
  National Languages
  Official Languages

Language Shift
DC 43750
SN A change in language use in which speakers of one language substitute another language in certain contexts or situations, culminating in the abandonment of the first language.
HN Added, 1992.
BT Language Use
RT Bilingualism
Cultural Change
Diachronic Linguistics
Diglossia
Indigenous Languages
Language
Language Contact
Language Death
Language Maintenance
Language of Instruction
Language Planning
Language Policy
Minority Languages
Social Factors
Sociolinguistics

Language Situation
Use Language Status

Language Speech Distinction
Use Langue and Parole

Language Standardization
DC 43900
SN The development of a standard dialect and/or standard written form of a language by language planning, normative instruction, spontaneous change, or other means.
HN Added, 1992.
UF Codification (of Language)
BT Language Change
Language Planning
RT Dialectology
Dialects
Diglossia
Language
Language Diversity
Language Modernization
Language Policy
Language Rights
Language Usage
Languages
Minority Languages
National Languages
Nonstandard Dialects
Official Languages
Orthography Reform
Social Factors
Sociolinguistics
Standard Dialects
Terminology

Language Status
DC 43920
SN A characterization of the users, circumstances of use, and perceived value of a language within a community or polity; includes legal or other formal rules defining or governing the use of a language.
HN Added, 1992.
UF Language Situation
RT Cultural Factors
Descriptive Linguistics
Diachronic Linguistics
Indigenous Languages
International Languages
Language Attitudes
Language Culture Relationship

Language Status (cont'd)
RT Language Death
Language Maintenance
Language Modernization
Language Planning
Language Policy
Language Rights
Minority Languages
National Languages
Nonstandard Dialects
Official Languages
Social Factors
Sociolinguistics
Standard Dialects

Language Styles
DC 43930
SN Variations in language usage (eg, vocabulary, sounds, structures) that are characteristic of different users, registers, and literacy styles.
HN Added, 1992.
UF Linguistic Styles
RT Colloquial Language
Idioms
Language Diversity
Language for Special Purposes
Language Patterns
Language Usage
Legal Language
Literary Language
Medical Language
Occupations
Political Discourse
Pragmatics
Registers (Sociolinguistics)
Scientific Technical Language
Slang
Terminology

Language Tasks
Use Verbal Tasks

Language Teaching Materials
DC 43950
HN Formerly (1973-1991) DC la6.
BT Teaching Materials
NT Authentic Texts
Language Textbooks
RT Audiovisual Language Teaching
Bilingual Teaching Materials
Dictionaries

Language Teaching Methods
DC 44100
HN Formerly (1973-1991) DC la7.
BT Teaching Methods
NT Audiolingual Language Teaching
Audiovisual Language Teaching
Communicative Language Teaching
Direct Method of Language Teaching
Grammar Translation Method of Language Teaching
Language Experience Approach
Pattern Drills
Suggestopedia
Whole Language Approach
RT Applied Linguistics
Language Arts
Language Laboratories
Native Language Instruction
Oral Language Instruction
Second Language Instruction
Written Language Instruction

Language Tests
DC 44250
HN Added, 1992.
BT Tests
NT Second Language Tests
RT Achievement Tests
Cloze Procedure
Communicative Competence
Error Analysis (Language)
Illinois Test of Psycholinguistic Abilities
Language
Peabody Picture Vocabulary Test
Reading Tests
Speech Tests
Writing Tests

Language Textbooks
DC 44300
HN Added, 1992.
UF Foreign Language Textbooks
Second Language Textbooks
BT Language Teaching Materials
RT Authentic Texts
Second Language Instruction

Language Therapy
DC 44400
HN Formerly (1973-1991) DC la7a.
BT Therapy
RT Aphasia
Applied Linguistics
Autism
Delayed Language Acquisition
Language
Learning Disabilities
Nervous System Disorders
Reading Deficiencies
Speech Pathology
Speech Therapy
Writing Disorders

Language Thought Relationship
DC 44410
HN Added, 1992.
UF Cognition Language Relationship
Thought Language Relationship
RT Associative Processes
Brain
Cognitive Development
Cognitive Style
Comprehension
Decoding (Cognitive Process)
Encoding (Cognitive Process)
Imagery
Information Processing
Inner Speech
Intelligence
Language Processing
Learning Disabilities
Learning Processes
Learning Theories
Memory
Metacognition
Metalanguage
Perception
Psycholinguistics
Reading Processes
Stereotypes

Language Typology
DC 44450
SN Classification of languages according to their structural characteristics, eg, word order, parts of speech, and phonological systems.
HN Formerly (1973-1991) DC ty2, Typology of Language.
UF Typology of Language (1973-1991)
BT Language Classification
RT Areal Linguistics
Comparative Linguistics

Language Typology (cont'd)
- **RT** Descriptive Linguistics
  - Etymology
  - Language Universals
  - Languages
  - Morphology
  - Phonemes
  - Phonemics
  - Phonology
  - Port Royal School
  - Synchronic Linguistics
  - Syntax
  - Taxonomic Approaches

Language Units
- **Use** Linguistic Units

Language Universals
- **DC** 44550
- **SN** Structural patterns or properties that occur in all languages.
- **HN** Formerly (1973-1991) DC la8.
- **UF** Linguistic Universals
  - Universals (Language)
- **RT** Artificial Languages
  - Case
  - Diachronic Linguistics
  - Distinctive Features
  - Form (Language Structure)
  - Language
  - Language Acquisition
  - Language Patterns
  - Language Typology
  - Languages
  - Linguistic Theories
  - Markedness
  - Negation
  - Pro Drop Parameter
  - Structuralist Linguistics
  - Transformational Generative Grammar
  - Universal Grammar

Language Usage
- **DC** 44600
- **SN** Patterns in the use of a particular language in speech or writing. For language of use in a particular context, use Language Use.
- **HN** Added, 1992.
- **NT** Phraseology
- **RT** Borrowing
  - Code Switching
  - Cohesion
  - Colloquial Language
  - Creativity (Linguistics)
  - Descriptive Linguistics
  - Discourse Analysis
  - Ellipsis
  - Error Analysis
  - Ethnographic Linguistics
  - Feminism
  - Grammaticality
  - Language
  - Language for Special Purposes
  - Language Maintenance
  - Language Patterns
  - Language Processing
  - Language Rights
  - Language Standardization
  - Language Styles
  - Linguistics
  - Miscue Analysis
  - Native Nonnative Speaker Communication
  - Neologisms
  - Obscenities
  - Oral Language

Language Usage (cont'd)
- **RT** Pragmatics
  - Registers (Sociolinguistics)
  - Sexism
  - Slang
  - Social Class
  - Social Factors
  - Sociolinguistics
  - Speech Communities
  - Spoken Written Language Relationship
  - Standard Dialects
  - Statistical Analysis of Style
  - Stylistics
  - Synchronic Linguistics
  - Turn Taking
  - Written Language

Language Use
- **DC** 44610
- **SN** Patterns in the use of different languages within particular speech communities or geographical areas; for variations or patterns in the use of a particular language, use Language Usage.
- **HN** Added, 1992.
- **NT** Diglossia
  - Language Shift
- **RT** Bilingualism
  - Code Switching
  - Creoles
  - Diachronic Linguistics
  - Dialectology
  - Dialects
  - Indigenous Languages
  - Language
  - Language Death
  - Language Diversity
  - Language Maintenance
  - Language of Instruction
  - Language Patterns
  - Language Planning
  - Language Policy
  - Language Rights
  - Languages
  - Minority Languages
  - Multilingualism
  - National Languages
  - Native Language
  - Native Language Instruction
  - Native Nonnative Speaker Communication
  - Native Speakers
  - Official Languages
  - Secret Languages
  - Sociolinguistics
  - Trade Languages

Languages
- **DC** 44700
- **HN** Added, 1992.
- **NT** African Languages
  - Altaic Languages
  - Amerindian Languages
  - Artificial Languages
  - Australian Macro Phylum
  - Austro Asiatic Languages
  - Austronesian Languages
  - Caucasian Languages
  - Chukchee Kamchatkan Languages
  - Click Languages
  - Creoles
  - Dialects
  - Dravidian Languages
  - Indigenous Languages
  - Indo European Languages
  - Indo Pacific Languages

Languages (cont'd)
- **NT** International Languages
  - Language Isolates
  - Minority Languages
  - Non Western Languages
  - Nonverbal Languages
  - Pidgins
  - Scandinavian Languages
  - Secret Languages
  - Sino Tibetan Languages
  - Unknown Languages
  - Uralic Languages
- **RT** Bilingualism
  - Dialectology
  - Fluency
  - Idioms
  - Intelligibility
  - Language
  - Language Classification
  - Language Death
  - Language Diversity
  - Language Laboratories
  - Language Maintenance
  - Language Modernization
  - Language of Instruction
  - Language Planning
  - Language Policy
  - Language Standardization
  - Language Typology
  - Language Universals
  - Language Usage
  - Language Use
  - Linguistics
  - Monolingualism
  - Multilingualism
  - Second Language Instruction
  - Second Languages
  - Translation

Languages without Classification (1979-1991)
- **HN** DC la8aa.
- **Use** Language Isolates

Langue and Parole
- **DC** 44900
- **SN** A distinction made by Ferdinand de Saussure in defining the field of linguistics as the study of the language system shared by a speech community (langue) and the actual use of that language by individuals (parole).
- **HN** Formerly (1973-1991) DC la9.
- **UF** Language Speech Distinction
- **RT** Language
  - Linguistic Competence
  - Linguistic Performance
  - Linguistic Theories
  - Speech

Lao
- **Use** Sino Tibetan Languages

Laos
- **DC** 45100
- **HN** Added, 1992.
- **BT** Southeast Asia

Lapland
- **DC** 45150
- **HN** Added, 1992.
- **BT** Scandinavia
- **RT** Arctic Regions

Lappic Languages
- **Use** Finno Ugric Languages

Laryngectomy
DC 45250
HN Formerly (1973-1991) DC la11.
BT Surgery
RT Esophageal Speech
Laryngology
Phonation Structures

Laryngology
DC 45350
HN Formerly (1973-1991) DC la12.
BT Medicine
RT Laryngectomy
Phonation Disorders
Phonation Structures
Speech Pathology
Speech Therapy
Voice Disorders

Larynx
Use Phonation Structures

Lateral Dominance
Use Cerebral Dominance

Laterality
Use Cerebral Dominance

Latin
DC 45400
HN Formerly (1977-1991) DC la14.
BT Italic Languages
RT Romance Languages

Latin America
DC 45500
HN Added, 1992.
NT Caribbean
Central America
Mexico
South America
RT Latin American Cultural Groups
North America

Latin American Cultural Groups
DC 45600
HN Added, 1992.
UF South American Cultural Groups
BT Cultural Groups
NT Caribbean Cultural Groups
RT American Indians
Latin America
North American Cultural Groups

Latvia
DC 45650
HN Added, 1992.
BT Baltic States
Commonwealth of Independent
States
RT Union of Soviet Socialist Republics

Latvian
Use Lettish

Law and Language
Use Legal Language

Learning
DC 45750
HN Added, 1992.
NT Discrimination Learning
Second Language Learning
Transfer (Learning)
Verbal Learning
RT Academic Achievement
Cognitive Development
Concept Formation
Conditioning

Learning (cont'd)
RT Education
Educational Activities
Feedback
Instruction
Interference (Learning)
Learning Processes
Learning Theories
Problem Solving
Recall (Memory)
Retention (Memory)
Socialization

Learning Activities
Use Educational Activities

Learning Cycles
Use Learning Processes

Learning Disabilities
DC 45850
HN Formerly (1973-1991) DC la16.
BT Disorders
NT Dyslexia
RT Aphasia
Attention Deficit Disorders
Cognitive Processes
Diagnostic Tests
Emotional Disturbances
Handicapped
Language Pathology
Language Therapy
Language Thought Relationship
Nervous System Disorders
Reading Deficiencies
Recall (Memory)
Recognition
Remedial Reading
Special Education (Handicapped)
Writing Disorders

Learning Processes
DC 45950
HN Added, 1992.
UF Learning Cycles
Von Restorff Effect (1973-1991)
BT Cognitive Processes
NT Concept Formation
Generalization
Memorization
RT Associative Processes
Cognitive Style
Conditioning
Conservation (Concept)
Encoding (Cognitive Process)
Imitation
Information Processing
Interference (Learning)
Interlanguage
Judgment
Language Processing
Language Thought Relationship
Learning
Learning Theories
Listening Comprehension
Logic
Mediation Theory
Memory
Metacognition
Recall (Memory)
Recognition
Principles and Parameters Approach
Writing Processes

Learning Style
Use Cognitive Style

Learning Theories
DC 46100
HN Formerly (1973-1991) DC le1.
RT Behavioristic Linguistic Theory
Cognitive Processes
Conditioning
Context Effects (Perception)
Generalization
Information Processing
Language Thought Relationship
Learning
Learning Processes
Linguistic Theories
Paired Associate Learning
Principles and Parameters Approach
Serial Learning

Lebanon
DC 46200
HN Added, 1992.
BT Arab Countries
Mediterranean Countries
Middle East

Left Brain Dominance
Use Cerebral Dominance

Left Handedness
Use Handedness

Legal Education (Professional)
Use Professional Education

Legal Language
DC 46300
HN Added, 1992.
UF Judicial Language
Language of Law
Law and Language
BT Language for Special Purposes
RT Language Styles
Terminology

Leinster
Use Irish Gaelic

Lele
Use Gur Languages

Length (Phonological)
DC 46340
SN Relative durations of sounds and syl-
lables when they are linguistically
contrastive; eg, long and short vow-
els and consonants. For the physical
duration of a sound, use Sound Dura-
tion.
HN Added, 1992.
UF Gemination
Quantity (Phonological)
RT Consonants
Metrical Phonology
Mora
Phonology
Syllables
Time
Vowels

Lesotho
DC 46380
HN Added, 1992.
BT Sub Saharan Africa

Letter and Word Association
Use Word and Letter Association

Letter Association
Use Word and Letter Association

Letter Discrimination
Use Letter Recognition

Letter Recognition
DC 46400
HN Formerly (1973-1991) DC le2, Letter Recognition and Discrimination.
UF Character Recognition
Ideograph Recognition
Letter Discrimination
BT Recognition
RT Decoding (Reading)
Discrimination Learning
Dyslexia
Reading Processes
Sound Identification
Speech Perception
Visual Perception
Vowel Perception
Word and Letter Association

Letter Sound Correspondence
Use Grapheme Phoneme Correspondence

Letters (Alphabet)
Use Orthographic Symbols

Lettish
DC 46500
HN Added, 1992.
UF Latvian
BT Baltic Languages

Lévi-Strauss, Claude
DC 46600
SN Born 1908 - .
HN Formerly (1973-1991) DC le3, Levi Strauss.

Lexemes
Use Lexicon

Lexical Ambiguity
Use Ambiguity

Lexical Borrowing
Use Borrowing

Lexical Change
Use Semantic Change

Lexical Creativity
Use Creativity (Linguistics)

Lexical Functional Grammar
DC 46650
SN Generative models of language developed by Joan Bresnan and others in the late 1970s and 1980s under the constraint that grammar theory conform to results of psycholinguistic research. Computational information-processing techniques are used to derive competence-based models of linguistic performance that claim to be psychologically realistic and unify research in linguistics, language acquisition, and language processing.
HN Added, 1992.
BT Generative Grammar
RT Form Classes
Functional Grammar
Lexicon
Natural Language Processing
Syntax
Words

Lexical Items
Use Lexicon

Lexical Meaning
Use Word Meaning

Lexical Phonology
DC 46750
SN A model of generative phonology characterized by two levels of representation, lexical & postlexical.
HN Added, 1992.
BT Phonology
RT Generative Grammar
Lexicon
Morphology
Words

Lexical Semantics
DC 46770
HN Added, 1992.
BT Semantics
RT Lexicology
Lexicon
Linguistic Theories
Semantic Analysis
Semantic Features
Word Meaning

Lexical Structure
Use Word Structure

Lexical Tasks
Use Verbal Tasks

Lexical Theory (1987-1991)
HN DC le3a, deleted 1992. See now Lexicon or Linguistic Theories.

Lexicography
DC 46800
SN The compiling of dictionaries or thesauri.
HN Added, 1992.
RT Applied Linguistics
Dictionaries
Etymology
Lexicology
Lexicon

Lexicology
DC 46900
HN Formerly (1973-1991) DC le5.
RT Borrowing
Comparative Linguistics
Componential Analysis
Diachronic Linguistics
Dictionaries
Etymology
Language Arts
Lexical Semantics
Lexicography
Lexicon
Morphology
Onomastics
Semantic Features
Syntagmatic Relations

Lexicon
DC 47150
SN The component of language that consists of a more or less structured, open set of individual units having both semantic content and phonological form, and usable in specified morphosyntactic functions.
HN Added, 1992.
UF Lexemes
Lexical Items

Lexicon (cont'd)
UF Vocabulary (1973-1991)
NT Acronyms
Antonyms
Clitics
Cognates
Homographs
Homonyms
Homophones
Idioms
Neologisms
Obscenities
Phraseologisms
Slang
Synonyms
Terminology
RT Borrowing
Code Switching
Compound Words
Dictionaries
Etymology
Form Classes
Functional Grammar
Language
Lexical Functional Grammar
Lexical Phonology
Lexical Semantics
Lexicography
Lexicology
Semantic Fields
Semantics
Statistical Analysis of Style
Stylistics
Syntagmatic Relations
Syntax
Vocabulary Instruction
Word Formation
Word Frequency
Word Meaning
Word Recognition
Words

Liberia
DC 47240
HN Added, 1992.
BT Sub Saharan Africa

Libya
DC 47250
HN Added, 1992.
BT Arab Countries
Mediterranean Countries
North Africa

Liechtenstein
DC 47300
HN Added, 1992.
BT Western Europe

Limen
Use Thresholds

Limited English Proficiency
DC 47330
HN Added, 1992.
RT Bilingual Education
Bilingualism
Communicative Competence
English as a Second Language
English for Special Purposes
Linguistic Competence
Linguistic Performance
Minority Languages
Second Language Learning

Linear Learning
　Use　Serial Learning

Lingala
　Use　Bantoid Languages

Lingua Franca
　Use　Trade Languages

Linguistic Accommodation
　DC　47340
　HN　Added, 1992
　BT　Language Patterns
　RT　Adult Child Interaction
　　　　Baby Talk
　　　　Cross Cultural Communication
　　　　Intelligibility
　　　　Maternal Speech
　　　　Native Nonnative Speaker Communi-
　　　　　cation
　　　　Native Speakers
　　　　Nonverbal Communication
　　　　Pronunciation
　　　　Registers (Sociolinguistics)
　　　　Speech Rate

Linguistic Anthropology
　Use　Anthropological Linguistics

Linguistic Attitudes
　Use　Language Attitudes

Linguistic Borrowing
　Use　Borrowing

Linguistic Change
　Use　Language Change

Linguistic Comparison
　Use　Comparative Linguistics

Linguistic Competence
　DC　47400
　HN　Added, 1992. Prior to 1992 see DC
　　　　co7, Competence and Performance.
　UF　Competence (Linguistic)
　RT　Communicative Competence
　　　　Generative Grammar
　　　　Generative Phonology
　　　　Grammaticality
　　　　Interlanguage
　　　　Language Acquisition
　　　　Langue and Parole
　　　　Limited English Proficiency
　　　　Linguistic Performance
　　　　Threshold Levels (Language)
　　　　Transformational Generative Gram-
　　　　　mar
　　　　Well Formedness

Linguistic Creativity
　Use　Creativity (Linguistics)

Linguistic Geography
　Use　Areal Linguistics

Linguistic Interference
　DC　47500
　SN　Errors in speaking a second lan-
　　　　guage, attributed to the effects of
　　　　the speaker's native language or an-
　　　　other language in which the speaker
　　　　has had some experience.
　HN　Formerly (1973-1991) DC li1.
　UF　Communicative Interference
　BT　Interference (Learning)
　　　　Language Processing
　RT　Bilingualism
　　　　Code Switching
　　　　Comparative Linguistics

Linguistic Interference (cont'd)
　RT　Error Analysis (Language)
　　　　Foreign Accent
　　　　Interlanguage
　　　　Language Contact
　　　　Psycholinguistics
　　　　Second Language Learning

Linguistic Minorities
　Use　Minority Languages

Linguistic Paleontology
　Use　Paleolinguistics

Linguistic Patterns
　Use　Language Patterns

Linguistic Performance
　DC　47550
　HN　Added, 1992. Prior to 1992, see DC
　　　　co7, Competence and Performance.
　UF　Performance (Linguistic)
　RT　Fluency
　　　　Generative Grammar
　　　　Interlanguage
　　　　Language Acquisition
　　　　Language Processing
　　　　Langue and Parole
　　　　Limited English Proficiency
　　　　Linguistic Competence
　　　　Slips of the Tongue
　　　　Speech
　　　　Transformational Generative Gram-
　　　　　mar
　　　　Well Formedness

Linguistic Philosophy
　Use　Philosophy of Language

Linguistic Policy
　Use　Language Policy

Linguistic Relativity
　DC　47650
　SN　A theory advanced by the anthropo-
　　　　logical linguists Eduard Sapir and
　　　　Benjamin Lee Whorf that the struc-
　　　　ture of a language governs in whole
　　　　or in part its native speakers' view of
　　　　the world.
　HN　Formerly (1973-1991) DC li2.
　UF　Relativity (Linguistics)
　　　　Sapir Whorf Hypothesis
　　　　Whorfian Hypothesis
　RT　Anthropological Linguistics
　　　　Beliefs
　　　　Linguistic Theories
　　　　Psycholinguistics

Linguistic Rights
　Use　Language Rights

Linguistic Styles
　Use　Language Styles

Linguistic Theories
　DC　47700
　HN　Added, 1992.
　NT　Behavioristic Linguistic Theory
　　　　Dialectical Materialistic Linguistic
　　　　　Theory
　　　　Functional Sentence Perspective
　　　　Grammar Theories
　　　　Montague Grammar
　　　　Nostratic Theory
　　　　Set Theory
　　　　Sign Theory
　　　　Trace Theory
　RT　Anthropological Linguistics
　　　　Applied Linguistics

Linguistic Theories (cont'd)
　RT　Areal Linguistics
　　　　Communicative Function of Lan-
　　　　　guage
　　　　Comparative Linguistics
　　　　Componential Analysis
　　　　Computational Linguistics
　　　　Descriptive Linguistics
　　　　Diachronic Linguistics
　　　　Distinctive Features
　　　　Ethnographic Linguistics
　　　　Ethnolinguistics
　　　　Expressive Function of Language
　　　　Functional Linguistics
　　　　Gestalt Theory
　　　　History of Linguistics
　　　　Langue and Parole
　　　　Language Universals
　　　　Learning Theories
　　　　Lexical Semantics
　　　　Linguistic Relativity
　　　　Linguistics
　　　　Linguistics Instruction
　　　　Logic of Language
　　　　London School
　　　　Mathematical Linguistics
　　　　Metalanguage
　　　　Neogrammarians
　　　　Neurolinguistics
　　　　Origin of Language
　　　　Paleolinguistics
　　　　Phonology
　　　　Poetics
　　　　Port Royal School
　　　　Prague School
　　　　Pro Drop Parameter
　　　　Psycholinguistics
　　　　Semantic Fields
　　　　Semantic Analysis
　　　　Semantics
　　　　Semiotics
　　　　Signifiant and Signifie
　　　　Sociolinguistics
　　　　Speech Acts
　　　　Structuralist Linguistics
　　　　Synchronic Linguistics
　　　　Systemic Linguistics
　　　　Taxonomic Approaches
　　　　Theoretical Linguistics

Linguistic Units
　DC　47800
　HN　Added, 1992.
　UF　Language Units
　　　　Units (Language)
　NT　Clauses
　　　　Morphemes
　　　　Paragraphs
　　　　Phrases
　　　　Predicate
　　　　Sentences
　　　　Subject (Grammatical)
　　　　Syllables
　　　　Words
　RT　Clitics
　　　　Coordination (Grammatical)
　　　　Form (Language Structure)
　　　　Form Classes
　　　　Grammatical Analysis
　　　　Grammatical Relations
　　　　Morphology
　　　　Reference (Grammatical)
　　　　Semantics
　　　　Structuralist Linguistics
　　　　Subordination (Grammatical)
　　　　Syntactic Structures
　　　　Syntagmatic Relations
　　　　Syntax
　　　　Word Order

Linguistic Universals
Use Language Universals

Linguistics
DC 47900
HN Formerly (1973-1991) DC ge1a, General Linguistics.
UF General Linguistics (1973-1991)
Philology
NT Anthropological Linguistics
Applied Linguistics
Areal Linguistics
Comparative Linguistics
Computational Linguistics
Descriptive Linguistics
Diachronic Linguistics
Dialectology
Ethnographic Linguistics
Ethnolinguistics
Functional Linguistics
Mathematical Linguistics
Neurolinguistics
Paleolinguistics
Paralinguistics
Phonology
Psycholinguistics
Semiotics
Sociolinguistics
Structuralist Linguistics
Synchronic Linguistics
Systemic Linguistics
Theoretical Linguistics
RT Dialectical Materialistic Linguistic Theory
History of Linguistics
Language
Language Patterns
Language Processing
Language Usage
Languages
Linguistic Theories
Linguistics Instruction
Logic of Language
London School
Metalanguage
Neogrammarians
Onomastics
Origin of Language
Orthography
Philosophy of Language
Phonemics
Phonetics
Port Royal School
Prague School
Speech
Syntax

Linguistics Instruction
DC 48200
HN Formerly (1981-1991) DC li2b, Linguistics, Teaching.
BT Instruction
RT Educational Activities
History of Linguistics
Linguistic Theories
Linguistics

Linguists
DC 48250
HN Added, 1992.
RT History of Linguistics

Lipreading
DC 48300
HN Formerly (1973-1991) DC li3.
UF Speech Reading
RT Hearing Disorders
Speech Perception
Visual Perception

Lips
Use Oral Cavity

Lisping
Use Articulation Disorders

Listening
DC 48400
HN Added, 1992.
BT Language Arts
RT Attention
Auditory Perception
Auditory Stimulation
Ear Preference
Hearing
Language Processing
Listening Comprehension
Motor Theory of Speech Perception
Receptive Language
Signal Detection
Silence
Turn Taking

Listening Comprehension
DC 48450
HN Formerly (1973-1991) DC li4.
UF Auditory Comprehension
Aural Comprehension
BT Comprehension
RT Auditory Perception
Decoding (Cognitive Process)
Language Processing
Learning Processes
Listening
Phonological Processing
Receptive Language
Second Language Learning
Verbal Learning

Literacy
DC 48550
HN Formerly (1973-1991) DC li5.
UF Illiteracy
NT Adult Literacy
Early Literacy
Functional Literacy
Reading
Writing
RT Literacy Programs
Reading Ability
Reading Achievement
Reading Writing Relationship

Literacy Programs
DC 48650
HN Added, 1992.
UF Universal Primary Education Programs
UPE Programs
RT Adult Literacy
Basic Writing
Education
Educational Activities
Functional Literacy
Literacy
Reading Ability

Literary Criticism
DC 48700
HN Formerly (1973-1991) DC li5a.
RT Content Analysis
Discourse Analysis
Literary Genres
Literary Theory
Literature
Narrative Structure
Novels
Stylistics

Literary Criticism (cont'd)
RT Text Analysis
Textual Criticism

Literary Genres
DC 48800
HN Formerly (1973-1991) DC li6.
NT Novels
RT Drama
Fiction
Humor
Literary Criticism
Literary Theory
Literature
Nonfiction
Poetry
Prose

Literary Language
DC 48950
HN Added, 1992.
BT Language
Language for Special Purposes
RT Colloquial Language
Language Styles
Literary Translation
Literature
Natural Language
Textual Criticism
Written Language

Literary Texts
Use Literature

Literary Theory
DC 49100
HN Formerly (1977-1991) DC li6a.
RT Literary Criticism
Literary Genres
Literature

Literary Translation
DC 49150
HN Added, 1992.
UF Literature Translation
Poetry Translation
BT Translation
RT Literary Language
Literature

Literature
DC 49250
HN Added, 1992.
UF Literary Texts
NT Childrens Literature
Drama
Poetry
Prose
RT Art
Authorship
Bible
Content Analysis
Fiction
Folklore
Humor
Imagery
Language Arts
Language Culture Relationship
Literary Criticism
Literary Genres
Literary Language
Literary Theory
Literary Translation
Metaphors
Mythology
Narrative Structure
Novels
Phonological Stylistics

Literature (cont'd)
RT   Religious Literature
      Rhetorical Figures
      Stylistics
      Symbolism
      Whole Language Approach
      Written Language

Literature Translation
Use   Literary Translation

Lithuania
DC   49340
HN   Added, 1992.
BT   Commonwealth of Independent
      States
RT   Union of Soviet Socialist Republics

Lithuanian
DC   49350
HN   Added, 1992.
BT   Baltic Languages

Little Russian
Use   Ukrainian

Loan (1975-1991)
HN   DC lo1.
Use   Borrowing

Loanword Borrowing
Use   Borrowing

Localization (Sound)
Use   Auditory Localization

Location
Use   Space

Locutionary Acts
Use   Speech Acts

Logic
DC   49540
HN   Added, 1992.
UF   Deductive Logic
      Formal Logic
      Inductive Logic
NT   Logic of Language
RT   Artificial Intelligence
      Associative Processes
      Cognitive Processes
      Generalization
      Learning Processes

Logic of Language
DC   49550
HN   Formerly (1973-1991) DC lo2.
UF   Modal Logic (1979-1991)
BT   Logic
      Philosophy of Language
RT   Entailment
      Extended Standard Theory
      Language
      Linguistic Theories
      Linguistics
      Logical Form
      Modality (Semantic)
      Montague Grammar
      Natural Language
      Port Royal School
      Presuppositions
      Private Language
      Quantifiers
      Semantics
      Semiotics
      Set Theory
      Syntax

Logical Form
DC   49600
SN   In government and binding theory, a
      level of representation derived by
      movement from S-structure (former-
      ly "Surface Structure") and serving
      as the interface between the gram-
      mar and a semantic interpreter.
HN   Formerly (1973-1991) DC lo2a.
BT   Form (Language Structure)
RT   Government Binding Theory
      Grammatical Analysis
      Grammatical Relations
      Logic of Language
      Modality (Semantic)
      Quantifiers
      Semantics
      Sentences
      Syntax

London School
DC   49700
HN   Added, 1992.
RT   History of Linguistics
      Linguistic Theories
      Linguistics
      Phonetics
      Phonology

Long Term Memory
DC   49800
HN   Formerly (1973-1991) DC lo3, Long-
      Term Memory.
UF   Delayed Recall
      LTM
BT   Memory
RT   Associative Processes
      Recall (Memory)
      Semantic Memory
      Short Term Memory

Longitudinal Studies
DC   49900
HN   Added, 1992.
UF   Follow Up Studies
RT   Case Studies
      Data Collection
      Language Acquisition
      Research Design
      Surveys

Loudness
Use   Intensity (Acoustics)

Louisiana
DC   49950
HN   Added, 1992.
BT   Southern States
      United States of America

Low Income Groups
DC   50100
HN   Added, 1992.
RT   Economic Factors
      Social Class
      Socioeconomic Status

Lower Class
Use   Social Class

Lozanov Method
Use   Suggestopedia

LTM
Use   Long Term Memory

Luganda
Use   Bantoid Languages

Luoravetlan
Use   Chukchee Kamchatkan Languages

Luwian
Use   Anatolian Languages

Luxembourg
DC   50150
HN   Added, 1992.
BT   Western Europe

Lycées
Use   Secondary Education

Lycian
Use   Anatolian Languages

Lydian
Use   Anatolian Languages

Maban Languages
Use   Nilo Saharan Languages

Macao
DC   50200
HN   Added, 1992.
BT   Far East

Macedonia
DC   50210
HN   Added, 1992.
BT   Eastern Europe

Macedonian
DC   50220
HN   Added, 1992.
BT   Slavic Languages

Machine Translation
DC   50250
HN   Formerly (1973-1991) DC ma1.
UF   Automatic Translation (Machine)
      Computer Assisted Translation
      Mechanical Translation
BT   Translation
RT   Computational Linguistics
      Computer Applications
      Computer Generated Language Anal-
      ysis
      Computer Software
      Natural Language Processing
      Word Processing

Macro Carib Phylum
Use   Ge Pano Carib Languages

Macro Chibchan Phylum
DC   50400
HN   Added, 1992.
UF   Chibchan Languages
      Inter Andine Languages
      Paez Coconuco Languages
BT   South Amerindian Languages

Macro Ge Bororo Phylum
Use   Ge Pano Carib Languages

Macro Panoan Phylum
Use   Ge Pano Carib Languages

Macro Siouan Phylum
DC   50450
HN   Added, 1992.
UF   Crow
      Dakota
      Iroquois
      Mohawk
      Siouan Languages
      Sioux
      Pawnee
BT   North Amerindian Languages

Macro Sudanic Languages
Use Chari Nile Languages

Macro Tucanoan Languages
Use Andean Equatorial Phylum

Madagascar
DC 50500
HN Added, 1992.
UF Malagasy Republic
BT Sub Saharan Africa

Madeira
DC 50550
HN Added, 1992.
BT Western Europe
RT North Africa

Maghreb
DC 50600
SN A region including northwest Africa, especially Morocco, Algeria, and Tunisia.
HN Added, 1992.
RT North Africa

Maine
DC 50650
HN Added, 1992.
BT Northern States
United States of America

Maipuran Languages
Use Andean Equatorial Phylum

Makua
Use Bantoid Languages

Malacca Languages
Use Austro Asiatic Languages

Malagasy Republic
Use Madagascar

Malawi
DC 50670
HN Added, 1992.
UF Nyasaland
BT Sub Saharan Africa

Malayalam
Use Dravidian Languages

Malayo Polynesian Languages
DC 50750
HN Added, 1992.
UF Philippine Languages
BT Austronesian Languages
NT Tagalog

Malaysia
DC 50800
HN Added, 1992.
BT Southeast Asia

Males
DC 50830
HN Added, 1992.
UF Men
RT Females
Sex Differences

Mali (Country)
DC 50840
HN Added, 1992.
BT Sub Saharan Africa

Mali Languages
Use Mande Languages

Malinke
Use Mande Languages

Malta
DC 50850
HN Added, 1992.
BT Mediterranean Countries
Western Europe

Mandarin
DC 50900
HN Added, 1992.
UF Northern Chinese
BT Chinese

Mande Languages
DC 50950
HN Added, 1992.
UF Bambara
Dyula
Mali Languages
Malinke
Mandingo Languages
BT Niger Congo Languages

Mandingo Languages
Use Mande Languages

Manitoba
DC 51100
HN Added, 1992.
BT Canada

Manufacturing
Use Business

Manuscripts
DC 51120
HN Added, 1992.
RT Diachronic Linguistics
Paleography
Printed Materials
Text Analysis
Textual Criticism
Written Language

Manx
Use Celtic Languages

Maori
Use Polynesian Languages

Marathi
Use Indic Languages

Markedness
DC 51150
SN A principle used to distinguish members of a set of units at any level of linguistic analysis (eg, phonology, morphology, syntax, or semantics) by means of the presence or absence of a specific feature or set of features.
HN Added, 1992.
RT Distinctive Features
Generative Grammar
Generative Phonology
Language Universals
Redundancy
Word Order

Markov Models
DC 51210
HN Added, 1992.
UF Hidden Markov Models
RT Computational Linguistics
Computer Generated Language Analysis

Markov Models (cont'd)
RT Mathematical Linguistics
Neural Networks
Research Design
Statistical Analysis

Markov, Andrey Andreyevich
DC 51200
SN Born 1856 - Died 1922.
HN Formerly (1973-1991) DC ma2, Markov.

Married Couples
Use Spouses

Martinet, André
DC 51250
SN Born 1908 - .
HN Formerly (1973-1991) DC ma3, Martinet.

Marxist Analysis
DC 51350
HN Added, 1992. Prior to 1992, see DC di2a, Dialectical Materialistic Linguistic Theory.
UF Marxist Leninist Analysis
RT Dialectical Materialistic Linguistic Theory
Economic Factors
Language Culture Relationship
Social Class
Social Factors
Sociolinguistics

Marxist Leninist Analysis
Use Marxist Analysis

Maryland
DC 51400
HN Added, 1992.
BT Northern States
United States of America

Masking
DC 51450
HN Formerly (1984-1991) DC ma3a.
UF Backward Masking
Forward Masking
Visual Masking
NT Auditory Masking
RT Perception
Signal Detection
Stimulation
Visual Stimulation

Mass Communication
Use Mass Media

Mass Media
DC 51500
HN Formerly (1973-1991) DC ma4.
UF Communications Media
Mass Communication
NT Films
Newspapers
Radio
Television
RT Advertisements
Communication
Content Analysis
Music
Political Discourse
Registers (Sociolinguistics)

Massachusetts
DC 51550
HN Added, 1992.
BT Northern States
 United States of America

Mastoidectomy (1973-1991)
HN DC ma5.
Use Surgery

Maternal Speech
DC 51650
HN Added, 1992.
BT Adult Language
 Speech
RT Adult Child Interaction
 Age Differences
 Baby Talk
 Child Language
 Children
 Females
 Infants
 Language Acquisition
 Linguistic Accommodation
 Parent Child Interaction
 Parents
 Sex Differences

Mathematical Linguistics
DC 51700
HN Added, 1992. Prior to 1992, see DC
 co7b, Computational Linguistics.
UF Algebraic Linguistics
BT Linguistics
RT Computational Linguistics
 Linguistic Theories
 Markov Models
 Mathematics
 Set Theory
 Statistical Analysis
 Word Frequency

Mathematics
DC 51850
HN Formerly (1973-1991) DC ma6.
UF Arithmetic
RT Computational Linguistics
 Mathematical Linguistics
 Numerals
 Scientific Technical Language

Mauritania
DC 51880
HN Added, 1992.
BT Sub Saharan Africa

Mauritius
DC 51890
HN Added, 1992.
BT Sub Saharan Africa

Mayan Languages
DC 51900
HN Added, 1992.
UF Quiche
 Yucatan (Language)
 Yucatec
BT Mexican Amerindian Languages
 North Amerindian Languages

Mean Length of Utterance
DC 52100
HN Added, 1992.
UF MLU
RT Child Language
 Discourse Analysis
 Language Acquisition
 Morphemes
 Speech Duration

Mean Ray Technology
Use Radiography

Meaning
DC 52200
HN Formerly (1973-1991) DC me1.
UF Denotation
 Semantic Value
NT Connotation
 Implicature
 Word Meaning
RT Ambiguity
 Anaphora
 Antonyms
 Componential Analysis
 Comprehension
 Context Clues
 Deixis
 Discourse Analysis
 Form (Language Structure)
 Homographs
 Homonyms
 Homophones
 Idioms
 Modality (Semantic)
 Pragmatics
 Reference (Grammatical)
 Semantic Analysis
 Semantic Differential
 Semantic Processing
 Semantics
 Semiotics
 Signifiant and Signifie
 Space
 Speech Acts
 Symbolism
 Synonyms
 Time
 Topic and Comment

Measures (Instruments)
DC 52300
HN Added, 1992.
UF Assessment Instruments
 Inventories (Measures)
 Scales
NT Miscue Analysis
 Personality Measures
 Projective Techniques
 Rating Scales
 Tests
RT Classroom Observation
 Interviews
 Research Design
 Surveys
 Test Validity and Reliability
 Thresholds

Mechanical Translation
Use Machine Translation

Mediation (1973-1991)
HN DC me2.
Use Mediation Theory

Mediation Theory
DC 52350
HN Formerly (1973-1991) DC me2, Me-
 diation.
UF Cognitive Mediation
 Mediation (1973-1991)
 Verbal Mediation
RT Cognitive Processes
 Generalization
 Learning Processes
 Recall (Memory)
 Retention (Memory)
 Verbal Learning

Medical Education
Use Professional Education

Medical Language
DC 52400
SN Terminology and prose used in medi-
 cine and related fields.
HN Added, 1992.
UF Language of Medicine
BT Language for Special Purposes
RT Language Styles
 Medicine
 Physicians
 Practitioner Patient Relationship
 Scientific Technical Language
 Technical Translation
 Terminology

Medical Patients
Use Patients

Medical Sciences
Use Medicine

Medicine
DC 52500
HN Added, 1992.
UF General Medicine
 Medical Sciences
NT Audiology
 Language Pathology
 Laryngology
 Speech Pathology
 Surgery
RT Anatomical Systems
 Biology
 Disorders
 Drug Effects
 Genetics
 Medical Language
 Patients
 Physicians
 Practitioner Patient Relationship
 Radiography
 Therapy

Mediterranean Countries
DC 52550
HN Added, 1992.
NT Algeria
 Cyprus
 Egypt
 France
 Greece
 Israel
 Italy
 Lebanon
 Libya
 Malta
 Monaco
 Morocco
 Spain
 Syria
 Tunisia
 Turkey
RT Arab Countries
 Europe
 Middle East
 North Africa
 Palestine

Medium of Instruction (Language)
Use Language of Instruction

Melanesia
DC 52600
SN One of the three principal divisions
 of Oceania, comprising the island
 groups in the South Pacific Ocean
 northeast of Australia.

Melanesia (cont'd)
- **HN** Added, 1992.
- **BT** Oceania
- **NT** Fiji Islands

Melanesian Languages
- **Use** Indo Pacific Languages

Memorization
- **DC** 52700
- **HN** Added, 1992.
- **BT** Learning Processes
- **RT** Memory
  - Pattern Drills
  - Recall (Memory)
  - Rehearsal (Verbal Learning)
  - Retention (Memory)
  - Serial Learning
  - Verbal Learning

Memory
- **DC** 52750
- **HN** Formerly (1973-1991) DC me3.
- **UF** Forgetting (1973-1991)
  - Memory Trace Theory (1973-1991)
  - Remembering
- **BT** Cognitive Processes
- **NT** Long Term Memory
  - Recall (Memory)
  - Recognition
  - Retention (Memory)
  - Semantic Memory
  - Short Term Memory
- **RT** Anomalous Strings
  - Associative Processes
  - Brain
  - Conditioning
  - Encoding (Cognitive Process)
  - Information Processing
  - Interference (Learning)
  - Language Thought Relationship
  - Learning Processes
  - Memorization
  - Memory Disorders
  - Metacognition
  - Neurolinguistics
  - Nonsense Syllables
  - Psycholinguistics
  - Semantic Processing

Memory Disorders
- **DC** 52800
- **HN** Added, 1992.
- **UF** Amnesia
- **BT** Disorders
- **RT** Alzheimers Disease
  - Aphasia
  - Brain
  - Brain Damage
  - Memory

Memory Trace Theory (1973-1991)
- **HN** DC me4.
- **Use** Memory

Men
- **Use** Males

Ménières Disease
- **DC** 52850
- **HN** Formerly (1973-1991) DC me5.
- **BT** Hearing Disorders

Meningitis
- **Use** Nervous System Disorders

Mental Development
- **Use** Cognitive Development

Mental Disorders
- **DC** 52900
- **HN** Added, 1992.
- **UF** Mental Illness
  - Psychiatric Disorders
- **BT** Disorders
- **NT** Emotional Disturbances
  - Mental Retardation
  - Neurosis
  - Psychosis
  - Schizophrenia
- **RT** Alzheimers Disease
  - Brain
  - Defense Mechanisms
  - Glossolalia
  - Nervous System Disorders
  - Psychoanalysis
  - Psychotherapy

Mental Illness
- **Use** Mental Disorders

Mental Retardation
- **DC** 52950
- **HN** Formerly (1973-1991) DC me7.
- **UF** Mentally Handicapped
  - Retardation (Mental)
- **BT** Mental Disorders
- **NT** Downs Syndrome
- **RT** Brain Damage
  - Handicapped
  - Intelligence
  - Nervous System Disorders
  - Special Education (Handicapped)

Mentally Handicapped
- **Use** Mental Retardation

Merchants
- **DC** 53000
- **HN** Added, 1992.
- **RT** Business
  - Occupations

Mesoamerican Indian Languages
- **Use** Mexican Amerindian Languages

Metacognition
- **DC** 53100
- **HN** Added, 1992.
- **BT** Cognitive Processes
- **RT** Comprehension
  - Language Thought Relationship
  - Learning Processes
  - Memory
  - Self Evaluation
  - Social Perception

Metalanguage
- **DC** 53150
- **SN** Any symbolic system used in the description of language, and the structure of such a system.
- **HN** Added, 1992.
- **RT** Applied Linguistics
  - Cognitive Processes
  - Language
  - Language Thought Relationship
  - Linguistic Theories
  - Linguistics
  - Philosophy of Language
  - Psycholinguistics
  - Terminology

Metaphors
- **DC** 53250
- **HN** Added, 1992.
- **BT** Rhetorical Figures
- **RT** Imagery
  - Literature
  - Semantics
  - Semiotics
  - Symbolism

Meter
- **Use** Rhythm

Metric Structure (Phonology)
- **Use** Metrical Phonology

Metrical Grids
- **Use** Metrical Phonology

Metrical Phonology
- **DC** 53270
- **HN** Added, 1992.
- **UF** Metric Structure (Phonology)
  - Metrical Grids
- **BT** Phonology
- **RT** Autosegmental Phonology
  - Juncture
  - Length (Phonological)
  - Mora
  - Stress
  - Syllables
  - Words

Metyibo
- **Use** Akan

Mexican Americans
- **DC** 53300
- **HN** Formerly (1973-1991) DC me8, Mexican American.
- **UF** Chicanos
- **BT** Hispanic Americans

Mexican Amerindian Languages
- **DC** 53400
- **HN** Formerly (1973-1991) DC me9.
- **UF** Mesoamerican Indian Languages
  - Olmeca Otomangue Languages
  - Oto Manguean Languages
  - Otomi
- **BT** Central Amerindian Languages
- **NT** Mayan Languages
- **RT** Uto Aztecan Languages

Mexico
- **DC** 53450
- **HN** Added, 1992.
- **BT** Latin America
  - North America
- **RT** Central America

Miao Yao Languages
- **Use** Sino Tibetan Languages

Michigan
- **DC** 53550
- **HN** Added, 1992.
- **BT** Midwestern States
  - United States of America

Micronesia
- **DC** 53600
- **SN** One of the three principal divisions of Oceania, comprising the small Pacific islands north of the equator and east of the Philippines, whose main groups are the Mariana Islands, the Caroline Islands, and the Marshall Islands.
- **HN** Added, 1992.

Micronesia (cont'd)
BT   Oceania

Middle Class
Use   Social Class

Middle Ear (1973-1991)
HN   DC mi1.
Use   Auditory System

Middle East
DC   53650
HN   Added, 1992.
BT   Asia
NT   Afghanistan
      Bahrain
      Cyprus
      Iran
      Iraq
      Israel
      Jordan
      Kuwait
      Lebanon
      Oman
      Palestine
      Qatar
      Republic of Yemen
      Saudi Arabia
      Syria
      Turkey
      United Arab Emirates
RT   Arab Countries
      Arab Cultural Groups
      Mediterranean Countries
      Middle Eastern Cultural Groups

Middle Eastern Cultural Groups
DC   53750
HN   Added, 1992.
BT   Cultural Groups
RT   Arab Cultural Groups
      Middle East

Middle English
DC   53800
HN   Added, 1992.
BT   English

Middle High German
Use   German

Middle School Education
Use   Junior High School Education

Middle Voice
Use   Voice (Grammatical)

Midwestern States
DC   53950
HN   Added, 1992.
NT   Illinois
      Indiana
      Iowa
      Kansas
      Michigan
      Minnesota
      Missouri
      Nebraska
      North Dakota
      Ohio
      South Dakota
      Wisconsin
RT   United States of America

Migrant Workers
DC   54000
HN   Added, 1992.
BT   Migrants
RT   Occupations

Migrants
DC   54030
HN   Added, 1992.
NT   Migrant Workers
RT   Acculturation
      Gypsies
      Immigrants
      Minority Groups
      Refugees

Military Personnel
Use   Armed Forces

Minnesota
DC   54100
HN   Added, 1992.
BT   Midwestern States
      United States of America

Minnesota Multiphasic Personality Inventory
DC   54200
HN   Added, 1992.
UF   MMPI
BT   Personality Measures

Minority Groups
DC   54240
HN   Added, 1992.
UF   Ethnic Minorities
      Racial Minorities
RT   Bilingualism
      Cross Cultural Communication
      Cultural Differences
      Cultural Groups
      Ethnolinguistics
      Foreigners
      Immigrants
      Indigenous Populations
      Migrants
      Minority Languages
      Refugees
      Religions
      Sociolinguistics

Minority Languages
DC   54250
HN   Added, 1992.
UF   Language Minorities
      Linguistic Minorities
BT   Languages
RT   Indigenous Languages
      Language Attitudes
      Language Contact
      Language Death
      Language Diversity
      Language Maintenance
      Language Policy
      Language Rights
      Language Shift
      Language Standardization
      Language Status
      Language Use
      Limited English Proficiency
      Minority Groups
      National Languages
      Official Languages
      Social Factors
      Sociolinguistics

Miscue Analysis
DC   54300
HN   Added, 1992.
BT   Measures (Instruments)
RT   Context Clues
      Decoding (Reading)
      Grapheme Phoneme Correspondence
      Language Usage

Miscue Analysis (cont'd)
RT   Oral Reading
      Reading
      Reading Instruction
      Reading Processes
      Reading Tests

Mississippi
DC   54350
HN   Added, 1992.
BT   Southern States
      United States of America

Missouri
DC   54450
HN   Added, 1992.
BT   Midwestern States
      United States of America

Misspelling
Use   Spelling Errors

MLU
Use   Mean Length of Utterance

MMPI
Use   Minnesota Multiphasic Personality Inventory

Modal Logic (1979-1991)
HN   DC ml1.
Use   Logic of Language

Modal Verbs
DC   54600
SN   Verbs expressing the modality of a proposition, ie, its possibility, desirability, necessity, propriety, compulsory or obligatory nature.
HN   Added, 1992.
BT   Verbs
RT   Auxiliary Verbs
      Conditional Clauses
      Modality (Semantic)
      Mood (Grammatical)
      Tense

Modality (Semantic)
DC   54610
HN   Added, 1992. Formerly (1973-1991) included in DC mo1, Mode.
RT   Logic of Language
      Logical Form
      Meaning
      Modal Verbs
      Semantic Categories
      Semantics

Mode (1973-1992)
HN   DC mo1, deleted 1992. See now Modality (Semantic) or Mood (Grammatical).

Modeling
Use   Imitation

Mohawk
Use   Macro Siouan Phylum

Moldova
DC   54640
HN   Added, 1992.
BT   Commonwealth of Independent States
RT   Union of Soviet Socialist Republics

Mon Khmer Languages
  Use Austro Asiatic Languages

Monaco
  DC 54650
  HN Added, 1992.
  BT Mediterranean Countries
       Western Europe

Monaural Stimulation
  DC 54670
  HN Formerly (1973-1991) DC mo3.
  BT Auditory Stimulation
  RT Binaural Stimulation
       Ear Preference

Mongol Languages
  Use Mongolian Languages

Mongolia
  DC 54700
  HN Added, 1992.
  BT Far East

Mongolian Languages
  DC 54750
  HN Added, 1992.
  UF Mongol Languages
  BT Altaic Languages

Mongolism
  Use Downs Syndrome

Monkeys
  Use Primates

Monolingualism
  DC 54850
  HN Added, 1992.
  RT Bilingualism
       Child Language
       Languages
       Multilingualism
       Native Language
       Native Speakers
       Second Language Learning
       Social Factors
       Sociolinguistics

Monophthongs
  Use Vowels

Montague Grammar
  DC 54900
  HN Formerly (1979-1991) DC mo4a.
  BT Linguistic Theories
  RT Categorial Grammar
       Grammatical Analysis
       Logic of Language
       Semantic Analysis
       Semantics
       Syntax

Montana
  DC 54950
  HN Added, 1992.
  BT United States of America
       Western States

Montenegro
  DC 55100
  HN Added, 1992.
  BT Balkan States
       Eastern Europe
  RT Yugoslavia

Mood (Grammatical)
  DC 55150
  SN In morphology, a category of verb in-
       flection (eg, indicative, subjunctive,
       optative) expressing contrasts in the
       stance of the speaker toward the
       content of a predicate (eg, assertion,
       wish, doubt, command).
  HN Added, 1992. Formerly (1973-1991)
       included in DC mo1, Mode.
  UF Modality
  BT Grammatical Categories
  NT Subjunctive
  RT Aspect
       Auxiliary Verbs
       Conditional Clauses
       Conjugation
       Declarative Sentences
       Imperative Sentences
       Interrogative Sentences
       Modal Verbs
       Morphology
       Semantics
       Syntax
       Tense
       Verbs

Mora
  DC 55200
  SN A unit of phonological length or met-
       rical time used to account for phe-
       nomena of syllabification, tone, and
       accentuation in certain languages.
  HN Added, 1992.
  RT Generative Phonology
       Length (Phonological)
       Metrical Phonology
       Phonemes
       Phonology
       Rhythm
       Stress
       Suprasegmentals
       Syllables

Morocco
  DC 55300
  HN Added, 1992.
  BT Arab Countries
       Mediterranean Countries
       North Africa

Morphemes
  DC 55350
  SN The smallest distinctive units of
       grammar in many systems of linguis-
       tic description.
  HN Added, 1992.
  UF Allomorphs
       Morphological Units
  BT Linguistic Units
  NT Affixes
       Roots (Morphology)
  RT Compound Words
       Mean Length of Utterance
       Morphology
       Morphophonemics
       Negation
       Number (Grammatical)
       Phonemes
       Syntactic Structures
       Syntagmatic Relations
       Syntax
       Tense
       Word Formation

Morphological Change
  DC 55400
  SN Change over time in the system of
       inflection, derivation, and word for-
       mation of a language.
  HN Added, 1992.
  BT Language Change
  RT Analogy (Language Change)
       Diachronic Linguistics
       Etymology
       Grammatical Change
       Morphology
       Semantic Change
       Sound Change
       Word Formation
       Word Structure

Morphological Units
  Use Morphemes

Morphology
  DC 55500
  SN Study of the structure, formation,
       and classes of words.
  HN Formerly (1973-1991) DC mo5.
  NT Morphophonemics
  RT Acronyms
       Affixes
       Aspect
       Autolexical Grammar
       Borrowing
       Case
       Code Switching
       Conjugation
       Deixis
       Derivation (Morphology)
       Form (Language Structure)
       Form Classes
       Gender (Grammatical)
       Government (Grammatical)
       Grammatical Analysis
       Grammatical Categories
       Incorporation (Grammatical)
       Inflection (Morphology)
       Intonation
       Juncture
       Language
       Language Patterns
       Language Typology
       Lexical Phonology
       Lexicology
       Linguistic Units
       Mood (Grammatical)
       Morphemes
       Morphological Change
       Number (Grammatical)
       Person
       Phonology
       Reflexivity
       Roots (Morphology)
       Rule Ordering
       Stress
       Suprasegmentals
       Surface Structure
       Syntax
       Tense
       Tone
       Voice (Grammatical)
       Word Formation
       Word Structure
       Words

Morphophonemics
  DC 55550
  SN In certain varieties of structural lin-
       guistics, the description of pat-
       terned, morphologically conditioned
       phonemic alternations, especially
       those observed in more than one
       morpheme. Used in other schools of
       linguistics to describe various phono-
       logical distributions that cannot be
       explained by reference to observable
       phonological features. Use this de-
       scriptor for the relation between
       phonology and morphology.

Morphophonemics (cont'd)
- **HN** Added, 1992.
- **UF** Morphophonology
- **BT** Morphology
  - Phonemics
- **RT** Affixes
  - Morphemes
  - Phonemes
  - Phonetics
  - Phonology
  - Prague School
  - Sandhi
  - Stress
  - Suprasegmentals
  - Surface Structure
  - Tone
  - Vowel Harmony

Morphophonology
- **Use** Morphophonemics

Mossi
- **Use** Gur Languages

Mother Tongue
- **Use** Native Language

Mothers
- **Use** Parents

Motion Pictures
- **Use** Films

Motor Cortex
- **Use** Brain

Motor Theory of Speech Perception
- **DC** 55600
- **HN** Formerly (1973-1991) DC mo6.
- **RT** Brain
  - Listening
  - Perceptual Motor Skills
  - Speech
  - Speech Perception

Mouth
- **Use** Oral Cavity

Movement (Grammatical)
- **DC** 55610
- **SN** In government and binding theory and related models of generative grammar, the mapping of D-structure (deep structure) onto S-structure (surface structure) and S-structure onto logical form.
- **HN** Added, 1992.
- **UF** Permutation (Grammatical)
  - Reordering (Grammatical)
- **RT** Generative Grammar
  - Government Binding Theory
  - Grammar Theories
  - Grammatical Analysis
  - Incorporation (Grammatical)
  - Noun Phrases
  - Syntax
  - Trace Theory
  - Transformation Rules
  - Transformational Generative Grammar
  - Wh Phrases

Movies
- **Use** Films

Mozambique
- **DC** 55620
- **HN** Added, 1992.
- **BT** Sub Saharan Africa

Multilingualism
- **DC** 55650
- **HN** Formerly (1973-1991) DC pl1, Plurilingualism.
- **UF** Plurilingualism (1973-1991)
- **RT** Bilingual Education
  - Bilingualism
  - Code Switching
  - Cross Cultural Communication
  - Diglossia
  - Indigenous Languages
  - Language Contact
  - Language Diversity
  - Language Maintenance
  - Language Planning
  - Language Policy
  - Language Rights
  - Language Use
  - Languages
  - Monolingualism
  - Psycholinguistics
  - Second Language Learning
  - Second Languages
  - Social Factors
  - Sociolinguistics

Multiple Sclerosis
- **Use** Nervous System Disorders

Munda Languages
- **Use** Austro Asiatic Languages

Munster
- **Use** Irish Gaelic

Muscular Disorders
- **DC** 55750
- **HN** Formerly (1973-1991) DC mu2a.
- **UF** Muscular Dystrophy
  - Myasthenia Gravis
- **BT** Disorders
- **NT** Parkinsons Disease
- **RT** Drug Effects
  - Handicapped
  - Nervous System Disorders
  - Phonation Disorders
  - Speech Pathology
  - Voice Disorders

Muscular Dystrophy
- **Use** Muscular Disorders

Music
- **DC** 55800
- **HN** Formerly (1973-1991) DC mu3.
- **RT** Art
  - Folklore
  - Mass Media
  - Poetry
  - Rhythm
  - Singing
  - Suggestopedia
  - Videotape Recordings

Muskogean Languages
- **DC** 55850
- **HN** Added, 1992.
- **UF** Choctaw
  - Hitchiti
  - Koasiti
  - Muskogee
  - Seminole
- **BT** North Amerindian Languages

Muskogee
- **Use** Muskogean Languages

Mutism
- **Use** Speech Pathology

Myanmar
- **DC** 55880
- **HN** Added, 1992.
- **UF** Burma
- **BT** Southeast Asia

Myasthenia Gravis
- **Use** Muscular Disorders

Mythology
- **DC** 55900
- **HN** Added, 1992.
- **RT** Folklore
  - Literature
  - Religions
  - Symbolism

Na Dene Phylum
- **DC** 56100
- **HN** Added, 1992.
- **UF** Athapascan
  - Navajo
- **BT** North Amerindian Languages

Nahua
- **Use** Uto Aztecan Languages

Nahuatl
- **Use** Uto Aztecan Languages

Names
- **Use** Onomastics

Namibia
- **DC** 56130
- **HN** Added, 1992.
- **UF** South West Africa
- **BT** Sub Saharan Africa

Narrative Structure
- **DC** 56150
- **SN** Recurrent patterns occuring in the representation of characters, events, and setting in literary or conversational narratives.
- **HN** Formerly (1988-1991) DC my3.
- **RT** Discourse Analysis
  - Literary Criticism
  - Literature
  - Story Grammar
  - Structuralist Linguistics
  - Text Analysis
  - Text Structure

Nasal Consonants
- **Use** Nasalization

Nasal Structures (1973-1991)
- **HN** DC na1, deleted 1991. See now Respiratory System or Nasalization.

Nasal Vowels
- **Use** Nasalization

Nasalization
- **DC** 56250
- **HN** Added, 1992. Prior to 1992, see DC na1, Nasal Structures.
- **UF** Nasal Consonants
  - Nasal Vowels
- **RT** Air Flow
  - Consonants
  - Place of Articulation
  - Respiratory System
  - Phonation Structures
  - Vowels

National Languages
- **DC** 56300
- **HN** Formerly (1973-1991) DC na1a.
- **BT** Official Languages
- **RT** Language Diversity
  Language Maintenance
  Language Planning
  Language Policy
  Language Rights
  Language Standardization
  Language Status
  Language Use
  Minority Languages
  Native Language
  Native Speakers
  Social Factors
  Sociolinguistics
  Speech Communities

Native Americans
- **Use** American Indians

Native Language
- **DC** 56390
- **HN** Added, 1992.
- **UF** First Language
  Mother Tongue
- **BT** Language
- **RT** Bilingualism
  Dialects
  Language Acquisition
  Language Use
  Monolingualism
  National Languages
  Native Language Instruction
  Native Speakers
  Nonstandard Dialects
  Regional Dialects
  Second Language Instruction
  Second Languages
  Speech Communities
  Standard Dialects
  Transformational Generative Grammar

Native Language Instruction
- **DC** 56400
- **HN** Formerly (1973-1991) DC na2.
- **BT** Instruction
- **RT** Bilingual Education
  Educational Activities
  Grammar Instruction
  Language Acquisition
  Language Arts
  Language Teaching Methods
  Language Use
  Native Language
  Native Speakers
  Nonstandard Dialects
  Oral Language Instruction
  Standard Dialects
  Written Language Instruction

Native Nonnative Speaker Communication
- **DC** 56420
- **HN** Added, 1992.
- **UF** Foreigner Talk
- **BT** Cross Cultural Communication
  Interpersonal Communication
- **RT** Intelligibility
  Language Patterns
  Language Usage
  Language Use
  Linguistic Accommodation
  Native Speakers
  Nonverbal Communication
  Pronunciation

Native Nonnative Speaker Communication (cont'd)
- **RT** Repair
  Second Languages
  Speech
  Speech Rate

Native Speakers
- **DC** 56450
- **HN** Formerly (1973-1991) DC na3, Native Speaker.
- **RT** Bilingual Education
  Bilingualism
  Creoles
  Dialects
  Grammaticality
  Immersion Programs
  Language Death
  Language Maintenance
  Language of Instruction
  Language Patterns
  Language Use
  Linguistic Accommodation
  Monolingualism
  National Languages
  Native Language
  Native Language Instruction
  Native Nonnative Speaker Communication
  Natural Language
  Nonstandard Dialects
  Official Languages
  Regional Dialects
  Second Language Instruction
  Second Languages
  Sociolinguistics
  Speech Communities
  Standard Dialects

Natural Generative Phonology
- **Use** Generative Phonology

Natural Language
- **DC** 56500
- **HN** Formerly (1973-1991) DC na3a.
- **BT** Language
- **RT** Artificial Languages
  Computer Generated Language Analysis
  Entailment
  Language Processing
  Literary Language
  Logic of Language
  Native Speakers
  Natural Language Processing
  Voice Recognition

Natural Language Processing
- **DC** 56550
- **SN** Use of computers to analyze textual materials in natural human languages; does not include literary and linguistic computing.
- **HN** Added, 1992.
- **UF** NLP
- **BT** Computational Linguistics
- **RT** Artificial Intelligence
  Computer Applications
  Computer Generated Language Analysis
  Computer Software
  Discourse Analysis
  Generalized Phrase Structure Grammar
  Lexical Functional Grammar
  Machine Translation
  Natural Language
  Neural Networks
  Pragmatics
  Semantic Analysis
  Syntactic Processing

Natural Phonology
- **DC** 56600
- **SN** A school of phonology based on a theory of natural processes in the acquisition of speech sounds and suppression of specific processes as the phonological system is acquired.
- **HN** Formerly (1979-1991) DC na3aa.
- **BT** Phonology
- **RT** Baby Talk
  Child Language
  Generative Phonology
  Language Acquisition
  Speech Therapy

Navajo
- **Use** Na Dene Phylum

Nebraska
- **DC** 56650
- **HN** Added, 1992.
- **BT** Midwestern States
  United States of America

Negation
- **DC** 56700
- **HN** Formerly (1973-1991) DC ne1, see Negative Statement.
- **UF** Negative Sentences
  Negative Statement (1973-1991)
- **RT** Interrogative Sentences
  Language Universals
  Morphemes
  Semantics
  Sentences
  Syntax
  Tagmemics

Negative Feedback
- **Use** Feedback

Negative Reinforcement
- **Use** Reinforcement

Negative Sentences
- **Use** Negation

Negative Statement (1973-1991)
- **HN** DC ne1.
- **Use** Negation

Negative Transfer
- **Use** Transfer (Learning)

Neogrammarians
- **DC** 56750
- **SN** A group of late nineteenth-century scholars, mostly German, who developed the comparative method of diachronic linguistics; they advanced the principle of regularity in sound change and provided the foundation for structural linguistics and the concept of the phoneme.
- **HN** Added, 1992.
- **UF** Junggrammatiker
- **RT** Comparative Linguistics
  Diachronic Linguistics
  History of Linguistics
  Linguistic Theories
  Linguistics

Neologisms
- **DC** 56850
- **SN** Words that have only recently appeared in the lexicon of a language as the result of linguistic creativity or word formation, and are not borrowings from another language or dialect.
- **HN** Formerly (1973-1991) DC ne2, Neologism.

Neologisms (cont'd)
- **BT** Lexicon
- **RT** Compound Words
  - Creativity (Linguistics)
  - Language Usage
  - Phraseologisms
  - Syntagmatic Relations
  - Word Formation

Nepal
- **DC** 56900
- **HN** Added, 1992.
- **BT** Himalayan States
  - South Asia

Nepalese
- **Use** Indic Languages

Nervous System Disorders
- **DC** 57100
- **HN** Formerly (1973-1991) DC ne3, Nervous System Pathology.
- **UF** Brain Disease
  - Cerebral Palsy
  - Encephalitis
  - Epilepsy
  - Meningitis
  - Multiple Sclerosis
  - Neurological Disorders
  - Paralysis (1973-1991)
- **BT** Disorders
- **NT** Alzheimers Disease
  - Aphasia
  - Brain Damage
- **RT** Attention Deficit Disorders
  - Behavior Disorders
  - Brain
  - Handicapped
  - Language Pathology
  - Language Therapy
  - Learning Disabilities
  - Mental Disorders
  - Mental Retardation
  - Muscular Disorders
  - Parkinsons Disease

Netherlandic
- **Use** Dutch

Netherlands
- **DC** 57150
- **HN** Added, 1992.
- **UF** Holland
- **BT** Western Europe

Network Grammar
- **Use** Generative Grammar

Neural Networks
- **DC** 57240
- **HN** Added, 1992.
- **RT** Artificial Intelligence
  - Cognitive Processes
  - Computational Linguistics
  - Computer Generated Language Analysis
  - Markov Models
  - Natural Language Processing
  - Neurolinguistics
  - Parallel Distributed Processing Models
  - Speech Synthesis
  - Voice Recognition

Neurolinguistics
- **DC** 57250
- **SN** Study of the neurological bases of language development, use, and disorders, with particular focus on the function and structure of the brain.

Neurolinguistics (cont'd)
- **HN** Formerly (1977-1991) DC ne3a.
- **UF** Neurological Linguistics
- **BT** Linguistics
- **RT** Aphasia
  - Brain
  - Brain Damage
  - Language Pathology
  - Language Processing
  - Linguistic Theories
  - Memory
  - Neural Networks
  - Psycholinguistics
  - Semantic Processing
  - Slips of the Tongue
  - Speech Pathology
  - Syntactic Processing

Neurological Disorders
- **Use** Nervous System Disorders

Neurological Linguistics
- **Use** Neurolinguistics

Neurosis
- **DC** 57300
- **HN** Formerly (1973-1991) DC ne4, Neurotic Disorders.
- **UF** Neurotic Disorders (1973-1991)
  - Psychoneurosis
- **BT** Mental Disorders
- **RT** Emotional Disturbances

Neurotic Disorders (1973-1991)
- **HN** DC ne4.
- **Use** Neurosis

Nevada
- **DC** 57350
- **HN** Added, 1992.
- **BT** United States of America
  - Western States

New Brunswick
- **DC** 57450
- **HN** Added, 1992.
- **BT** Canada

New England
- **Use** Northern States

New Guinea Non Austronesian Languages
- **Use** Indo Pacific Languages

New Hampshire
- **DC** 57460
- **HN** Added, 1992.
- **BT** Northern States
  - United States of America

New Jersey
- **DC** 57470
- **HN** Added, 1992.
- **BT** Northern States
  - United States of America

New Mexico
- **DC** 57500
- **HN** Added, 1992.
- **BT** United States of America
  - Western States

New Norse
- **Use** Norwegian

New York
- **DC** 57550
- **HN** Added, 1992.

New York (cont'd)
- **BT** Northern States
  - United States of America

New Zealand
- **DC** 57650
- **HN** Added, 1992.
- **BT** Australasia

Newfoundland
- **DC** 57700
- **HN** Added, 1992.
- **BT** Canada

Newspapers
- **DC** 57800
- **HN** Added, 1992.
- **BT** Mass Media
- **RT** Printed Materials
  - Reading Materials

Nicaragua
- **DC** 57850
- **HN** Added, 1992.
- **BT** Central America

Nicobarese Languages
- **Use** Austro Asiatic Languages

Niger (Country)
- **DC** 57880
- **HN** Added, 1992.
- **BT** Sub Saharan Africa

Niger Chad Languages
- **Use** Chadic Languages

Niger Congo Languages
- **DC** 57900
- **HN** Added, 1992.
- **UF** West Sudanic Languages
- **BT** Congo Kordofanian Languages
- **NT** Adamawa Eastern Phylum
  - Benue Congo Phylum
  - Gur Languages
  - Kwa Languages
  - Mande Languages
  - West Atlantic Languages

Nigeria
- **DC** 57910
- **HN** Added, 1992.
- **BT** Sub Saharan Africa

Nilo Saharan Languages
- **DC** 57950
- **HN** Formerly (1975-1991) DC ni1, Nilo-Saharan Languages.
- **UF** Coman Languages
  - Fur (Language)
  - Koman Languages
  - Maban Languages
  - Saharan Languages
  - Songhai
- **BT** African Languages
- **NT** Chari Nile Languages

NLP
- **Use** Natural Language Processing

Noise
- **DC** 58100
- **HN** Formerly (1973-1991) DC no1.
- **UF** Environmental Noise (1977-1991)
  - White Noise
- **RT** Acoustics
  - Auditory Masking
  - Auditory Perception
  - Auditory Stimulation

Noise (cont'd)
RT Hearing
Hearing Conservation
Intensity (Acoustics)
Psychoacoustics
Silence

Nominal Phrases
Use Noun Phrases

Nominalization
Use Nouns

Non Western Languages
DC 58150
HN Formerly (1973-1991) DC ex1, Exotic Languages.
UF Exotic Languages (1973-1991)
BT Languages

Nonfiction
DC 58200
HN Added, 1992.
BT Prose
RT Fiction
Literary Genres
Reading Materials

Nonsense Sentences
Use Anomalous Strings

Nonsense Syllables
DC 58250
HN Formerly (1973-1991) DC no2.
UF CVC Trigrams
Trigrams (1973-1991)
BT Anomalous Strings
Syllables
RT Memory
Nonsense Words
Psycholinguistics
Recognition
Verbal Learning

Nonsense Words
DC 58350
HN Formerly (1973-1991) DC no3.
UF Nonwords
BT Anomalous Strings
Words
RT Nonsense Syllables
Psycholinguistics
Verbal Learning
Word Recognition

Nonstandard Dialects
DC 58400
HN Formerly (1973-1991) DC no4, Nonstandard Dialect.
BT Dialects
RT Black English
Colloquial Language
Dialectology
Diglossia
Language Diversity
Language Maintenance
Language Standardization
Language Status
Native Language Instruction
Native Language
Native Speakers
Obscenities
Regional Dialects
Slang
Sociolinguistics
Standard Dialects

Nonverbal Communication
DC 58500
HN Formerly (1979-1991) DC no4a.
BT Communication
NT Facial Expressions
Gestures
RT Animal Communication
Communicative Competence
Eye Movements
Infant Vocalization
Infants
Interpersonal Communication
Kinesics
Linguistic Accommodation
Native Nonnative Speaker Communication
Nonverbal Languages
Paralinguistics
Sign Language
Silence

Nonverbal Languages
DC 58550
HN Formerly (1973-1991) DC no5.
UF Drum Languages
Whistle Languages
BT Languages
NT Sign Language
RT Facial Expressions
Gestures
Nonverbal Communication
Paralinguistics
Secret Languages

Nonwords
Use Nonsense Words

Nordic Countries
Use Scandinavia

Normative Grammar
Use Prescriptive Grammar

North Africa
DC 58600
HN Added, 1992.
BT Africa
NT Algeria
Egypt
Libya
Morocco
Sudan
Tunisia
RT Arab Countries
Canary Islands
Madeira
Maghreb
Mediterranean Countries
Sub Saharan Africa

North African Cultural Groups
DC 58650
HN Added, 1992.
BT African Cultural Groups
RT Arab Cultural Groups
Southern African Cultural Groups

North America
DC 58750
HN Added, 1992.
NT Bermuda
Canada
Greenland
Mexico
United States of America
RT Latin America
North American Cultural Groups

North American Cultural Groups
DC 58800
HN Added, 1992.
BT Cultural Groups
NT American Indians
Anglo Americans
Asian Americans
Black Americans
Hispanic Americans
Jewish Americans
RT Caribbean Cultural Groups
Jewish Cultural Groups
Latin American Cultural Groups
North America

North Amerindian Languages
DC 58900
HN Formerly (1973-1991) DC no6.
UF Hokan Phylum
Penutian Phylum
Salish Languages
Wakashan Languages
BT Amerindian Languages
NT Algonquian Languages
Eskimo Aleut Languages
Macro Siouan Phylum
Mayan Languages
Muskogean Languages
Na Dene Phylum
Uto Aztecan Languages
RT Central Amerindian Languages

North Carolina
DC 58950
HN Added, 1992.
BT Southern States
United States of America

North Dakota
DC 59100
HN Added, 1992.
BT Midwestern States
United States of America

North Korea
DC 59150
HN Added, 1992.
BT Far East

North Vietnam
Use Vietnam

Northern Chinese
Use Mandarin

Northern Ireland
DC 59200
HN Added, 1992.
BT United Kingdom
RT Ireland

Northern Rhodesia
Use Zambia

Northern States
DC 59250
HN Added, 1992.
UF New England
NT Connecticut
Delaware
Maine
Maryland
Massachusetts
New Hampshire
New Jersey
New York
Pennsylvania
Rhode Island
Vermont
RT United States of America

Northwest Territories
DC   59350
HN   Added, 1992.
BT   Canada
RT   Arctic Regions

Norway
DC   59400
HN   Added, 1992.
BT   Scandinavia

Norwegian
DC   59450
HN   Added, 1992.
UF   Dano Norwegian
     New Norse
BT   Germanic Languages
     Scandinavian Languages

Nostratic Theory
DC   59500
SN   A hypothesis that the Indo-European
     languages are genetically related to
     several other families of languages,
     including Uralic, Caucasian, and/or
     Afro-Asiatic.
HN   Formerly (1981-1991) DC no6c,
     Nostratic.
BT   Linguistic Theories
RT   Archaeological Evidence
     Comparative Linguistics
     Diachronic Linguistics
     Paleolinguistics

Noun Phrases
DC   59600
SN   Sentence constituents that consist of
     a noun and, optionally, determiners,
     adjectives, and other modifiers, in-
     cluding modifying clauses and
     phrases.
HN   Formerly (1973-1991) DC no8, Noun
     Phrase.
UF   Nominal Phrases
BT   Phrases
RT   Movement (Grammatical)
     Nouns
     Relative Clauses
     Subject (Grammatical)
     Syntax
     Thematic Roles
     Wh Phrases

Nouns
DC   59650
HN   Formerly (1973-1991) DC no7,
     Noun.
UF   Nominalization
     Substantives
BT   Form Classes
RT   Adjectives
     Animacy and Inanimacy
     Articles
     Case
     Gender (Grammatical)
     Incorporation (Grammatical)
     Noun Phrases
     Number (Grammatical)
     Prepositions
     Pronouns
     Quantifiers
     Valence
     Voice (Grammatical)

Nova Scotia
DC   59700
HN   Added, 1992.
BT   Canada

Novels
DC   59800
HN   Added, 1992.
BT   Fiction
     Literary Genres
RT   Literary Criticism
     Literature
     Reading Materials

Number (Grammatical)
DC   59850
HN   Formerly (1973-1991) DC nu1, Num-
     ber.
UF   Plural Forms
     Pluralization
     Singular Forms
BT   Grammatical Categories
RT   Adjectives
     Agreement
     Conjugation
     Form Classes
     Gender (Grammatical)
     Inflection (Morphology)
     Morphemes
     Morphology
     Nouns
     Person
     Pronouns
     Syntax
     Verbs

Numbers
Use Numerals

Numerals
DC   59950
HN   Formerly (1973-1991) DC nu2, Nu-
     meral.
UF   Digits (Numbers)
     Numbers
BT   Quantifiers
RT   Determiners
     Mathematics
     Written Language

Numic
Use Uto Aztecan Languages

Nupe
Use Kwa Languages

Nursery School Children
Use Preschool Children

Nursery School Education
Use Preschool Education

Nyasaland
Use Malawi

Obscenities
DC   60100
HN   Added, 1992.
UF   Profanity
     Swearwords
     Vulgarisms
BT   Lexicon
RT   Language Usage
     Nonstandard Dialects
     Slang

Obstruents
Use Consonants

Occipital Lobe
Use Brain

Occitan
Use Provencal

Occlusives
Use Stops

Occupations
DC   60200
HN   Added, 1992.
UF   Careers
     Jobs
     Professions
     Vocations
RT   Armed Forces
     Business
     Economic Factors
     Language for Special Purposes
     Language Styles
     Merchants
     Migrant Workers
     Registers (Sociolinguistics)
     Social Class
     Socioeconomic Status
     Scientific Technical Language

Oceania
DC   60300
SN   Islands of the central and south Pa-
     cific regions.
HN   Added, 1992.
NT   Melanesia
     Micronesia
     Polynesia
RT   Oceanic Cultural Groups

Oceanic Cultural Groups
DC   60350
HN   Added, 1992.
UF   Pacific Island Cultural Groups
BT   Cultural Groups
RT   Oceania

Oceanic Languages
DC   60400
HN   Added, 1992.
UF   Eastern Austronesian Languages
BT   Austronesian Languages
NT   Polynesian Languages

Oculomotor Responses
Use Eye Movements

Oesphageal Speech
Use Esophageal Speech

Official Languages
DC   60500
HN   Added, 1992.
BT   Language
NT   National Languages
RT   Bilingual Education
     Language Diversity
     Language Maintenance
     Language of Instruction
     Language Planning
     Language Policy
     Language Rights
     Language Standardization
     Language Status
     Language Use
     Minority Languages
     Native Speakers
     Social Factors
     Sociolinguistics

Ohio
- **DC** 60550
- **HN** Added, 1992.
- **BT** United States of America

Ojibwa
- **Use** Algonquian Languages

Oklahoma
- **DC** 60600
- **HN** Added, 1992.
- **BT** United States of America
-       Western States
- **RT** Ozark Mountains

Old Aramaic
- **Use** Aramaic

Old Church Slavic
- **DC** 60750
- **HN** Added, 1992.
- **UF** Church Slavonic
-       Old Church Slavonic
- **BT** Slavic Languages

Old English
- **DC** 60800
- **HN** Added, 1992.
- **UF** Anglo Saxon
- **BT** English

Old High German
- **Use** German

Older Adults
- **Use** Elderly

Olmeca Otomangue Langues
- **Use** Mexican Amerindian Languages

Oman
- **DC** 60850
- **HN** Added, 1992.
- **BT** Middle East

Omotic Languages
- **Use** Cushitic Languages

Onomastics
- **DC** 60900
- **SN** The branch of linguistics concerned with the names of individuals, families, and other sociocultural units, political entities, places, and provenances; For placenames, use the more precise term Toponymy.
- **HN** Formerly (1973-1991) DC on1a, Onomatology, Onomastics (Name, Naming).
- **UF** Anthroponomastics
-       Anthroponymy
-       Names
-       Proper Nouns
- **NT** Toponymy
- **RT** Archaeological Evidence
-       Descriptive Linguistics
-       Diachronic Linguistics
-       Etymology
-       Language
-       Lexicology
-       Linguistics

Onomatology, Onomastics (Name, Naming) (1973-1991)
- **HN** DC on1a, deleted 1992. See now Onomastics or Typonymy.

Onomatopoeia
- **DC** 60950
- **HN** Added, 1992.
- **UF** Sound Symbolism
- **RT** Phonological Stylistics
-       Poetry

Ontario
- **DC** 61100
- **HN** Added, 1992.
- **BT** Canada

Opacity
- **DC** 61150
- **HN** Formerly (1973-1991) DC on1b.
- **UF** Transparency
- **RT** Generative Phonology
-       Semantics
-       Syntax

Open Juncture
- **Use** Juncture

Operant Conditioning
- **Use** Conditioning

Operations (Surgery)
- **Use** Surgery

Opinions (1973-1991)
- **HN** DC op1.
- **Use** Attitudes

Oral Air Flow
- **Use** Air Flow

Oral Cavity
- **DC** 61200
- **HN** Formerly (1973-1991) DC or2, Oral Structures.
- **UF** Lips
-       Mouth
-       Oral Structures (1973-1991)
-       Palate
-       Teeth
-       Tongue
- **BT** Anatomical Systems
- **RT** Articulatory Phonetics
-       Cleft Palate
-       Phonation Structures
-       Place of Articulation

Oral Language
- **DC** 61300
- **HN** Formerly (1973-1991) DC op2.
- **UF** Spoken Language
- **BT** Language
- **RT** Adolescent Language
-       Adult Language
-       Child Language
-       Colloquial Language
-       Dialects
-       Discourse Analysis
-       Expressive Function of Language
-       Intelligibility
-       Foreign Accent
-       Interpersonal Communication
-       Language Acquisition
-       Language Patterns
-       Language Usage
-       Oral Language Instruction
-       Pronunciation
-       Pauses
-       Rhetoric
-       Rhythm
-       Second Language Learning
-       Speech
-       Speech Communities
-       Spoken Written Language Relationship
-       Story Telling
-       Written Language

Oral Language Instruction
- **DC** 61350
- **HN** Formerly (1973-1991) DC or1, Oral Language Teaching.
- **BT** Instruction
- **RT** Communicative Competence
-       Conversation Courses
-       Direct Method of Language Teaching
-       Educational Activities
-       Language Teaching Methods
-       Native Language Instruction
-       Oral Language
-       Pronunciation Accuracy
-       Second Language Instruction
-       Written Language Instruction

Oral Language Written Language Relationship
- **Use** Spoken Written Language Relationship

Oral Reading
- **DC** 61450
- **HN** Formerly (1973-1991) DC or1a.
- **UF** Reading Aloud
- **BT** Reading
- **RT** Decoding (Reading)
-       Miscue Analysis
-       Reading Instruction
-       Silent Reading

Oral Structures (1973-1991)
- **HN** DC or2.
- **Use** Oral Cavity

Oral Written Language Differences
- **Use** Spoken Written Language Relationship

Ordering of Rules
- **Use** Rule Ordering

Oregon
- **DC** 61500
- **HN** Added, 1992.
- **BT** United States of America
-       Western States

Oriental Cultural Groups
- **Use** Asian Cultural Groups

Origin of Language
- **DC** 61550
- **HN** Formerly (1973-1991) DC or4.
- **UF** Language Origin
- **RT** Animal Communication
-       Anthropological Linguistics
-       Archaeological Evidence
-       Diachronic Linguistics
-       Language
-       Linguistic Theories
-       Linguistics
-       Paleolinguistics
-       Unknown Languages

Originality
- **Use** Creativity (Psychology)

Orthoepy
- **Use** Pronunciation Accuracy

Orthographic Errors
- **Use** Spelling Errors

Orthographic Symbols
- **DC** 61700
- **HN** Added, 1992.
- **UF** Diacritical Marks
-       Diacritics

Orthographic Symbols (cont'd)
- **UF** Letters (Alphabet)
- **BT** Written Language
- **RT** Alphabets
  Consonants
  Grapheme Phoneme Correspondence
  Graphemics
  Ideographs
  Orthography
  Phonetic Transcription
  Phonetics
  Pronunciation
  Punctuation
  Reading
  Vowels
  Writing Systems

Orthography
- **DC** 61750
- **HN** Formerly (1973-1991) DC or5.
- **UF** Spelling
- **RT** Alphabets
  Dictionaries
  Grapheme Phoneme Correspondence
  Graphemics
  Homographs
  Language Arts
  Linguistics
  Orthographic Symbols
  Orthography Reform
  Phonotactics .
  Punctuation
  Spelling Errors
  Spelling Instruction
  Writing
  Written Language

Orthography Instruction
- **Use** Spelling Instruction

Orthography Reform
- **DC** 61850
- **HN** Added, 1992.
- **UF** Spelling Reform
- **RT** Language Modernization
  Language Planning
  Language Standardization
  Orthography

Oscan
- **Use** Italic Languages

Ossetic
- **Use** Iranian Languages

Other Repair
- **Use** Repair

Oto Manguean Languages
- **Use** Mexican Amerindian Languages

Otomi
- **Use** Mexican American Languages

Outer Ear, Pinna, Auricle (1978-1991)
- **HN** DC ou1.
- **Use** Auditory System

Outpatients
- **Use** Patients

Overgeneralization
- **Use** Generalization

Ozark Mountains
- **DC** 61900
- **HN** Added, 1992.
- **RT** Arkansas
  Missouri
  Oklahoma

Pacific Island Cultural Groups
- **Use** Oceanic Cultural Groups

Paelignian
- **Use** Italic Languages

Paez Coconuco Languages
- **Use** Macro Chibchan Phylum

Paired Associate Learning
- **DC** 62100
- **HN** Formerly (1973-1991) DC pa1.
- **BT** Verbal Learning
- **RT** Associative Processes
  Discrimination Learning
  Learning Theories
  Perception
  Recall (Memory)
  Rehearsal (Verbal Learning)
  Serial Learning
  Transfer (Learning)

Paiute Languages
- **Use** Uto Aztecan Languages

Pakistan
- **DC** 62200
- **HN** Added, 1992.
- **BT** South Asia

Palaeography
- **Use** Paleography

Palaic
- **Use** Anatolian Languages

Palatalization
- **DC** 62250
- **SN** In articulatory phonetics, the articulation of any speech sound with the lamina of the tongue raised toward or touching the hard palate. In phonology, a distinctive feature realized by this form of coarticulation.
- **HN** Added, 1992.
- **RT** Assimilation (Language Change)
  Consonants
  Phonology
  Place of Articulation

Palate
- **Use** Oral Cavity

Paleography
- **DC** 62300
- **SN** Study of ancient ways of writing, particularly the decipherment of texts.
- **HN** Added, 1992. Prior to 1992, see Paleolinguistics.
- **UF** Epigraphy
  Palaeography
- **RT** Archaeological Evidence
  Diachronic Linguistics
  Manuscripts
  Paleolinguistics
  Writing
  Writing Systems

Paleolinguistics
- **DC** 62400
- **SN** The reconstruction of features of a hypothesized prehistoric language, or protolanguage.
- **HN** Formerly (1984-1991) DC pa1aa.

Paleolinguistics (cont'd)
- **UF** Linguistic Paleontology
- **BT** Linguistics
- **RT** Anthropological Linguistics
  Archaeological Evidence
  Diachronic Linguistics
  Linguistic Theories
  Nostratic Theory
  Origin of Language
  Paleography
  Proto Indo European
  Textual Criticism
  Unknown Languages

Palestine
- **DC** 62410
- **HN** Added, 1992.
- **BT** Arab Countries
  Middle East
- **RT** Israel
  Jordan
  Mediterranean Countries

Pama Nyungan
- **Use** Australian Macro Phylum

Pamiguan Languages
- **Use** Andean Equatorial Phylum

Panama
- **DC** 62450
- **HN** Added, 1992.
- **BT** Central America

Panjabi
- **Use** Indic Languages

Pano Languages
- **Use** Ge Pano Carib Languages

Papua New Guinea
- **DC** 62550
- **HN** Added, 1992.
- **BT** Southeast Asia

Papuan Languages
- **Use** Indo Pacific Languages

Paradigmatic Relations
- **Use** Grammatical Relations

Paragraphs
- **DC** 62600
- **HN** Added, 1992.
- **BT** Linguistic Units
- **RT** Discourse Analysis
  Sentences
  Syntax
  Writing

Paraguay
- **DC** 62650
- **HN** Added, 1992.
- **BT** South America

Paralanguage
- **Use** Paralinguistics

Paralinguistics
- **DC** 62750
- **SN** Study of vocal and nonvocal forms of communication other than language, such as intonation, eye and head movements, gestures, and facial expressions, that may express agreement or disagreement or affect the meaning of utterances.
- **HN** Formerly (1973-1991) DC pa2.
- **UF** Paralanguage
- **BT** Linguistics
- **RT** Gestures
  Intonation

Paralinguistics (cont'd)
- **RT** Kinesics
  - Nonverbal Communication
  - Nonverbal Languages
  - Speech
  - Stress
  - Suprasegmentals

Parallel Distributed Processing Models
- **DC** 62755
- **HN** Added, 1992.
- **UF** Connectionist Models
  - PDP Models
- **RT** Computational Linguistics
  - Language Processing
  - Neural Networks

Paralysis (1973-1991)
- **HN** DC pa3.
- **Use** Nervous System Disorders

Parametric Approach (Grammatical)
- **Use** Principles and Parameters Approach

Parent Child Interaction
- **DC** 62760
- **HN** Added, 1992.
- **UF** Child Parent Interaction
- **BT** Adult Child Interaction
- **RT** Baby Talk
  - Children
  - Dyadic Interaction
  - Infants
  - Interpersonal Communication
  - Maternal Speech
  - Parents

Parents
- **DC** 62770
- **HN** Added, 1992.
- **UF** Fathers
  - Mothers
- **RT** Adult Child Interaction
  - Adults
  - Maternal Speech
  - Parent Child Interaction
  - Spouses

Parietal Lobe
- **Use** Brain

Parkinsons Disease
- **DC** 62800
- **HN** Added, 1992.
- **BT** Muscular Disorders
- **RT** Nervous System Disorders

Parsing
- **DC** 62850
- **SN** The process of identifying the morphological and syntactic functions and class memberships of elements of an utterance; often extended to include the description of the syntactic structure of the utterance.
- **HN** Added, 1992.
- **BT** Grammatical Analysis
- **RT** Computational Linguistics
  - Generative Grammar
  - Grammatical Categories
  - Grammatical Relations
  - Syntax

Partial Sight
- **Use** Vision Disorders

Parts of Speech
- **Use** Form Classes

Pashto
- **Use** Iranian Languages

Passive Voice
- **DC** 62900
- **SN** A verb inflection indicating that the subject, if one is present, is the sentence constituent that would otherwise appear as an indirect or direct object.
- **HN** Added, 1992.
- **BT** Voice (Grammatical)
- **RT** Agent Patient Relationship (Grammatical)
  - Clauses
  - Sentences
  - Subject (Grammatical)
  - Surface Structure
  - Verbs

Pathologies
- **Use** Disorders

Patient Agent Relationship (Grammatical)
- **Use** Agent Patient Relationship (Grammatical)

Patient Practitioner Relationship
- **Use** Practitioner Patient Relationship

Patients
- **DC** 62950
- **HN** Added, 1992.
- **UF** Medical Patients
  - Outpatients
- **RT** Disorders
  - Medicine
  - Practitioner Patient Relationship
  - Therapy

Pattern Drills
- **DC** 63000
- **HN** Added, 1992.
- **UF** Drills (Language Patterns)
  - Substitution Drills
- **BT** Language Teaching Methods
- **RT** Memorization
  - Second Language Instruction

Patterns (Language) (1977-1991)
- **HN** DC pa4b.
- **Use** Language Patterns

Pauses
- **DC** 63100
- **HN** Formerly (1973-1991) DC pa5.
- **UF** Filled Pauses
  - Speech Pauses
- **RT** Discourse Analysis
  - Oral Language
  - Punctuation
  - Rhythm
  - Silence
  - Speech
  - Turn Taking

Pawnee
- **Use** Macro Siouan Phylum

PB Lists
- **Use** Phonetically Balanced Lists

PDP Models
- **Use** Parallel Distributed Processing Models

Peabody Picture Vocabulary Test
- **DC** 63150
- **SN** Test designed to estimate verbal intelligence based on hearing vocabulary.
- **HN** Formerly (1973-1991) DC pe1.
- **BT** Intelligence Tests
- **RT** Language Tests

Pedagogy
- **Use** Instruction

Peirce, Charles Sanders
- **DC** 63200
- **SN** Born 1839 - Died 1941.
- **HN** Formerly (1973-1991) DC pe2, Peirce.

Pemba
- **Use** Swahili

Pennsylvania
- **DC** 63300
- **HN** Added, 1992.
- **BT** Northern States
  - United States of America
- **RT** Appalachia

Penutian Phylum
- **Use** North Amerindian Languages

Peoples Republic of China
- **DC** 63350
- **HN** Added, 1992.
- **BT** Far East
- **NT** Tibet
- **RT** Hong Kong

Perception
- **DC** 63450
- **HN** Formerly (1973-1991) DC pe3.
- **UF** Awareness
  - Cross Modality Matching
  - Sensation
- **BT** Cognitive Processes
- **NT** Auditory Perception
  - Proprioception
  - Social Perception
  - Speech Perception
  - Tactual Perception
  - Visual Perception
- **RT** Attention
  - Cerebral Dominance
  - Context Effects (Perception)
  - Credibility
  - Encoding (Cognitive Process)
  - Familiarity
  - Gestalt Theory
  - Identification
  - Language Thought Relationship
  - Masking
  - Paired Associate Learning
  - Perceptual Motor Skills
  - Recognition
  - Self Concept
  - Sensory Systems
  - Stimulation
  - Thresholds

Perceptual Defense
- **Use** Defense Mechanisms

Perceptual Identification of Speech
- **Use** Sound Identification

Perceptual Motor Skills
- **DC** 63550
- **HN** Formerly (1973-1991) DC pe4.
- **UF** Sensory Motor Skills
- **RT** Motor Theory of Speech Perception
  - Perception

Perceptual Stimulation
  Use Stimulation

Perceptual Style
  Use Cognitive Style

Perceptual Systems
  Use Sensory Systems

Performance (Linguistic)
  Use Linguistic Performance

Performative Utterances
  DC 63650
  HN Formerly (1973-1991) DC pe5, Performance Utterance.
  BT Speech
  RT Discourse Analysis
     Persuasion
     Politeness
     Pragmatics
     Semantic Analysis
     Semantics
     Speech Acts
     Verbs

Perlocutionary Acts
  Use Speech Acts

Permic Languages
  Use Finno Ugric Languages

Permutation (Grammatical)
  Use Movement (Grammatical)

Persia
  Use Iran

Persian
  DC 63700
  HN Added, 1992.
  UF Farsi
  BT Iranian Languages

Person
  DC 63750
  HN Formerly (1973-1991) DC pe6.
  UF Grammatical Person
  BT Grammatical Categories
  RT Auxiliary Verbs
     Conjugation
     Deixis
     Gender (Grammatical)
     Morphology
     Number (Grammatical)
     Pronouns
     Syntax
     Verbs

Person Perception
  Use Social Perception

Personal Accounts
  Use Verbal Accounts

Personal Identity
  Use Self Concept

Personality
  DC 63850
  HN Formerly (1973-1991) DC pe7, Personality and Personality Investigation.
  UF Character (Personality)
     Disposition (Personality)
  RT Cognitive Style
     Defense Mechanisms
     Emotions
     Personality Measures
     Self Concept

Personality Measures
  DC 63900
  SN Procedures or instruments used to obtain quantified descriptions of an individual's motivational and temperamental traits or behavior patterns.
  HN Added, 1992. Prior to 1992 see Personality and Personality Investigation.
  UF Kuder Preference Record
  BT Measures (Instruments)
  NT Minnesota Multiphasic Personality Inventory
  RT Diagnostic Tests
     Personality
     Projective Techniques
     Psychometric Analysis
     Self Concept
     Semantic Differential

Persuasion
  DC 63950
  HN Formerly (1973-1991) DC pe8.
  BT Communication
  RT Advertisements
     Beliefs
     Credibility
     Interpersonal Communication
     Performative Utterances
     Political Discourse
     Public Speaking
     Rhetoric

Peru
  DC 64100
  HN Added, 1992.
  BT South America

Pharyngeal Structures
  DC 64200
  HN Formerly (1973-1991) ph1.
  UF Pharynx
  BT Anatomical Systems
  RT Air Flow
     Fricatives
     Phonation Structures
     Place of Articulation

Pharynx
  Use Pharyngeal Structures

Philippine Languages
  Use Malayo Polynesian Languages

Philippines
  DC 64250
  HN Added, 1992.
  BT Southeast Asia

Philology
  Use Linguistics

Philosophical Linguistics
  Use Philosophy of Language

Philosophy of Language
  DC 64350
  HN Formerly (1973-1991) DC ph2.
  UF Linguistic Philosophy
     Philosophical Linguistics
  NT Logic of Language
  RT Language
     Linguistics
     Metalanguage
     Pragmatics
     Private Language
     Semantic Categories
     Semantics
     Semiotics
     Set Theory

Phonation
  DC 64400
  HN Formerly (1973-1991) DC ph3.
  NT Infant Vocalization
  RT Articulation
     Articulatory Phonetics
     Phonation Disorders
     Phonation Structures
     Singing
     Speech
     Voice Disorders
     Voicing

Phonation Disorders
  DC 64450
  HN Formerly (1973-1991) DC ph4.
  BT Disorders
  RT Applied Linguistics
     Articulation Disorders
     Handicapped
     Language Pathology
     Laryngology
     Muscular Disorders
     Phonation
     Phonation Structures
     Respiratory System
     Speech
     Speech Pathology
     Speech Therapy
     Voice Disorders

Phonation Structures
  DC 64550
  HN Formerly (1973-1991) DC ph5.
  UF Larynx
     Vocal Cords
     Vocal Folds
  BT Anatomical Systems
  RT Air Flow
     Articulation
     Articulatory Phonetics
     Laryngectomy
     Laryngology
     Nasalization
     Oral Cavity
     Pharyngeal Structures
     Phonation
     Phonation Disorders
     Respiratory System
     Voicing

Phoneme Grapheme Correspondence
  Use Grapheme Phoneme Correspondence

Phonemes
  DC 64600
  HN Formerly (1973-1991) DC ph5a.
  UF Allophones
     Phonological Units
  NT Consonants
     Diphthongs
     Vowels
  RT Comparative Linguistics
     Distinctive Features
     Grapheme Phoneme Correspondence
     Graphemics
     Intonation
     Juncture
     Language Patterns
     Language Typology
     Mora
     Morphemes
     Morphophonemics
     Phonemic Transcription
     Phonemics

Phonemes (cont'd)
- **RT** Phonetic Transcription
  Phonetics
  Phonological Analysis
  Phonological Processing
  Phonology
  Phonotactics
  Place of Articulation
  Sound Change
  Sound Duration (Phonetics)
  Suprasegmentals
  Syllables
  Syntagmatic Relations
  Voicing

Phonemic Transcription
- **DC** 64650
- **HN** Formerly (1973-1991) DC ph6.
- **RT** Grapheme Phoneme Correspondence
  Phonemes
  Phonetic Transcription
  Phonemics
  Phonetics
  Sound Duration (Phonetics)
  Writing Systems

Phonemics
- **DC** 64670
- **SN** The description of contrastive categories of speech sounds (phonemes) in terms of distinctive features present in the sounds; also, the process of segmenting utterances and classifying the segments into phonemes based on observed contrasts between utterances.
- **HN** Added, 1992.
- **BT** Phonology
- **NT** Morphophonemics
- **RT** Comparative Linguistics
  Descriptive Linguistics
  Diachronic Linguistics
  Generative Phonology
  Grapheme Phoneme Correspondence
  Graphemics
  Language Patterns
  Language Typology
  Linguistics
  Phonemes
  Phonemic Transcription
  Phonetic Transcription
  Phonetics
  Sound Change
  Speech
  Stratificational Grammar
  Taxanomic Approaches

Phonetic Change
- **Use** Sound Change

Phonetic Symbolism
- **Use** Speech Perception

Phonetic Transcription
- **DC** 64700
- **HN** Formerly (1973-1991) DC ph7.
- **RT** Alphabets
  International Phonetic Alphabet
  Orthographic Symbols
  Phonemes
  Phonemic Transcription
  Phonemics
  Phonetics
  Phonology
  Writing Systems
  Written Language

Phonetically Balanced Lists
- **DC** 64800
- **HN** Formerly (1973-1991) DC ph8.
- **UF** PB Lists
- **RT** Articulation Disorders
  Audiometry
  Diagnostic Testing
  Hearing Disorders
  Speech Perception

Phonetics
- **DC** 64850
- **SN** The scientific study of human speech sounds, their production (articulatory phonetics), their nature (acoustic phonetics), and their perception (auditory phonetics).
- **HN** Formerly (1973-1991) DC ph9.
- **NT** Acoustic Phonetics
  Articulatory Phonetics
- **RT** Articulation
  Assimilation (Language Change)
  Computational Linguistics
  Consonants
  Distinctive Features
  Generative Phonology
  Linguistics
  London School
  Morphophonemics
  Orthographic Symbols
  Phonemes
  Phonemic Transcription
  Phonemics
  Phonetic Transcription
  Phonics
  Phonology
  Place of Articulation
  Sound Duration (Phonetics)
  Speech
  Speech Perception
  Stress
  Tone
  Voice Quality
  Vowels

Phonic Method
- **Use** Phonics

Phonics
- **DC** 64900
- **HN** Formerly (1982-1991) DC ph10.
- **UF** Phonic Method
- **RT** Basal Reading
  Beginning Reading
  Decoding (Reading)
  Grapheme Phoneme Correspondence
  Initial Teaching Alphabet
  Phonetics
  Phonology
  Reading Instruction

Phonological Analysis
- **DC** 64950
- **SN** An analysis of the phonological structure of language data, using any of several models of phonology.
- **HN** Formerly (1973-1991) DC ph11.
- **RT** Assimilation (Language Change)
  Comparative Linguistics
  Computer Generated Language Analysis
  Descriptive Linguistics
  Phonemes
  Phonological Processing
  Phonology
  Place of Articulation
  Rhythm

Phonological Borrowing
- **Use** Borrowing

Phonological Change
- **DC** 65100
- **HN** Added, 1992.
- **BT** Language Change
- **RT** Assimilation (Language Change)
  Diachronic Linguistics
  Etymology
  Generative Phonology
  Phonology
  Sound Change

Phonological Processing
- **DC** 65110
- **HN** Added, 1992.
- **BT** Language Processing
- **RT** Anomalous Strings
  Applied Linguistics
  Decoding (Cognitive Process)
  Encoding (Cognitive Process)
  Language Acquisition
  Listening Comprehension
  Phonemes
  Phonological Analysis
  Phonology
  Phonotactics
  Reading Processes

Phonological Stylistics
- **DC** 65150
- **HN** Formerly (1973-1991) DC ph12.
- **UF** Alliteration
  Assonance
  Consonance
- **BT** Stylistics
- **NT** Rhyme
- **RT** Expressive Function of Language
  Literature
  Onomatopoeia
  Phonology
  Poetics
  Poetry
  Rhythm

Phonological Units
- **Use** Phonemes

Phonology
- **DC** 65250
- **SN** Branch of linguistics that studies the range, function, and rules governing the sounds in a specific language.
- **HN** Formerly (1973-1991) DC ph13.
- **BT** Linguistics
- **NT** Autosegmental Phonology
  Generative Phonology
  Lexical Phonology
  Metrical Phonology
  Natural Phonology
  Phonemics
- **RT** Accentuation
  Anomalous Strings
  Borrowing
  Comparative Linguistics
  Componential Analysis
  Consonants
  Descriptive Linguistics
  Diphthongs
  Distinctive Features
  Foreign Accent
  Grapheme Phoneme Correspondence
  Intonation
  Language Typology
  Length (Phonological)
  Linguistic Theories

Phonology (cont'd)
RT London School
  Mora
  Morphology
  Morphophonemics
  Palatalization
  Phonemes
  Phonetic Transcription
  Phonetics
  Phonics
  Phonological Analysis
  Phonological Change
  Phonological Processing
  Phonological Stylistics
  Phonotactics
  Place of Articulation
  Rule Ordering
  Sound Spectrographs
  Speech
  Stress
  Structuralist Linguistics
  Suprasegmentals
  Surface Structure
  Syllables
  Tagmemics
  Taxonomic Approaches
  Tone
  Voicing
  Vowel Harmony
  Vowels
  Word Structure

Phonotactics
DC 65300
SN The sequential arrangements of pho-
  nemes that occur in a language and
  the rules determining possible se-
  quences.
HN Added, 1992.
RT Orthography
  Phonemes
  Phonological Processing
  Phonology
  Pronounceability
  Sandhi
  Stratificational Grammar
  Syllables

Photography
Use Art

Phrase Structure Grammar
DC 65400
SN A model of generative grammar that
  describes sentence structure in
  terms of phrase structure rules that
  are capable of generating strings and
  can also provide a constituent analy-
  sis of the strings.
HN Formerly (1987-1991) DC ph13a.
BT Generative Grammar
NT Generalized Phrase Structure Gram-
  mar
RT Context Free Grammar
  Context Sensitive Grammar
  Deep Structure
  Form Classes
  Grammatical Analysis
  Phrases
  Surface Structure
  Syntactic Structures
  Syntax
  Transformation Rules
  Transformational Generative Gram-
  mar

Phraseologism, Phraseology (1973-
1991)
HN DC ph14, deleted 1992. See now
  Phraseologisms or Phraseology.

Phraseologisms
DC 65450
HN Added, 1992. Formerly (1985-1991)
  included in DC ph14, Phraseologism,
  Phraseology.
UF Proverbs
  Sayings
BT Lexicon
RT Colloquial Language
  Folklore
  Idioms
  Neologisms
  Phraseology

Phraseology
DC 65550
HN Added, 1992. Formerly (1985-1991)
  included in DC ph14, Phraseologism,
  Phraseology.
BT Language Usage
RT Idioms
  Phraseologisms
  Phrases
  Pragmatics
  Stylistics
  Words

Phrases
DC 65600
HN Added, 1992.
BT Linguistic Units
NT Noun Phrases
  Wh Phrases
RT Clauses
  Generalized Phrase Structure Gram-
  mar
  Grammatical Analysis
  Phrase Structure Grammar
  Phraseology
  Prepositions
  Sentence Structure
  Sentences
  Syntactic Structures
  Syntagmatic Relations
  Syntax
  Word Order

Physicians
DC 65640
HN Added, 1992.
UF Doctors (Medical)
RT Medical Language
  Medicine
  Practitioner Patient Relationship
  Professional Education

Physiological Phonetics
Use Articulatory Phonetics

Piaget, Jean
DC 65700
SN Born 1896 - Died 1980.
HN Formerly (1973-1991) DC pi1, Pia-
  get.

Piaroan Languages
Use Andean Equatorial Phylum

Pictographs
Use Writing Systems

Pictorial Images
Use Visual Media

Picture, Visual Media (1977-1991)
HN DC pi1aa.
Use Visual Media

Pictures
Use Visual Media

Pidgins
DC 65850
SN Contact languages, usually with limit-
  ed vocabulary and simplified gram-
  matical structure, and no native
  speakers; typically resulting from the
  incorporation of vocabulary from one
  or more languages into a simplified
  form of another language.
HN Added, 1992.
BT Languages
RT Borrowing
  Creoles
  Cross Cultural Communication
  Indigenous Languages
  Language Contact
  Language Diversity
  Trade Languages

Pike, Kenneth L.
DC 65900
SN Born 1912 - .
HN Prior to 1992, users were instructed
  to see Tagmemics.

Pinna
Use Auditory System

Pitch (Acoustics)
Use Frequency (Acoustics)

Pitch (Phonology)
DC 65950
SN The relative frequency of the voice,
  either as measured acoustically or as
  organized by the phonology of a lan-
  guage into distinctive levels and con-
  tours.
HN Formerly (1973-1991) DC pi2, Pitch.
RT Accentuation
  Fundamental Frequency
  Intonation
  Suprasegmentals
  Tone
  Voice Quality

Place of Articulation
DC 66100
SN Point in the speech tract where a
  speech sound is produced.
HN Added, 1992.
UF Articulation Point
  Point of Articulation
RT Articulation
  Articulatory Phonetics
  International Phonetic Alphabet
  Nasalization
  Oral Cavity
  Palatalization
  Pharyngeal Structures
  Phonemes
  Phonetics
  Phonological Analysis
  Phonology

Placenames
Use Toponymy

Plattdeutsch
  Use German

Plays (Theatrical)
  Use Drama

Plosives
  Use Stops

Plural Forms
  Use Number (Grammatical)

Pluralization
  Use Number (Grammatical)

Plurilingualism (1973-1991)
  HN DC pl1.
  Use Multilingualism

Poetics
  DC 66140
  SN The study of the structure of poetic language and poetic discourse.
  HN Added, 1992.
  RT Creative Writing
    Creativity (Psychology)
    Foregrounding
    Linguistic Theories
    Phonological Stylistics
    Poetry
    Rhetorical Figures
    Rhyme
    Rhythm
    Symbolism

Poetry
  DC 66150
  HN Formerly (1973-1991) DC pl2.
  BT Literature
  RT Authorship
    Creative Writing
    Drama
    Fiction
    Folklore
    Literary Genres
    Music
    Onomatopoeia
    Phonological Stylistics
    Poetics
    Prose
    Rhetorical Figures
    Rhyme
    Rhythm
    Symbolism

Poetry Translation
  Use Literary Translation

Point of Articulation
  Use Place of Articulation

Poland
  DC 66200
  HN Added, 1992.
  BT Eastern Europe

Polish
  DC 66300
  HN Formerly (1977-1991) DC pl3.
  BT Slavic Languages

Politeness
  DC 66350
  HN Added, 1992.
  UF Courtesy
  RT Address Forms
    Cultural Factors
    Discourse Analysis
    Interpersonal Behavior
    Performative Utterances
    Registers (Sociolinguistics)
    Turn Taking

Political Discourse
  DC 66450
  HN Added, 1992.
  UF Language of Politics
  BT Discourse Analysis
  RT Advertisements
    Language for Special Purposes
    Language Styles
    Mass Media
    Persuasion
    Pragmatics
    Public Speaking
    Registers (Sociolinguistics)

Polynesia
  DC 66500
  SN One of the three principal divisions of Oceania, comprising those island groups in the Pacific Ocean lying east of Melanesia and Micronesia and extending from Hawaii south to New Zealand.
  HN Added, 1992.
  BT Oceania
  NT American Samoa
    French Polynesia
    Hawaii
    Western Samoa

Polynesian Languages
  DC 66550
  HN Added, 1992.
  UF Hawaiian
    Maori
    Samoan
  BT Oceanic Languages

Polysemy
  DC 66560
  SN The attribution of more than one meaning or complex of meanings to the same word or other linguistic item.
  HN Added, 1992.
  RT Etymology
    Homonyms
    Semantic Analysis
    Semantics
    Word Meanings

Port Royal School
  DC 66650
  HN Formerly (1979-1991) DC po1a, Port-Royal School.
  UF Grammaire generale et raisonnee
  RT Grammatical Analysis
    History of Linguistics
    Language Typology
    Linguistic Theories
    Linguistics
    Logic of Language
    Semiotics

Portugal
  DC 66750
  HN Added, 1992.
  BT Western Europe

Portuguese
  DC 66800
  HN Added, 1992.
  UF Galician
  BT Romance Languages
  NT Brazilian Portuguese

Positional Reference
  Use Space

Positive Feedback
  Use Feedback

Positive Reinforcement
  Use Reinforcement

Positive Transfer
  Use Transfer (Learning)

Postsecondary Education
  Use Higher Education

Practice (Verbal Learning)
  Use Rehearsal (Verbal Learning)

Practitioner Patient Relationship
  DC 66830
  HN Added, 1992.
  UF Patient Practitioner Relationship
  RT Interpersonal Communication
    Medical Language
    Medicine
    Patients
    Physicians
    Psychotherapy
    Therapy

Pragmatics
  DC 66850
  SN Study of the use of language in communication, particularly in relation to the influence of social context and language structure on meaning.
  HN Formerly (1978-1991) DC pq1.
  RT Communicative Function of Language
    Conversation
    Discourse Analysis
    Foregrounding
    Functional Grammar
    Functional Linguistics
    Implicature
    Interpersonal Communication
    Language for Special Purposes
    Language Patterns
    Language Styles
    Language Usage
    Meaning
    Natural Language Processing
    Performative Utterances
    Philosophy of Language
    Phraseology
    Political Discourse
    Rheme
    Semantic Analysis
    Semantics
    Semiotics
    Social Factors
    Sociolinguistics
    Speech
    Speech Acts
    Syntax
    Truth

Prague School
  DC 67150
  HN Formerly (1973-1991) DC pr1.
  RT Focus
    Functional Linguistics
    Functional Sentence Perspective
    History of Linguistics
    Linguistic Theories
    Linguistics
    Morphophonemics
    Rheme
    Structuralist Linguistics

Prague School (cont'd)
RT   Synchronic Linguistics

Predicate
DC   67200
HN   Added, 1992.
UF   Verb Phrases
BT   Linguistic Units
RT   Agent Patient Relationship (Grammatical)
     Clauses
     Grammatical Categories
     Grammatical Relations
     Sentences
     Subject (Grammatical)
     Topic and Comment
     Verbs

Prefixation
Use   Prefixes

Prefixes
DC   67250
HN   Formerly (1973-1984) DC pr2, Prefix. Between 1984-1991, see DC af1, Affix.
UF   Prefixation
BT   Affixes
RT   Suffixes
     Word Formation

Prepositions
DC   67300
HN   Formerly (1973-1991) DC pr3, Preposition.
BT   Form Classes
RT   Function Words
     Grammatical Categories
     Nouns
     Phrases
     Pronouns

Preprimary Education
Use   Preschool Education

Presbyacusis
Use   Hearing Disorders

Preschool Children
DC   67350
HN   Added, 1992.
UF   Nursery School Children
BT   Children
RT   Early Literacy
     Kindergarten
     Preschool Education

Preschool Education
DC   67400
HN   Formerly (1977-1991) DC pr3aa, Preschool.
UF   Nursery School Education
     Preprimary Education
BT   Education
RT   Early Literacy
     Kindergarten
     Preschool Children

Preschool Literacy
Use   Early Literacy

Prescriptive Grammar
DC   67450
SN   Any treatment of a language that imposes a view of most correct or best usage.
HN   Added, 1992.
UF   Normative Grammar
BT   Grammar Theories
RT   Grammaticality
     Syntax

Presuppositions
DC   67500
HN   Formerly (1982-1991) DC pr3b, Presupposition.
UF   Assumptions
BT   Beliefs
RT   Entailment
     Logic of Language
     Truth

Primary Memory
Use   Short Term Memory

Primary School Education
Use   Elementary Education

Primary School Students
Use   Elementary School Students

Primates
DC   67650
HN   Added, 1992.
UF   Monkeys
RT   Animal Communication
     Interspecies Communication

Prince Edward Island
DC   67700
HN   Added, 1992.
BT   Canada

Principles and Parameters Approach
DC   67710
SN   The approach to language developed by Noam Chomsky during the 1980s, in which the human ability to speak is explained by a biologically programmed universal grammar, consisting of principles common to all languages and specific parameters along which individual languages vary. Children learn a language by discovering its parameter settings.
HN   Added, 1992.
UF   Parametric Approach (Grammatical)
BT   Grammar Theories
RT   Child Language
     Generalized Phrase Structure Grammar
     Generative Grammar
     Government Binding Theory
     Grammatical Analysis
     Language Acquisition
     Learning Processes
     Learning Theories
     Psycholinguistics
     Syntax
     Universal Grammar

Printed Materials
DC   67720
HN   Formerly (1973-1991) DC pr4, Printed Type.
UF   Fonts
     Typography
RT   Manuscripts
     Newspapers
     Reading Materials
     Textual Criticism
     Writing Systems
     Written Language

Printscript (Handwriting)
Use   Handwriting

Private Language
DC   67750
SN   Language in which the words are defined to refer to the private sensations of the user, and whose meanings can be known only to him or her. The logical possibility of such a language is in contention.

Private Language (cont'd)
HN   Formerly (1973-1991) DC pr4a, Private Languages.
BT   Language
RT   Inner Speech
     Logic of Language
     Philosophy of Language

Pro Drop Parameter
DC   67800
SN   A parameter used in government and binding theory to account for the difference between languages such as Spanish that allow unexpressed (null) subjects & those that do not.
HN   Added, 1992.
RT   Generative Grammar
     Government Binding Theory
     Incorporation (Grammatical)
     Language Universals
     Linguistic Theories
     Pronouns

Problem Solving
DC   67850
HN   Formerly (1973-1991) DC pr4aa.
BT   Cognitive Processes
RT   Creativity (Psychology)
     Intelligence
     Judgment
     Learning
     Word Games

Productivity (Linguistics)
Use   Creativity (Linguistics)

Profanity
Use   Obscenities

Professional Education
DC   67900
HN   Formerly (1973-1991) included in DC gr1, Graduate and Professional Schools.
UF   Legal Education (Professional)
     Medical Education
BT   Higher Education
NT   Teacher Education
RT   Graduate Education
     Physicians

Professions
Use   Occupations

Prognoses
Use   Prognostic Tests

Prognostic Tests
DC   68150
SN   Tests used to predict the outcome or success of educational, medical, or psychological treatment programs.
HN   Formerly (1977-1991) DC pr4b.
UF   Prognoses
BT   Tests
RT   Diagnostic Tests
     Reading Readiness
     Special Education (Handicapped)
     Therapy

Programmed Instruction
DC   68200
HN   Formerly (1973-1991) DC pr5.
UF   Autoinstructional Methods
BT   Instruction
NT   Computer Assisted Instruction
RT   Educational Activities
     Feedback
     Language Laboratories

Programming Languages
  Use Computer Languages

Projective Techniques
  DC 68300
  SN Procedures or devices for studying
       attitudes or personality by observing
       a person's response to a standard-
       ized set of ambiguous, unstructured,
       test stimuli (eg, being asked to give
       the meaning of inkblots or cloud pic-
       tures).
  HN Formerly (1973-1991), DC pr6.
  UF Bender Gestalt Test
       Rorschach Tests
  BT Measures (Instruments)
  RT Diagnostic Tests
       Personality Measures

Pronominals
  Use Pronouns

Pronounceability
  DC 68350
  HN Formerly (1973-1991) DC pr8.
  UF Unpronounceable Words
  RT Articulatory Phonetics
       Phonotactics
       Pronunciation
       Pronunciation Accuracy
       Intelligibility

Pronouns
  DC 68400
  HN Formerly (1973-1991) DC pr7, Pro-
       noun.
  UF Pronominals
  BT Form Classes
  RT Address Forms
       Anaphora
       Case
       Clitics
       Deixis
       Demonstratives
       Gender (Grammatical)
       Nouns
       Number (Grammatical)
       Person
       Prepositions
       Pro Drop Parameter
       Reflexivity
       Relative Clauses

Pronunciation
  DC 68500
  HN Added, 1992.
  BT Speech
  RT Articulation
       Articulatory Phonetics
       Child Language
       Foreign Accent
       Imitation
       Intelligibility
       International Phonetic Alphabet
       Linguistic Accommodation
       Native Nonnative Speaker Communi-
         cation
       Oral Language
       Orthographic Symbols
       Pronounceability
       Pronunciation Accuracy
       Sound Change
       Sound Duration (Phonetics)
       Speech Tests

Pronunciation Accuracy
  DC 68550
  HN Formerly (1973-1991) DC pr9.
  UF Orthoepy
  RT Articulatory Phonetics
       Foreign Accent
       Intelligibility
       Oral Language Instruction
       Pronounceability
       Pronunciation
       Second Language Instruction
       Vocabulary Instruction
       Speech Tests

Proper Nouns
  Use Onomastics

Proprioception
  DC 68600
  HN Formerly (1974-1991) DC pr11.
  UF Proprioceptive Perception
  BT Perception
  RT Hearing Disorders
       Tactual Perception

Proprioceptive Perception
  Use Proprioception

Prose
  DC 68700
  HN Added, 1992.
  BT Literature
  NT Fiction
       Nonfiction
  RT Creative Writing
       Drama
       Literary Genres
       Poetry
       Rhythm
       Writing
       Written Language

Prosodic Features
  Use Suprasegmentals

Prosody
  Use Suprasegmentals

Prostheses
  Use Prosthetic Devices

Prosthetic Devices
  DC 68750
  HN Formerly (1973-1991) DC pr12.
  UF Prostheses
  NT Hearing Aids
  RT Cleft Palate
       Esophageal Speech
       Surgery
       Therapy

Proto Indo European
  DC 68850
  HN Added, 1992.
  BT Indo European Languages
  RT Archaeological Evidence
       Diachronic Linguistics
       Paleolinguistics

Provençal
  DC 68860
  HN Added, 1992.
  UF Occitan
       South French
  BT Romance Languages
  RT French

Proverbs
  Use Phraseologisms

Psychiatric Disorders
  Use Mental Disorders

Psychoacoustics
  DC 68900
  SN Discipline concerned with the phys-
       ics and perception of sound and the
       physiological and psychological foun-
       dations of hearing.
  HN Formerly (1973-1991) DC ps1.
  BT Acoustics
  RT Auditory Localization
       Auditory Perception
       Auditory Stimulation
       Auditory System
       Hearing
       Noise
       Psycholinguistics
       Sound Identification

Psychoanalysis
  DC 69100
  HN Added, 1992. Prior to 1992, see Psy-
       choanalysis and Psychotherapy.
  RT Behavior Disorders
       Emotional Disturbances
       Mental Disorders
       Psychotherapy

Psychoanalysis and Psychotherapy
(1973-1991)
  HN DC ps2, deleted 1992. See now Men-
       tal Disorders, Psychoanalysis, or Psy-
       chotherapy.

Psycholinguistics
  DC 69200
  HN Formerly (1973-1991) DC ps3.
  UF Psychology of Language
  BT Linguistics
  RT Anomalous Strings
       Behavioristic Linguistic Theory
       Bilingualism
       Child Language
       Cognitive Processes
       Context Effects (Perception)
       Creativity (Linguistics)
       Generative Grammar
       Gestalt Theory
       Grammaticality
       Interlanguage
       Language Acquisition
       Language Attitudes
       Language Processing
       Language Thought Relationship
       Linguistic Interference
       Linguistic Relativity
       Linguistic Theories
       Memory
       Metalanguage
       Multilingualism
       Neurolinguistics
       Nonsense Syllables
       Nonsense Words
       Principles and Parameters Approach
       Psychoacoustics
       Psychometric Analysis
       Receptive Language
       Repair
       Semantic Categories
       Semantic Processing
       Signal Detection
       Slips of the Tongue
       Social Factors
       Social Perception

Psycholinguistics (cont'd)
RT   Sociolinguistics
Speech Perception
Syntactic Processing
Topic and Comment
Universal Grammar
Verbal Learning

Psychological Conditioning
Use   Conditioning

Psychology of Language
Use   Psycholinguistics

Psychometric Analysis
DC   69210
SN   The measurement of psychological traits, abilities, and processes using standard devices such as intelligence and personality tests.
HN   Added, 1992.
UF   Psychometry
RT   Cognitive Processes
Intelligence Tests
Personality Measures
Psycholinguistics
Statistical Analysis

Psychometry
Use   Psychometric Analysis

Psychoneurosis
Use   Neurosis

Psychosis
DC   69250
HN   Formerly (1973-1991) DC ps4, Psychotic Disorders.
UF   Insanity
Psychotic Disorders (1973-1991)
BT   Mental Disorders
NT   Autism
Schizophrenia
RT   Emotional Disturbances

Psychosomatic Disorders
Use   Emotional Disturbances

Psychotherapy
DC   69300
HN   Added, 1992. Prior to 1992, see Psychoanalysis and Psychotherapy.
UF   Behavioral Therapy
Gestalt Therapy
Reality Therapy
BT   Therapy
RT   Emotional Disturbances
Mental Disorders
Practitioner Patient Relationship
Psychoanalysis
Self Concept

Psychotic Disorders (1973-1991)
HN   DC ps4.
Use   Psychosis

Public Speaking
DC   69450
HN   Formerly (1973-1991) DC pu1.
BT   Language Arts
RT   Persuasion
Political Discourse
Rhetoric
Speech
Spontaneous Speech

Puerto Rico
DC   69500
HN   Added, 1992.
BT   Caribbean

Punctuation
DC   69550
HN   Formerly (1973-1991) DC pu2.
BT   Written Language
RT   Graphemics
Orthographic Symbols
Orthography
Pauses
Sentence Structure

Punishment
Use   Reinforcement

Punjabi
Use   Indic Languages

Puns
Use   Word Play

Pure Tone Audiometry
Use   Audiometry

Qatar
DC   69650
HN   Added, 1992.
BT   Arab Countries
Middle East

Quantification (1973-1991)
HN   DC pu2c.
Use   Quantifiers

Quantifiers
DC   69700
SN   In logic, terms that specify universality or existence; in grammar, a noun-phrase determiner that expresses distinctive quantity; in semantics, both senses intersect in use.
HN   Formerly (1973-1991) DC pu2c, Quantification.
UF   Quantification (1973-1991)
BT   Form Classes
NT   Numerals
RT   Adjectives
Determiners
Logic of Language
Logical Form
Nouns

Quantity (Phonological)
Use   Length (Phonological)

Quebec
DC   69800
HN   Added, 1992.
BT   Canada

Quebec French
Use   Canadian French

Quechua
DC   69900
HN   Added, 1992.
UF   Kechua
Quichua
BT   Andean Equatorial Phylum

Questions
Use   Interrogative Sentences

Quiche
Use   Mayan Languages

Quichua
Use   Quechua

Quine, Willard Van Orman
DC   69950
SN   Born 1908 -.
HN   Formerly (1973-1991) DC qu1, Quine.

Rabbinical Literature
Use   Religious Literature

Racial Minorities
Use   Minority Groups

Radio
DC   70100
HN   Added, 1992.
BT   Mass Media
RT   Frequency (Acoustics)
Television

Radiocinematography
Use   Radiography

Radiography
DC   70200
HN   Formerly (1973-1991) DC ra1, Radiograph.
UF   Cineradiography
Mean Ray Technology
Radiocinematography
Roentgenography
X Ray Technology
RT   Articulatory Phonetics
Medicine
Speech Pathology

Rajasthani
Use   Indic Languages

Rapid Eye Movements
Use   Eye Movements

Rate of Speech
Use   Speech Rate

Rating Scales
DC   70250
HN   Formerly (1973-1991) DC ra2, Rating Scale.
BT   Measures (Instruments)
NT   Semantic Differential
RT   Familiarity
Judgment
Test Validity and Reliability

Readability
DC   70350
HN   Formerly (1975-1991) DC ra2a.
UF   Readability Formulas
RT   Cloze Procedure
Content Analysis
Content Area Reading
Reading Comprehension
Reading Instruction
Reading Materials
Reading Rate
Story Grammar
Text Structure

Readability Formulas
Use   Readability

Readers (Materials)
Use   Reading Materials

Reading
DC 70400
HN Added, 1992.
BT Language Arts
Literacy
NT Basal Reading
Beginning Reading
Cloze Procedure
Content Area Reading
Oral Reading
Remedial Reading
Silent Reading
RT Context Clues
Decoding (Reading)
Grapheme Phoneme Correspondence
Initial Teaching Alphabet
Language Processing
Miscue Analysis
Orthographic Symbols
Reading Ability
Reading Achievement
Reading Aids for the Blind
Reading Comprehension
Reading Deficiencies
Reading Instruction
Reading Materials
Reading Processes
Reading Rate
Reading Readiness
Reading Strategies
Reading Writing Relationship
Tachistoscopes
Verbal Tasks
Vision
Writing
Written Language

Reading Ability
DC 70500
HN Formerly (1973-1991) DC re1.
UF Reading Skills
NT Reading Rate
RT Adult Literacy
Decoding (Reading)
Functional Literacy
Literacy
Literacy Programs
Reading
Reading Achievement
Reading Comprehension
Reading Deficiencies
Reading Instruction
Reading Processes
Reading Readiness
Reading Strategies
Word and Letter Association

Reading Achievement
DC 70600
HN Formerly (1973-1991) DC re2.
RT Literacy
Reading
Reading Ability
Reading Comprehension
Reading Tests

Reading Aids for the Blind
DC 70700
HN Formerly (1973-1991) DC re2a.
UF Braille
Kurzweil Reading Machine
RT Reading
Reading Instruction
Reading Materials
Tactual Perception
Vision Disorders

Reading Aloud
Use Oral Reading

Reading Comprehension
DC 70750
HN Formerly (1973-1991) DC re2b.
BT Comprehension
RT Cloze Procedure
Content Area Reading
Context Clues
Decoding (Reading)
Language Experience Approach
Readability
Reading
Reading Ability
Reading Achievement
Reading Processes
Reading Rate
Reading Strategies
Reading Tests
Receptive Language
Story Grammar
Text Structure
Word Recognition

Reading Deficiencies
DC 70900
HN Formerly (1973-1991) DC re3, Reading Deficiency.
UF Reading Difficulties
Reading Disorders
Reading Problems
BT Disorders
NT Dyslexia
RT Language Pathology
Language Therapy
Learning Disabilities
Reading
Reading Ability
Remedial Reading
Writing Disorders

Reading Difficulties
Use Reading Deficiencies

Reading Disorders
Use Reading Deficiencies

Reading in Content Areas
Use Content Area Reading

Reading Instruction
DC 70950
HN Formerly (1973-1990) DC re4.
BT Instruction
NT Basal Reading
Content Area Reading
Remedial Reading
Second Language Reading Instruction
RT Educational Activities
Initial Teaching Alphabet
Language Experience Approach
Miscue Analysis
Oral Reading
Phonics
Readability
Reading
Reading Ability
Reading Aids for the Blind
Reading Materials
Reading Readiness
Reading Strategies
Reading Tests
Silent Reading
Story Grammar
Tachistoscopes
Vocabulary Instruction
Whole Language Approach

Reading Materials
DC 71100
HN Formerly (1973-1991) DC re5.
UF Readers (Materials)
RT Basal Reading
Childrens Literature
Newspapers
Nonfiction
Novels
Printed Materials
Readability
Reading
Reading Aids for the Blind
Reading Instruction
Teaching Materials
Visual Media

Reading Problems
Use Reading Deficiencies

Reading Processes
DC 71150
HN Formerly (1973-1991) DC re6.
BT Cognitive Processes
NT Context Effects (Perception)
Decoding (Reading)
RT Eye Movements
Language Processing
Language Thought Relationship
Letter Recognition
Miscue Analysis
Phonological Processing
Reading
Reading Ability
Reading Comprehension
Reading Strategies
Reading Writing Relationship
Receptive Language
Semantic Processing
Word Recognition

Reading Rate
DC 71250
HN Formerly (1975-1991) DC re6a.
UF Reading Speed
BT Reading Ability
RT Readability
Reading
Reading Comprehension
Reading Tests
Silent Reading

Reading Readiness
DC 71350
HN Formerly (1975-1991) DC re6b.
RT Beginning Reading
Early Literacy
Prognostic Tests
Reading
Reading Ability
Reading Instruction

Reading Skills
Use Reading Ability

Reading Speed
Use Reading Rate

Reading Strategies
DC 71400
HN Added, 1992.
RT Reading
Reading Ability
Reading Comprehension
Reading Instruction
Reading Processes

Reading Tests
- **DC** 71550
- **HN** Formerly (1973-1991) DC re6c, Reading Testing.
- **BT** Tests
- **RT** Achievement Tests
  Cloze Procedure
  Language Tests
  Miscue Analysis
  Reading Achievement
  Reading Comprehension
  Reading Instruction
  Reading Rate
  Speech Tests
  Writing Tests

Reading Writing Relationship
- **DC** 71650
- **HN** Added, 1992.
- **UF** Writing Reading Relationship
- **RT** Language Arts
  Literacy
  Reading
  Reading Processes
  Story Grammar
  Text Structure
  Whole Language Approach
  Writing
  Writing Processes

Realistic Grammar
- **Use** Generative Grammar

Reality Therapy
- **Use** Psychotherapy

Reasoning
- **Use** Cognitive Processes

Recall (Memory)
- **DC** 71700
- **HN** Added, 1992.
- **BT** Memory
- **NT** Aided Recall
  Unaided Recall
- **RT** Encoding (Cognitive Process)
  Familiarity
  Learning
  Learning Disabilities
  Learning Processes
  Long Term Memory
  Mediation Theory
  Memorization
  Paired Associate Learning
  Recognition
  Retention (Memory)
  Short Term Memory
  Verbal Tasks

Receptive Aphasia
- **Use** Aphasia

Receptive Language
- **DC** 71800
- **HN** Formerly (1978-1991) DC re6d.
- **BT** Language Processing
- **RT** Aphasia
  Communication
  Decoding (Cognitive Process)
  Language
  Language Acquisition
  Language Pathology
  Listening
  Listening Comprehension
  Psycholinguistics
  Reading Comprehension
  Reading Processes

Recipient Agent Relationship (Grammatical)
- **Use** Agent Patient Relationship (Grammatical)

Recognition
- **DC** 71850
- **HN** Added, 1992.
- **BT** Memory
- **NT** Letter Recognition
  Word Recognition
- **RT** Aided Recall
  Associative Processes
  Encoding (Cognitive Process)
  Familiarity
  Identification
  Learning Disabilities
  Learning Processes
  Nonsense Syllables
  Perception
  Recall (Memory)
  Retention (Memory)
  Signal Detection
  Tachistoscopes

Reduced Constructions
- **Use** Ellipsis

Redundancy
- **DC** 71950
- **HN** Formerly (1973-1991) DC re7.
- **RT** Distinctive Features
  Grammatical Analysis
  Markedness
  Semantics
  Syntax
  Word Formation

Reference (Grammatical)
- **DC** 71970
- **SN** The relation of a word or other linguistic element to the specific entity or set/class of entities that it represents in a given instance. Distinguish meaning, characterizable in some semantic models as the set of possible references of a linguistic unit. Also distinguish anaphora, which denotes one type of relationship between two linguistic units having the same reference.
- **HN** Added, 1992.
- **UF** Arbitrary Reference
  Referential Expression
- **NT** Anaphora
- **RT** Deixis
  Government Binding Theory
  Grammatical Analysis
  Grammatical Relations
  Linguistic Units
  Meaning Deixis
  Semantics
  Syntax

Referential Expression
- **Use** Reference (Grammatical)

Reflexivity
- **DC** 71980
- **HN** Added, 1992.
- **RT** Affixes
  Anaphora
  Case
  Generative Grammar
  Government Binding Theory
  Grammatical Analysis
  Morphology
  Pronouns
  Transformational Generative Grammar

Reflexivity (cont'd)
- **RT** Verbs

Refugees
- **DC** 72000
- **HN** Added, 1992.
- **RT** Acculturation
  Foreigners
  Immigrants
  Migrants
  Minority Groups

Regional Dialects
- **DC** 72100
- **HN** Added, 1992.
- **UF** Geographical Dialects
  Regional Variety
- **BT** Dialects
- **RT** Areal Linguistics
  Black English
  Dialectology
  Idioms
  Native Language
  Native Speakers
  Nonstandard Dialects
  Standard Dialects

Regional Variety
- **Use** Regional Dialects

Register (Phonology)
- **Use** Voice Quality

Registers (Sociolinguistics)
- **DC** 72250
- **SN** Linguistically distinct activities requiring special terminology, norms, and conventions. For the language varieties associated with particular registers, see Language for Special Purposes and its associated terms.
- **HN** Formerly (1973-1991) DC re8, Register.
- **RT** Address Forms
  Adult Child Interaction
  Armed Forces
  Baby Talk
  Business
  Colloquial Language
  Conversation
  Diglossia
  Language
  Language for Special Purposes
  Language Patterns
  Language Styles
  Language Usage
  Linguistic Accommodation
  Mass Media
  Occupations
  Politeness
  Political Discourse
  Secret Languages
  Sex Differences
  Slang
  Social Factors
  Speech Communities
  Sports
  Terminology

Rehearsal (Verbal Learning)
- **DC** 72400
- **HN** Formerly (1973-1991) DC re8a.
- **UF** Practice (Verbal Learning)
- **RT** Memorization
  Paired Associate Learning
  Serial Learning
  Verbal Learning

Reinforcement
- **DC** 72450
- **HN** Formerly (1973-1991) DC re9.
- **UF** Negative Reinforcement
  Positive Reinforcement
  Punishment
  Reward
- **RT** Conditioning
  Educational Activities
  Feedback
  Teaching Methods

Relation (Grammatical) (1973-1991)
- **HN** DC re9c.
- **Use** Grammatical Relations

Relational Grammar
- **DC** 72600
- **SN** A theory of grammar developed in the 1970s that rejects the linear order and dominance elements of transformational-generative grammar. Clause structure is represented via grammatical relations, taken to be the primitive elements of syntax; distinct syntactic levels are posited.
- **HN** Added, 1992.
- **BT** Generative Grammar
- **RT** Grammatical Relations
  Subject (Grammatical)
  Syntax

Relative Clauses
- **DC** 72650
- **HN** Added, 1992.
- **BT** Clauses
- **RT** Noun Phrases
  Pronouns
  Sentences
  Subordination (Grammatical)
  Syntax

Relativity (Linguistics)
- **Use** Linguistic Relativity

Reliability (Tests)
- **Use** Test Validity and Reliability

Religions
- **DC** 72750
- **HN** Added, 1992.
- **RT** Beliefs
  Bible
  Cultural Groups
  Culture
  Ethnolinguistics
  Folklore
  Glossolalia
  Minority Groups
  Mythology
  Religious Literature
  Sociolinguistics

Religious Literature
- **DC** 72800
- **HN** Added, 1992.
- **UF** Koran
  Rabbinical Literature
  Sacred Literature
  Talmud
- **NT** Bible
- **RT** Literature
  Religions

Remedial Reading
- **DC** 72900
- **HN** Added, 1992.
- **BT** Reading
  Reading Instruction
- **RT** Basic Writing
  Dyslexia
  Initial Teaching Alphabet
  Learning Disabilities
  Reading Deficiencies

Remedial Writing
- **Use** Basic Writing

Remembering
- **Use** Memory

Remote Associates
- **Use** Associative Processes

Reordering (Grammatical)
- **Use** Movement (Grammatical)

Repair
- **DC** 72920
- **HN** Added, 1992.
- **UF** Error Repair
  Other Repair
  Self Repair
  Speech Error Repair
- **RT** Cognitive Processes
  Comprehension
  Conversation
  Discourse Analysis
  Error Analysis (Language)
  Language Patterns
  Native Nonnative Speaker Communication
  Psycholinguistics
  Slips of the Tongue
  Speech
  Speech Acts
  Speech Perception

Republic of China
- **Use** Taiwan

Republic of Yemen
- **DC** 72930
- **SN** Country formed by the merger of the Yemen Arab Republic and the People's Democratic Republic of Yemen.
- **HN** Added, 1992.
- **UF** Aden
  Yemen
- **BT** Arab Countries
  Middle East

Research Design
- **DC** 72950
- **HN** Formerly (1973-1991) DC re11, Research Design and Instrumentation.
- **UF** Experimental Design
- **RT** Case Studies
  Componential Analysis
  Data Collection
  Data Processing
  Databases
  Fieldwork
  Interviews
  Longitudinal Studies
  Markov Models
  Measures (Individuals)
  Research Subjects
  Statistical Analysis
  Surveys

Research Subjects
- **DC** 72970
- **HN** Added, 1992.
- **UF** Control Subjects
  Experimental Subjects
  Human Subjects (Research)
- **RT** Research Design
  Respondents

Resonants
- **Use** Consonants

Respiration and Respiratory Structures (1973-1991)
- **HN** DC re12.
- **Use** Respiratory System

Respiratory System
- **DC** 73100
- **HN** Formerly (1973-1991) DC re12, Respiration and Respiratory Structures.
- **UF** Respiration and Respiratory Structures (1973-1991)
- **BT** Anatomical Systems
- **RT** Air Flow
  Nasalization
  Phonation Disorders
  Phonation Structures
  Stuttering
  Voice Disorders

Respondent Conditioning
- **Use** Conditioning

Respondents
- **DC** 73120
- **HN** Added, 1992.
- **UF** Informants
  Interviewees
- **RT** Interviews
  Research Subjects
  Surveys

Retardation (Mental)
- **Use** Mental Retardation

Retarded Speech Development
- **Use** Delayed Language Acquisition

Retention (Memory)
- **DC** 73150
- **HN** Added, 1992.
- **BT** Memory
- **RT** Encoding (Cognitive Process)
  Familiarity
  Interference (Learning)
  Learning
  Mediation Theory
  Memorization
  Recall (Memory)
  Recognition
  Short Term Memory
  Unaided Recall

Réunion
- **DC** 73170
- **HN** Added, 1992.
- **BT** Sub Saharan Africa

Reward
- **Use** Reinforcement

Rheme
- **DC** 73250
- **SN** Part of the theme/rheme division of sentences in functional linguistics, especially functional sentence perspective; all components of the sentence that contribute to the communication of new information belong to the rheme, the rest of the sentence constituting the theme.
- **HN** Formerly (1977-1991) DC re17.
- **RT** Discourse Analysis
  Focus
  Foregrounding
  Functional Sentence Perspective
  Pragmatics

Rheme (cont'd)
RT   Prague School
     Semantic Analysis
     Semantics
     Sentences
     Text Structure

Rhetoric
DC   73300
HN   Formerly (1973-1991) DC rh1.
BT   Language Arts
RT   Oral Language
     Persuasion
     Public Speaking
     Speech
     Writing

Rhetorical Figures
DC   73400
SN   Expressions or constructions deviating from standard usage or normal word order to achieve effect, eg, metaphor, simile, irony, or hyperbole.
HN   Formerly (1973-1991) DC rh2.
UF   Figurative Language
     Figures of Speech
     Hyperbole
     Simile
     Spoonerisms (Deliberate)
NT   Metaphors
RT   Ambiguity
     Creative Writing
     Imagery
     Literature
     Metaphors
     Poetics
     Poetry
     Stylistics
     Symbolism
     Text Analysis
     Word Play

Rhode Island
DC   73450
HN   Added, 1992.
BT   Northern States
     United States of America

Rhyme
DC   73550
HN   Added, 1992.
BT   Phonological Stylistics
RT   Poetics
     Poetry

Rhythm
DC   73600
HN   Formerly (1977-1991) DC rh3a.
UF   Meter
RT   Accentuation
     Mora
     Music
     Oral Language
     Pauses
     Phonological Analysis
     Phonological Stylistics
     Poetics
     Poetry
     Prose
     Stress

Riddles
Use   Word Play

Riff
Use   Berber Languages

Right Brain Dominance
Use   Cerebral Dominance

Right Handedness
Use   Handedness

Right to Left Learning
Use   Serial Learning

Roentgenography
Use   Radiography

Romance Languages
DC   73750
HN   Formerly (1973-1991) DC ro1.
BT   Indo European Languages
NT   Catalan
     French
     Italian
     Portuguese
     Provençal
     Romanian
     Spanish
RT   Italic Languages
     Latin

Romani (Language)
Use   Romany (Language)

Romani (People)
Use   Gypsies

Romania
DC   73850
HN   Added, 1992.
UF   Rumania
BT   Balkan States
     Eastern Europe

Romanian
DC   73900
HN   Added, 1992.
UF   Balkan Romance
     Roumanian
     Rumanian
BT   Romance Languages

Romany (Language)
DC   73910
HN   Added, 1992.
UF   Gypsy (Language)
     Romani (Language)
BT   Indic Languages
RT   Gypsies

Roots (Diachronic Linguistics)
Use   Etymology

Roots (Morphology)
DC   74200
HN   Added, 1992.
UF   Base Forms
     Stems
BT   Morphemes
RT   Affixes
     Derivation (Morphology)
     Inflection (Morphology)
     Morphology
     Word Formation

Rorschach Tests
Use   Projective Techniques

Roumanian
Use   Romanian

Rule Ordering
DC   74300
SN   The application of grammatical rewrite rules in a distinctive sequence, rather than simultaneously; used especially to account for complex phonological alternations.

Rule Ordering (cont'd)
HN   Formerly (1977-1991) DC ro3.
UF   Ordering of Rules
RT   Morphology
     Phonology
     Sandhi
     Syntax
     Transformational Generative Grammar
     Transformation Rules

Rumania
Use   Romania

Rumanian
Use   Romanian

Russell, Bertrand Arthur William
DC   74350
SN   Born 1872 - Died 1970.
HN   Formerly (1973-1991) DC ru1, Russell.

Russia
DC   74400
HN   Added, 1992.
BT   Commonwealth of Independent States
RT   Union of Soviet Socialist Republics

Russian
DC   74450
HN   Formerly (1973-1991) DC ru2.
BT   Slavic Languages
NT   Russian as a Second Language

Russian as a Second Language
DC   74500
HN   Added, 1992.
BT   Russian
     Second Languages

Rwanda (Country)
DC   74510
HN   Added, 1992.
BT   Sub Saharan Africa

Rwanda (Language)
Use   Bantoid Languages

S Structure
Use   Surface Structure

Sabellian
Use   Italic Languages

Sacred Literature
Use   Religious Literature

Saharan Languages
Use   Nilo Saharan Languages

Salish Languages
Use   North Amerindian Languages

Salivan Languages
Use   Andean Equatorial Phylum

Samoan
Use   Polynesian Languages

Samoyed Languages
Use   Uralic Languages

San Marino
DC   74550
HN   Added, 1992.
BT   Western Europe
RT   Italy

Sandawe
   Use Khoisan Languages

Sandhi
   DC 74700
   SN Phonological alternations that can be
         predicted from the phonological
         characteristics of adjacent or nearby
         words. In some languages, sandhi
         phonemena occur between elements
         of compound words.
   HN Added, 1992.
   UF Tone Sandhi
   RT Morphophonemics
         Phonology
         Phonotactics
         Rule Ordering
         Tone

Sango
   Use Adamawa Eastern Phylum

Sanskrit
   DC 74750
   HN Added, 1992.
   UF Vedic Sanskrit
   BT Indic Languages

São Tome and Príncipe
   DC 74760
   HN Added, 1992.
   BT Sub Saharan Africa

Sapir Whorf Hypothesis
   Use Linguistic Relativity

Sapir, Eduard
   DC 74800
   SN Born 1884 - Died 1939.
   HN Formerly (1973-1991) DC sa1, Sapir.

Sardinia
   DC 74900
   HN Added, 1992.
   BT Italy

Saskatchewan
   DC 74950
   HN Added, 1992.
   BT Canada

Saudi Arabia
   DC 75100
   HN Added, 1992.
   BT Arab Countries
         Middle East

Saussure, Ferdinand de
   DC 75200
   SN Born 1857 - Died 1913.
   HN Formerly (1973-1991) DC sa2, Saus-
         sure.

Sayings
   Use Phraseologisms

Scales
   Use Measures (Instruments)

Scandinavia
   DC 75230
   HN Added, 1992.
   UF Nordic Countries
   BT Western Eurpoe
   NT Denmark
         Finland
         Greenland
         Iceland
         Lapland
         Norway
         Sweden

Scandinavian Languages
   DC 75240
   SN Usually, the North Germanic sub-
         group of the Germanic languages, di-
         vided into mainland Scandinavian
         languages (Swedish, Norwegian, Dan-
         ish) and insular Scandinavian lan-
         guages (Icelandic, Faeroese). May be
         used in some contexts to include
         non-Indo-European languages spoken
         in the region, eg, Lapp, Finnish.
   HN Added, 1992.
   BT Languages
   NT Danish
         Finnish
         Icelandic
         Norwegian
         Swedish
   RT Finno Ugric Languages
         Germanic Languages

Schizophrenia
   DC 75250
   HN Formerly (1973-1991) DC sc1.
   BT Mental Disorders
         Psychosis
   RT Autism
         Emotional Disturbances

Scholastic Achievement
   Use Academic Achievement

Schools
   Use Education

Scientific Technical Language
   DC 75350
   HN Added, 1992.
   UF Language of Science
         Technical Language
   BT Language for Special Purposes
   RT Business
         Business English
         Language Styles
         Mathematics
         Medical Language
         Occupations
         Technical Translation
         Terminology

Scotland
   DC 75400
   HN Added, 1992.
   BT Great Britain

Scottish Gaelic
   DC 75500
   HN Added, 1992.
   UF Gaelic (Scottish)
   BT Celtic Languages

Script Systems
   Use Writing Systems

Searle, John Rogers
   DC 75550
   SN Born 1932 - .
   HN Formerly (1973-1991) DC se1, Sear-
         le.

Second Dialect Learning
   DC 75650
   HN Formerly (1973-1991) DC se2.
   BT Second Language Learning
   RT Bilingualism
         Dialectology
         Dialects
         Standard Dialects

Second Language Conversation
Courses
   Use Conversation Courses

Second Language for Special Purposes
   Use Language for Special Purposes

Second Language Instruction
   DC 75700
   HN Added, 1992.
   UF Foreign Language Instruction
         Glottodidactics
   BT Instruction
   NT Second Language Reading Instruc-
         tion
         TESOL
   RT Applied Linguistics
         Audiolingual Language Teaching
         Bilingual Education
         Bilingual Teaching Materials
         Communicative Language Teaching
         Conversation Courses
         Direct Method of Language Teaching
         Educational Activities
         English for Special Purposes
         Error Analysis (Language)
         FLES
         Grammar Instruction
         Grammar Translation Method of Lan-
         guage Teaching
         Immersion Programs
         Language for Special Purposes
         Language Laboratories
         Language of Instruction
         Language Teaching Methods
         Language Textbooks
         Languages
         Native Language
         Native Speakers
         Oral Language Instruction
         Pattern Drills
         Pronunciation Accuracy
         Second Languages
         Suggestopedia
         Whole Language Approach
         Word Games
         Written Language Instruction

Second Language Learning
   DC 75850
   HN Formerly (1973-1991) DC se3.
   UF Foreign Language Learning
         Language Learning (Foreign)
   BT Learning
   NT Early Second Language Learning
         Second Dialect Learning
   RT Acculturation
         Audiolingual Language Teaching
         Bilingual Dictionaries
         Bilingual Education
         Bilingualism
         Communicative Competence
         Conversation Courses
         Direct Method of Language Teaching
         Error Analysis (Language)
         FLES
         Fluency
         Grammaticality
         Imitation
         Immersion Programs
         Immigrants
         Interlanguage
         Language of Instruction
         Language for Special Purposes
         Limited English Proficiency
         Linguistic Interference
         Listening Comprehension

Second Language Learning (cont'd)
- **RT** Language of Instruction
  - Monolingualism
  - Multilingualism
  - Oral Language
  - Second Languages
  - Threshold Level (Language)

Second Language Reading Instruction
- **DC** 75950
- **HN** Added, 1992.
- **UF** Foreign Language Reading Instruction
- **BT** Reading Instruction
  - Second Language Instruction
- **RT** Vocabulary Instruction

Second Language Tests
- **DC** 76150
- **HN** Formerly (1973-1991) DC se4, Second Language Testing.
- **UF** Foreign Language Tests
- **BT** Language Tests
- **NT** English as a Second Language Tests

Second Language Textbooks
- **Use** Language Textbooks

Second Languages
- **DC** 76200
- **HN** Added, 1992.
- **UF** Foreign Languages
- **BT** Language
- **NT** English as a Second Language
  - French as a Second Language
  - German as a Second Language
  - Russian as a Second Language
  - Spanish as a Second Language
- **RT** Applied Linguistics
  - Bilingualism
  - Foreign Accent
  - Immersion Programs
  - Interlanguage
  - Language for Special Purposes
  - Language of Instruction
  - Language Planning
  - Languages
  - Multilingualism
  - Native Language
  - Native Nonnative Speaker Communication
  - Native Speakers
  - Second Language Instruction
  - Second Language Learning

Secondary Education
- **DC** 76300
- **HN** Formerly (1973-1991) DC se5, Secondary School.
- **UF** Comprehensive Schools (British)
  - Gymnasium (German)
  - High School Education
  - Lycees
  - Volksschule
- **BT** Education
- **NT** Junior High School Education
- **RT** Junior High School Students
  - High School Students
  - Secondary School Students

Secondary School Students
- **DC** 76400
- **HN** Added, 1992.
- **UF** High School Students
- **BT** Students
- **NT** Junior High School Students
  - High School Students
- **RT** Adolescents
  - Junior High School Education
  - Secondary Education

Secret Languages
- **DC** 76420
- **SN** Autonomous, invented languages unintelligible to outsiders.
- **HN** Added, 1992.
- **BT** Languages
- **RT** Artificial Languages
  - Culture
  - Group Communication
  - Interpersonal Communication
  - Language Acquisition
  - Language Use
  - Nonverbal Languages
  - Registers (Sociolinguistics)

Self Assessment
- **Use** Self Evaluation

Self Concept
- **DC** 76500
- **HN** Added, 1992.
- **UF** Ego
  - Identity (Personal)
  - Personal Identity
  - Self Esteem
- **RT** Defense Mechanisms
  - Perception
  - Personality
  - Personality Measures
  - Psychotherapy
  - Self Evaluation
  - Social Perception

Self Esteem
- **Use** Self Concept

Self Evaluation
- **DC** 76550
- **HN** Added, 1992.
- **UF** Self Assessment
  - Self Rating
  - Self Report
- **RT** Metacognition
  - Self Concept

Self Perception (1973-1991)
- **HN** DC se6, deleted 1992. See now Self Concept or Self Evaluation.

Self Rating
- **Use** Self Evaluation

Self Repair
- **Use** Repair

Self Report
- **Use** Self Evaluation

Semantic Analysis
- **DC** 76570
- **HN** Added, 1992.
- **RT** Case Grammar
  - Comparative Linguistics
  - Componential Analysis
  - Computational Linguistics
  - Connotation
  - Decoding (Cognitive Process)
  - Deep Structure
  - Descriptive Linguistics
  - Discourse Analysis
  - Error Analysis (Language)
  - Focus
  - Generative Semantics
  - Grammatical Analysis
  - Implicature
  - Language
  - Language Patterns
  - Lexical Semantics
  - Linguistic Theories

Semantic Analysis (cont'd)
- **RT** Meaning
  - Montague Grammar
  - Natural Language Processing
  - Performative Utterances
  - Polysemy
  - Pragmatics
  - Rheme
  - Semantic Categories
  - Semantic Change
  - Semantic Features
  - Semantic Fields
  - Semantics
  - Syntax
  - Tagmemics
  - Taxonomic Approaches
  - Thematic Roles
  - Topic and Comment
  - Word Meaning

Semantic Categories
- **DC** 76580
- **HN** Added, 1992.
- **UF** Categories (Semantic)
- **RT** Agent Patient Relationship (Grammatical)
  - Modality (Semantic)
  - Philosophy of Language
  - Psycholinguistics
  - Semantic Analysis
  - Semantics
  - Thematic Roles
  - Time

Semantic Change
- **DC** 76600
- **SN** Change over time in the meaning of a word or other linguistic unit, or in the hypothesized semantic system of a language.
- **HN** Added, 1992.
- **UF** Lexical Change
- **BT** Language Change
- **RT** Diachronic Linguistics
  - Etymology
  - Morphological Change
  - Semantic Analysis
  - Semantics

Semantic Components
- **Use** Semantic Features

Semantic Differential
- **DC** 76700
- **SN** An attitude scale for measuring the subjective meaning of phenomena (persons, institutions, concepts, political issues, things) to an individual through the use of opposite adjectives (eg, strong-weak). Also, the techniques or methods in which the scale is used.
- **HN** Formerly (1973-1991) DC se7.
- **BT** Rating Scales
- **RT** Adjectives
  - Attitudes
  - Meaning
  - Personality Measures

Semantic Features
- **DC** 76705
- **HN** Added, 1992.
- **UF** Semantic Components
- **RT** Case Marking
  - Componential Analysis
  - Lexical Semantics
  - Lexicology
  - Semantic Analysis
  - Semantics
  - Word Meaning

Semantic Fields
DC   76710
SN   Specifiable areas of meaning and domains of reference expressed by sets of contrasting words or other linguistic units in a given language or across languages (eg, English hot/warm/cool/cold).
HN   Added, 1992.
RT   Lexicon
      Linguistic Theories
      Semantic Analysis
      Semantics
      Word Meaning

Semantic Memory
DC   76750
HN   Added, 1992.
BT   Memory
RT   Long Term Memory
      Word Recognition

Semantic Processing
DC   76760
HN   Added, 1992.
BT   Cognitive Processes
RT   Artificial Intelligence
      Associative Processes
      Decoding (Cognitive Process)
      Evoked Responses
      Information Processing
      Language Processing
      Meaning
      Memory
      Neurolinguistics
      Psycholinguistics
      Reading Processes
      Word Recognition

Semantic Roles
Use   Thematic Roles

Semantic Value
Use   Meaning

Semantics
DC   76850
SN   The branch of linguistics and/or the philosophy of language that investigates the relationship between linguistic forms and their meanings, the nature of meaning, and structures at the level of meaning that correspond to syntactic structures.
HN   Formerly (1973-1991) DC se9.
UF   Semasiology
NT   Generative Semantics
      Lexical Semantics
RT   Ambiguity
      Anaphora
      Animacy and Inanimacy
      Antonyms
      Case Grammar
      Comparative Linguistics
      Comparison
      Componential Analysis
      Computational Linguistics
      Connotation
      Decoding (Cognitive Process)
      Deep Structure
      Deixis
      Descriptive Linguistics
      Dictionaries
      Discourse Analysis
      Entailment
      Error Analysis (Language)
      Etymology
      Extended Standard Theory
      Focus

Semantics (cont'd)
RT   Grammatical Analysis
      Homographs
      Homonyms
      Homophones
      Idioms
      Implicature
      Language
      Language Patterns
      Lexicon
      Linguistic Theories
      Linguistic Units
      Logic of Language
      Logical Form
      Meaning
      Metaphors
      Modality (Semantic)
      Montague Grammar
      Mood (Grammatical)
      Negation
      Opacity
      Performative Utterances
      Philosophy of Language
      Polysemy
      Pragmatics
      Redundancy
      Reference (Grammatical)
      Rheme
      Semantic Analysis
      Semantic Categories
      Semantic Change
      Semantic Features
      Semantic Fields
      Semantics
      Semiotics
      Space
      Stratificational Grammar
      Synonyms
      Syntax
      Tagmemics
      Taxonomic Approaches
      Thematic Roles
      Time
      Topic and Comment
      Transformational Generative Grammar
      Word Meaning
      Words

Semasiology
Use   Semantics

Seminole
Use   Muskogean Languages

Semiology
Use   Semiotics

Semiotics
DC   77100
SN   Theory or study of signs and symbols, dealing especially with the semantic and pragmatic functions of language, in the context of all communication systems.
HN   Formerly (1973-1991) DC se11.
UF   Semiology
BT   Linguistics
RT   Language
      Language Patterns
      Linguistic Theories
      Logic of Language
      Meaning
      Metaphors
      Philosophy of Language
      Port Royal School
      Pragmatics
      Semantics
      Sign Theory

Semiotics (cont'd)
RT   Signifiant and Signifie
      Structuralist Linguistics
      Symbolism
      Syntax

Semitic Languages
DC   77200
HN   Added, 1992.
UF   Akkadian
      Tigrinya
BT   Afroasiatic Languages
NT   Amharic
      Arabic
      Aramaic
      Hebrew

Semito-Hamitic Languages
Use   Afroasiatic Languages

Senegal
DC   77280
HN   Added, 1992.
BT   Sub Saharan Africa

Senior Citizens
Use   Elderly

Sensation
Use   Perception

Sense Organs
Use   Sensory Systems

Sensory Motor Skills
Use   Perceptual Motor Skills

Sensory Systems
DC   77300
HN   Added, 1992.
UF   Perceptual Systems
      Sense Organs
BT   Anatomical Systems
NT   Hearing
      Vision
RT   Perception
      Tactual Perception
      Thresholds

Sentence Structure
DC   77400
SN   The overall pattern of elements in a sentence, based on recurrent distributional patterns in groups of sentences.
HN   Added, 1992.
RT   Clauses
      Cohesion
      Deep Structure
      Ellipsis
      Function Words
      Generative Grammar
      Generative Semantics
      Grammatical Analysis
      Phrases
      Punctuation
      Sentences
      Structuralist Linguistics
      Suprasegmentals
      Surface Structure
      Syntax
      Text Structure
      Well Formedness

Sentences
DC   77450
HN   Formerly (1973-1991) DC se13, Sentence.
BT   Linguistic Units
NT   Declarative Sentences
      Imperative Sentences

Sentences (cont'd)
- **NT** Interrogative Sentences
- **RT** Accentuation
  - Anomalous Strings
  - Clauses
  - Coordination (Grammatical)
  - Deep Structure
  - Discourse Analysis
  - Embedded Construction
  - Entailment
  - Focus
  - Functional Sentence Perspective
  - Grammatical Analysis
  - Intonation
  - Logical Form
  - Negation
  - Paragraphs
  - Passive Voice
  - Phrases
  - Predicate
  - Relative Clauses
  - Rheme
  - Sentence Structure
  - Subordination (Grammatical)
  - Syntactic Structures
  - Syntagmatic Relations
  - Syntax
  - Valence
  - Word Order
  - Writing

Senufo
- **Use** Gur Languages

Serbia
- **DC** 77550
- **HN** Added, 1992.
- **BT** Balkan States
  - Eastern Europe
- **RT** Yugoslavia

Serbian
- **Use** Serbo Croatian

Serbo Croatian
- **DC** 77600
- **HN** Added, 1992.
- **UF** Croatian
  - Serbian
- **BT** Slavic Languages

Serial Learning
- **DC** 77700
- **HN** Formerly (1973-1991) DC se14.
- **UF** Linear Learning
  - Right to Left Learning
- **BT** Verbal Learning
- **RT** Aided Recall
  - Associative Processes
  - Learning Theories
  - Memorization
  - Paired Associate Learning
  - Rehearsal (Verbal Learning)

Set Theory
- **DC** 77800
- **SN** A branch of mathematical logic concerned with the nature of, relations between, and operations on sets.
- **HN** Formerly (1979-1991) DC se14a.
- **BT** Linguistic Theories
- **RT** Computational Linguistics
  - Logic of Language
  - Mathematical Linguistics
  - Philosophy of Language

Sex Differences
- **DC** 77850
- **HN** Formerly (1974-1991) DC se15, Sexual Differences.
- **RT** Adult Child Interaction
  - Age Differences
  - Females
  - Males
  - Maternal Speech
  - Registers (Sociolinguistics)
  - Social Factors
  - Sociolinguistics

Sexism
- **DC** 77900
- **HN** Added, 1992.
- **UF** Sexist Language
- **RT** Attitudes
  - Feminism
  - Language Usage

Sexist Language
- **Use** Sexism

Seychelles
- **DC** 77910
- **HN** Added, 1992.
- **BT** Sub Saharan Africa

Shluh
- **Use** Berber Languages

Shona
- **Use** Bantoid Languages

Short Term Memory
- **DC** 78150
- **HN** Formerly (1973-1991) DC sh2, Short-Term Memory.
- **UF** Immediate Recall
  - Primary Memory
  - Short Term Store
  - STM
- **BT** Memory
- **RT** Long Term Memory
  - Recall (Memory)
  - Retention (Memory)

Short Term Store
- **Use** Short Term Memory

Shoshone
- **Use** Uto Aztecan Languages

Siberia
- **DC** 78200
- **HN** Added, 1992.
- **BT** Commonwealth of Independent States
  - Union of Soviet Socialist Republics
- **RT** Arctic Regions
  - Armenia
  - Azerbaijan
  - Belorus
  - Estonia
  - Georgia (Republic)
  - Kazakhstan
  - Kyrgyzstan
  - Latvia
  - Lithuania
  - Moldova
  - Russia
  - Tajikstan
  - Turkmenistan
  - Ukraine
  - Uzbekistan

Sibilants
- **Use** Fricatives

Siblings
- **DC** 78220
- **HN** Added, 1992.
- **UF** Brothers
  - Sisters
- **RT** Children

Sicily
- **DC** 78300
- **HN** Added, 1992.
- **BT** Italy

Side Effects (Drugs)
- **Use** Drug Effects

Sierra Leone
- **DC** 78350
- **HN** Added, 1992.
- **BT** Sub Saharan Africa

Sight
- **Use** Vision

Sign Language
- **DC** 78400
- **HN** Added, 1992.
- **BT** Nonverbal Languages
- **NT** American Sign Language
- **RT** Gestures
  - Hearing Disorders
  - Nonverbal Communication

Sign Theory
- **DC** 78500
- **HN** Formerly (1973-1991) DC si1.
- **UF** Content and Expression (1973-1991)
- **BT** Linguistic Theories
- **RT** Semiotics
  - Signifiant and Signifie

Signal Detection
- **DC** 78550
- **HN** Formerly (1973-1991) DC si2.
- **RT** Acoustic Phonetics
  - Acoustics
  - Cognitive Processes
  - Distortion of Speech Signal
  - Listening
  - Masking
  - Psycholinguistics
  - Recognition

Signal Distortion (Speech)
- **Use** Distortion of Speech Signal

Signifiant and Signifié
- **DC** 78600
- **HN** Formerly (1973-1991) DC si3.
- **UF** Signifier and Signified
- **RT** Linguistic Theories
  - Meaning
  - Semiotics
  - Sign Theory

Signifier and Signified
- **Use** Signifiant and Signifie

Silence
- **DC** 78700
- **HN** Added, 1992.
- **RT** Acoustics
  - Interpersonal Behavior
  - Listening
  - Noise
  - Nonverbal Communication
  - Pauses

Silence (cont'd)
RT   Speech
      Turn Taking

Silent Reading
DC   78800
HN   Added, 1992.
BT   Reading
RT   Inner Speech
      Oral Reading
      Reading Instruction
      Reading Rate

Silesian
Use   German

Simile
Use   Rhetorical Figures

Simultaneous Translation
Use   Translation

Sindhi
Use   Indic Languages

Singapore
DC   78900
HN   Added, 1992.
BT   Southeast Asia

Singing
DC   78950
HN   Formerly (1973-1991) DC si4.
UF   Chanting
      Songs
RT   Articulatory Phonetics
      Music
      Phonation
      Speech
      Voice Quality

Singular Forms
Use   Number (Grammatical)

Sinhalese
Use   Indic Languages

Sino Tibetan Languages
DC   79100
HN   Formerly (1979-1991) DC si4a, Sino-
      Tibetan.
UF   Hmong
      Lao
      Miao Yao Languages
BT   Languages
NT   Chinese
      Kam Tai Languages
      Tibeto Burman Languages

Siouan Languages
Use   Macro Siouan Phylum

Sioux
Use   Macro Siouan Phylum

SISI Test
Use   Audiometry

Sisters
Use   Siblings

Situational Determinants
Use   Context Effects (Perception)

Skinner, Burrhus Frederic
DC   79200
SN   Born 1904 - Died 1990.
HN   Formerly (1973-1991) DC sk1, Skin-
      ner.

Slang
DC   79250
HN   Added, 1992. Prior to 1992, see DC
      re8, Register.
UF   Argot
      Street Vernacular
BT   Lexicon
RT   Armed Forces
      Colloquial Language
      Idioms
      Language for Special Purposes
      Language Styles
      Language Usage
      Nonstandard Dialects
      Obscenities
      Registers (Sociolinguistics)
      Sports
      Terminology

Slavic Cultural Groups
DC   79340
HN   Added, 1992.
BT   Cultural Groups
RT   Commonwealth of Independent
      States Cultural Groups
      Eastern Europe
      Slavic Languages
      Union of Soviet Socialist Republics

Slavic Languages
DC   79350
HN   Formerly (1973-1991) DC sl1.
UF   Slavonic Languages
BT   Indo European Languages
NT   Belorussian
      Bulgarian
      Czech
      Macedonian
      Old Church Slavic
      Polish
      Russian
      Serbo Croatian
      Slovak
      Slovene
      Ukrainian
RT   Slavic Cultural Groups

Slavonic Languages
Use   Slavic Languages

Sleep
DC   79400
HN   Formerly (1973-1991) DC sl2.
RT   Eye Movements

Slips of the Tongue
DC   79450
HN   Formerly (1973-1991) DC sl3.
UF   Spoonerisms (Accidental)
      Tongue Slips
      Verbal Slips
RT   Cognitive Processes
      Error Analysis (Language)
      Linguistic Performance
      Neurolinguistics
      Psycholinguistics
      Repair
      Speech

Slovak
DC   79550
HN   Added, 1992.
BT   Slavic Languages

Slovene
DC   79600
HN   Added, 1992.
UF   Slovenian
BT   Slavic Languages

Slovenia
DC   79700
HN   Added, 1992.
BT   Balkan States
      Eastern Europe
RT   Yugoslavia

Slovenian
Use   Slovene

Smiles
Use   Facial Expressions

Social Class
DC   79900
HN   Added, 1992.
UF   Lower Class
      Middle Class
      Upper Class
      Working Class
RT   Economic Factors
      Language Usage
      Low Income Groups
      Marxist Analysis
      Occupations
      Social Factors
      Socioeconomic Status
      Sociolinguistics

Social Cognition
Use   Social Perception

Social Factors
DC   79910
HN   Added, 1992.
UF   Social Influences
RT   Age Differences
      Anthropological Linguistics
      Bilingualism
      Colloquial Language
      Cross Cultural Communication
      Cultural Factors
      Dialectical Materialistic Linguistic
      Theory
      Dialects
      Economic Factors
      Ethnographic Linguistics
      Ethnolinguistics
      Grammaticality
      Language Attitudes
      Language Contact
      Language Culture Relationship
      Language Death
      Language Diversity
      Language Maintenance
      Language Planning
      Language Policy
      Language Shift
      Language Standardization
      Language Status
      Language Usage
      Marxist Analysis
      Minority Languages
      Monolingualism
      Multilingualism
      National Languages
      Official Languages
      Pragmatics
      Psycholinguistics
      Registers (Sociolinguistics)
      Sex Differences
      Social Class
      Social Perception
      Socialization
      Socioeconomic Status
      Sociolinguistics
      Stereotypes

Social Influences
Use Social Factors

Social Perception
DC 79950
HN Added, 1992.
UF Interpersonal Perception
Person Perception
Social Cognition
BT Perception
RT Attitudes
Credibility
Interpersonal Behavior
Interpersonal Communication
Metacognition
Psycholinguistics
Self Concept
Social Factors
Socialization
Sociolinguistics
Stereotypes

Socialization
DC 80000
HN Added, 1992.
RT Adult Child Interaction
Cultural Factors
Education
Imitation
Interpersonal Behavior
Language Acquisition
Language Attitudes
Learning
Social Factors
Social Perception
Sociolinguistics

Socioeconomic Status
DC 80150
HN Formerly (1973-1991) DC so1.
RT Economic Factors
Education
Low Income Groups
Occupations
Social Class
Social Factors
Sociolinguistics

Sociolinguistics
DC 80200
SN Study of the effects of the social and
cultural context on the structure and
use of language, and of the effects of
early linguistic influences on patterns
of social relations.
HN Formerly (1973-1991) DC so2.
BT Linguistics
RT Address Forms
Age Differences
Anthropological Linguistics
Bilingualism
Borrowing
Code Switching
Colloquial Language
Cross Cultural Communication
Cultural Factors
Diachronic Linguistics
Dialectical Materialistic Linguistic
Theory
Dialectology
Dialects
Diglossia
Economic Factors
Ethnographic Linguistics
Ethnolinguistics
Folklore
Functional Linguistics
Graffiti

Sociolinguistics (cont'd)
RT Grammaticality
Indigenous Languages
Kinship Terminology
Language Attitudes
Language Change
Language Contact
Language Culture Relationship
Language Death
Language Diversity
Language Maintenance
Language of Instruction
Language Planning
Language Policy
Language Shift
Language Standardization
Language Status
Language Usage
Language Use
Linguistic Theories
Marxist Analysis
Minority Groups
Minority Languages
Monolingualism
Multilingualism
National Languages
Native Speakers
Nonstandard Dialects
Official Languages
Pragmatics
Psycholinguistics
Religions
Sex Differences
Social Class
Social Factors
Social Perception
Socialization
Socioeconomic Status
Speech Communities
Standard Dialects
Systemic Linguistics

Somali (Language)
Use Cushitic Languages

Somalia
DC 80220
HN Added, 1992.
BT Sub Saharan Africa

Somaliland
Use Djibouti

Songhai
Use Nilo Saharan Languages

Songs
Use Singing

Sonoran Languages
Use Uto Aztecan Languages

Sound
Use Acoustics

Sound Change
DC 80300
SN Change over time in the physical
sounds associated with units of pho-
nology (eg, phonemes, distinctive
features); refers to the production
and perception of sounds as well.
HN Formerly (1973-1991) DC so3.
UF Phonetic Change
BT Language Change
NT Assimilation (Language Change)
RT Diachronic Linguistics
Etymology
Morphological Change

Sound Change (cont'd)
RT Phonemes
Phonemics
Phonological Change
Pronunciation
Suprasegmentals

Sound Duration (Phonetics)
DC 80400
SN Physical duration of a sound. For rel-
ative durations of linguistically con-
trastive sounds, use Length (Phono-
logical).
HN Added, 1992. Prior to 1992, see
Time, Duration.
RT Phonemes
Phonemic Transcription
Phonetics
Pronunciation
Speech Duration
Time

Sound Identification
DC 80450
HN Added, 1992.
UF Consonant Identification
Perceptual Identification of Speech
Vowel Identification
BT Identification
RT Auditory Perception
Auditory Thresholds
Language Processing
Letter Recognition
Psychoacoustics
Speech Perception

Sound Localization
Use Auditory Localization

Sound Spectrographs
DC 80500
HN Formerly (1973-1991) DC so4,
Sound Spectrograph.
UF Spectrographs (Acoustics)
RT Acoustic Phonetics
Acoustics
Componential Analysis
Formants
Frequency (Acoustics)
Phonology
Speech
Speech Synthesis
Speech Therapy

Sound Symbolism
Use Onomatopoeia

Sound Transmission
Use Acoustics

Sound Waves
Use Acoustics

Source Credibility
Use Credibility

South Africa
DC 80590
HN Added, 1992.
BT Sub Saharan Africa

South America
DC 80600
HN Added, 1992.
BT Latin America
NT Argentina
Bolivia
Brazil
Chile

South America (cont'd)
- **NT** Colombia
  - Ecuador
  - French Guiana
  - Guyana
  - Paraguay
  - Peru
  - Surinam
  - Uruguay
  - Venezuela

South American Cultural Groups
- **Use** Latin American Cultural Groups

South Amerindian Languages
- **DC** 80700
- **HN** Formerly (1977-1991) DC so4a.
- **UF** Caribbean Amerindian Languages (1973-1982)
- **BT** Amerindian Languages
- **NT** Andean Equatorial Phylum
  - Ge Pano Carib Languages
  - Macro Chibchan Phylum
- **RT** Central Amerindian Languages

South Asia
- **DC** 80750
- **HN** Added, 1992.
- **BT** Asia
- **NT** Bangladesh
  - Bhutan
  - Himalayan States
  - India
  - Nepal
  - Pakistan
  - Sri Lanka
- **RT** Southeast Asia

South Asian Cultural Groups
- **DC** 80800
- **SN** Cultural groups of the Indian subcontinent.
- **HN** Added, 1992.
- **BT** Asian Cultural Groups
- **RT** Southeast Asian Cultural Groups

South Carolina
- **DC** 80850
- **HN** Added, 1992.
- **BT** Southern States
  - United States of America
- **RT** Appalachia

South Dakota
- **DC** 80900
- **HN** Added, 1992.
- **BT** Midwestern States
  - United States of America

South French
- **Use** Provençal

South Korea
- **DC** 81100
- **HN** Added, 1992.
- **BT** Far East

South Vietnam
- **Use** Vietnam

South West Africa
- **Use** Namibia

Southeast Asia
- **DC** 81200
- **HN** Added, 1992.
- **BT** Asia
- **NT** Brunei Darussalam
  - Cambodia

Southeast Asia (cont'd)
- **NT** Indonesia
  - Kampuchea
  - Laos
  - Malaysia
  - Myanmar
  - Papua New Guinea
  - Philippines
  - Singapore
  - Thailand
  - Vietnam
- **RT** South Asia

Southeast Asian Cultural Groups
- **DC** 81250
- **HN** Added, 1992.
- **BT** Asian Cultural Groups
- **RT** South Asian Cultural Groups

Southern African Cultural Groups
- **DC** 81300
- **HN** Added, 1992.
- **BT** African Cultural Groups
- **RT** North African Cultural Groups

Southern Rhodesia
- **Use** Zimbabwe

Southern States
- **DC** 81400
- **HN** Added, 1992.
- **NT** Alabama
  - Arkansas
  - Florida
  - Georgia (USA)
  - Kentucky
  - Louisiana
  - Mississippi
  - North Carolina
  - South Carolina
  - Tennessee
  - Virginia
  - West Virginia
- **RT** United States of America

Space
- **DC** 81600
- **HN** Formerly (1982-1991) DC so4b, Space, Spatial Position.
- **UF** Location
  - Positional Reference
  - Spatial Position
  - Spatial Representation
- **RT** Auditory Localization
  - Deixis
  - Meaning
  - Semantics
  - Time

Spain
- **DC** 81750
- **HN** Added, 1992.
- **BT** Mediterranean Countries
  - Western Europe
- **NT** Catalonia, Spain

Spanish
- **DC** 81800
- **HN** Formerly (1973-1991) DC so5.
- **BT** Romance Languages
- **NT** Spanish as a Second Language

Spanish Americans
- **Use** Hispanic Americans

Spanish as a Second Language
- **DC** 81950
- **HN** Added, 1992.
- **BT** Second Languages

Spanish as a Second Language (cont'd)
- **BT** Spanish

Spastic Dysphonia
- **Use** Voice Disorders

Spatial Position
- **Use** Space

Spatial Representation
- **Use** Space

Speaker Identification
- **Use** Speech Perception

Speaking in Tongues
- **Use** Glossolalia

Special Education (Handicapped)
- **DC** 82100
- **SN** Teaching methods and educational programs and services designed for individuals with physical, mental, emotional, or social handicaps for whom normal methods and materials are inappropriate.
- **HN** Formerly (1977-1991) DC so7.
- **BT** Education
- **NT** Behavior Disorders
  - Downs Syndrome
- **RT** Educational Activities
  - Handicapped
  - Hearing Disorders
  - Learning Disabilities
  - Mental Retardation
  - Prognostic Tests
  - Therapy
  - Vision Disorders

Special Languages (1973-1991)
- **HN** DC sp1.
- **Use** Language for Special Purposes

Specialized Vocabulary
- **Use** Terminology

Species Specific Communication (1975-1987)
- **HN** DC sp2. Between 1987 and 1991, see DC in13, Inter- and Interspecies Communication.
- **Use** Animal Communication

Spectrographs (Acoustics)
- **Use** Sound Spectrographs

Speech
- **DC** 82350
- **HN** Added, 1992.
- **NT** Baby Talk
  - Esophageal Speech
  - Inner Speech
  - Maternal Speech
  - Performative Utterances
  - Pronunciation
  - Spontaneous Speech
  - Whispering
- **RT** Acoustic Phonetics
  - Articulation
  - Articulation Disorders
  - Articulatory Phonetics
  - Colloquial Language
  - Discourse Analysis
  - Foreign Accent
  - Fundamental Frequency
  - Gestures
  - Intelligibility
  - Interpersonal Communication

Speech (cont'd)
RT Language
Language Patterns
Langue and Parole
Linguistic Performance
Linguistics
Motor Theory of Speech Perception
Native Nonnative Speaker Communication
Oral Language
Paralinguistics
Pauses
Phonation
Phonation Disorders
Phonemics
Phonetics
Phonology
Pragmatics
Public Speaking
Repair
Rhetoric
Silence
Singing
Slips of the Tongue
Sound Spectrographs
Speech Acts
Speech Communities
Speech Duration
Speech Pathology
Speech Perception
Speech Rate
Speech Synthesis
Speech Tests
Speech Therapy
Turn Taking
Verbal Accounts
Voice Disorders
Voice Quality
Voice Recognition
Word Frequency

Speech Acts
DC 82400
HN Formerly (1973-1991) DC sp2aa, Speech Act Theory.
UF Illocutionary Acts
Locutionary Acts
Perlocutionary Acts
Utterances
RT Communicative Function of Language
Discourse Analysis
Language Patterns
Linguistic Theories
Meaning
Performative Utterances
Pragmatics
Repair
Speech
Syntagmatic Relations
Turn Taking

Speech Audiometry
Use Audiometry

Speech Communities
DC 82410
SN Human groups identified by shared norms for speaking and, according to most definitions, a shared language or language variety.
HN Added, 1992.
RT Dialects
Interpersonal Behavior
Interpersonal Communication
Language Usage
Language Use
National Languages

Speech Communities (cont'd)
RT Native Language
Native Speakers
Oral Language
Registers (Sociolinguistics)
Sociolinguistics
Speech

Speech Discrimination
Use Speech Perception

Speech Duration
DC 82550
HN Formerly (1973-1991) DC sp3.
UF Duration of Speech
RT Articulatory Phonetics
Mean Length of Utterance
Sound Duration (Phonetics)
Speech
Time
Turn Taking

Speech Error Repair
Use Repair

Speech Identification
Use Speech Perception

Speech Intelligibility
Use Intelligibility

Speech Pathology
DC 82650
SN Study of speech abnormalities and disorders. Use Language Pathology for nervous system disorders affecting the reception, processing, or expression of language.
HN Formerly (1973-1991) DC sp5.
UF Mutism
BT Medicine
RT Aphasia
Applied Linguistics
Articulation Disorders
Cleft Palate
Esophageal Speech
Hearing Disorders
Language Pathology
Language Therapy
Laryngology
Muscular Disorders
Neurolinguistics
Phonation Disorders
Radiography
Speech
Speech Tests
Speech Therapy
Spontaneous Speech
Stuttering
Voice Disorders

Speech Pauses
Use Pauses

Speech Perception
DC 82700
SN The understanding and comprehension of speech. Not to be confused with Auditory Perception.
HN Formerly (1973-1991) DC sp6.
UF Phonetic Symbolism
Speaker Identification
Speech Discrimination
Speech Identification
BT Perception
NT Vowel Perception
RT Auditory Perception
Auditory Stimulation
Auditory Thresholds

Speech Perception (cont'd)
RT Ear Preference
Hearing
Language Processing
Letter Recognition
Lipreading
Motor Theory of Speech Perception
Phonetically Balanced Lists
Phonetics
Psycholinguistics
Repair
Sound Identification
Speech
Speech Rate
Voice Recognition

Speech Production
Use Articulation

Speech Rate
DC 82850
HN Formerly (1973-1991) DC sp7.
UF Accelerated Speech
Rate of Speech
Speed of Speech
RT Articulatory Phonetics
Intelligibility
Linguistic Accommodation
Native Nonnative Speaker Communication
Speech
Speech Perception

Speech Reading
Use Lipreading

Speech Reception Thresholds
Use Auditory Thresholds

Speech Recognition by Machine (1973-1991)
HN DC sp8.
Use Voice Recognition

Speech Signal Distortion
Use Distortion of Speech Signal

Speech Synthesis
DC 82900
HN Formerly (1973-1991) DC sp9.
UF Artificial Speech
Synthetic Speech
Voice Synthesis
RT Acoustic Phonetics
Computational Linguistics
Computer Applications
Neural Networks
Sound Spectrographs
Speech
Voice Recognition

Speech Tests
DC 83100
SN Tests of an individual's ability to communicate orally, including the ability to enunciate, pronounce, and articulate sounds. Also includes measures of pitch, harmonic scaling, and other characteristics of speech.
HN Formerly (1973-1991) DC sp12, Speech Testing.
BT Tests
RT Articulation
Articulation Disorders
Language Tests
Pronunciation
Pronunciation Accuracy
Reading Tests
Speech

Speech Tests (cont'd)
RT Speech Pathology
     Speech Therapy
     Spontaneous Speech
     Voice Disorders

Speech Therapy
DC 83200
HN Formerly (1973-1991) DC sp13.
BT Therapy
RT Applied Linguistics
     Articulation Disorders
     Cleft Palate
     Delayed Language Acquisition
     Esophageal Speech
     Hearing Disorders
     Language Therapy
     Laryngology
     Natural Phonology
     Phonation Disorders
     Sound Spectrographs
     Speech
     Speech Pathology
     Speech Tests
     Stuttering
     Voice Disorders

Speed of Speech
Use Speech Rate

Spelling
Use Orthography

Spelling Errors
DC 83250
HN Added, 1992.
UF Creative Spelling
     Invented Spelling
     Misspelling
     Orthographic Errors
RT Error Analysis (Language)
     Orthography
     Spelling Instruction

Spelling Instruction
DC 83350
HN Added, 1992.
UF Orthography Instruction
BT Instruction
RT Educational Activities
     Grapheme Phoneme Correspon-
     dence
     Orthography
     Spelling Errors
     Vocabulary Instruction

Spelling Reform
Use Orthography Reform

Spirants
Use Fricatives

Spoken Lanuguage
Use Oral Language

Spoken vs Written Communication
(1973-1991)
HN DC sp14.
Use Spoken Written Language Relation-
     ship

Spoken Written Language Relation-
ship
DC 83400
HN Formerly (1973-1991) DC sp14, Spo-
     ken vs Written Communication.
UF Oral Language Written Language Re-
     lationship
     Oral Written Language Differences

Spoken Written Language Relation-
ship (cont'd)
UF Spoken vs Written Communication
     (1973-1991)
     Written Language Spoken Language
     Relationship
RT Colloquial Language
     Communication
     Grammaticality
     Grapheme Phoneme Correspon-
     dence
     Language Usage
     Oral Language
     Written Language

Spontaneous Speech
DC 83500
HN Formerly (1973-1991) DC sp15.
BT Speech
RT Colloquial Language
     Inner Speech
     Interpersonal Communication
     Public Speaking
     Speech Tests

Spoonerisms (Accidental)
Use Slips of the Tongue

Spoonerisms (Deliberate)
Use Rhetorical Figures

Sports
DC 83550
HN Added, 1992.
UF Athletics
RT Registers (Sociolinguistics)
     Slang

Spouses
DC 83570
HN Added, 1992.
UF Husbands
     Married Couples
     Wives
RT Parents

Sri Lanka
DC 83650
HN Added, 1992.
UF Ceylon
BT South Asia

Stammering
Use Stuttering

Standard Dialects
DC 83800
HN Formerly (1973-1991) DC st1, Stan-
     dard Dialect.
UF Standard Spoken Usage
     Standard Variety
BT Dialects
RT Colloquial Language
     Dialectology
     Language Diversity
     Language Standardization
     Language Status
     Language Usage
     Native Language
     Native Language Instruction
     Native Speakers
     Nonstandard Dialects
     Regional Dialects
     Second Dialect Learning
     Sociolinguistics

Standard Spoken Usage
Use Standard Dialects

Standard Variety
Use Standard Dialects

Stanford Binet Test
Use Intelligence Tests

Stapedectomy (1973-1991)
HN DC st2.
Use Surgery

Statistical Analysis
DC 83850
HN Formerly (1988-1991) DC st2a.
UF Experimental Data Handling (1973-
     1991)
     Statistical Methods
     Stochastic Models (1973-1991)
NT Statistical Analysis of Style
RT Computational Linguistics
     Computer Applications
     Computer Generated Language Anal-
     ysis
     Computer Software
     Data Processing
     Databases
     Grammatical Analysis
     Markov Models
     Mathematical Linguistics
     Psychometric Analysis
     Research Design

Statistical Analysis of Style
DC 83950
HN Formerly (1973-1991) DC st3.
UF Stylometrics
     Stylostatistics
BT Statistical Analysis
RT Authorship
     Computational Linguistics
     Computer Generated Language Anal-
     ysis
     Language Usage
     Lexicon
     Stylistics
     Text Analysis
     Textual Criticism
     Word Frequency

Statistical Methods
Use Statistical Analysis

Stems
Use Roots (Morphology)

Stereotypes
DC 84050
HN Added, 1992.
BT Attitudes
RT Beliefs
     Interpersonal Behavior
     Language Attitudes
     Language Thought Relationship
     Social Factors
     Social Perception

Stimulation
DC 84150
HN Added, 1992.
UF Perceptual Stimulation
NT Auditory Stimulation
     Visual Stimulation
RT Conditioning
     Evoked Responses
     Feedback
     Masking
     Perception
     Thresholds

STM
Use Short Term Memory

Stochastic Models (1973-1991)
HN DC st4.
Use Statistical Analysis

Stops
DC 84300
SN Sounds that involve complete (if brief) stoppage of air flow through the oral and nasal cavities (eg, [p], [t], [k]).
HN Added, 1992.
UF Implosives
    Occlusives
    Plosives
BT Consonants

Story Grammar
DC 84350
HN Added, 1992.
UF Story Structure
RT Cohesion
    Discourse Analysis
    Narrative Structure
    Readability
    Reading Comprehension
    Reading Instruction
    Reading Writing Relationship
    Story Telling
    Text Analysis
    Text Structure
    Writing
    Written Language Instruction

Story Structure
Use Story Grammar

Story Telling
DC 84400
HN Added, 1992.
BT Language Arts
RT Folklore
    Oral Language
    Story Grammar

Stratificational Grammar
DC 84500
SN A model of language developed by Sydney M. Lamb and H. L. Gleason, Jr. during the 1960s as an alternative to transformational-generative grammar. A network of relations consisting of a sequence of similarly structured components, each containing a sign relation, an alternation pattern, and a tactic component, accounts for both competence and performance in encoding and decoding speech. The model includes phonetic and cognitive interfaces and a semiological component that treats discourse as a linguistic unit.
HN Added, 1992.
BT Grammar Theories
RT Grammatical Analysis
    History of Linguistics
    Phonemics
    Phonotactics
    Semantics
    Syntax

Street Vernacular
Use Slang

Stress
DC 84550
SN The relative intensity or amplitude of the voice, either as measured acoustically or as organized by the phonology of a language into distinctive degrees of intensity.

Stress (cont'd)
HN Formerly (1973-1991) DC st6.
UF Accent (Vocal Stress)
BT Suprasegmentals
RT Accentuation
    Intonation
    Juncture
    Metrical Phonology
    Mora
    Morphology
    Morphophonemics
    Paralinguistics
    Phonetics
    Phonology
    Rhythm
    Syllables

Stress Assignment
Use Accentuation

Stress Placement
Use Accentuation

Stroop Color Word Test
DC 84600
HN Formerly (1973-1991) DC st7.
BT Tests
RT Color
    Interference
    Language Processing

Structural Ambiguity
Use Ambiguity

Structural Linguistics
Use Structuralist Linguistics

Structuralist Linguistics
DC 84700
SN Any of several schools of linguistics, deriving from Ferdinand de Saussure's system of general linguistics & treating languages as formal systems; empirically & descriptively oriented, & often contrasted with generative grammar.
HN Formerly (1973-1991) DC st8, Structuralist Linguistic Theory.
UF Structural Linguistics
BT Linguistics
RT Comparative Linguistics
    Componential Analysis
    Context Free Grammar
    Context Sensitive Grammar
    Form (Language Structure)
    Functional Linguistics
    Grammatical Analysis
    Language Universals
    Linguistic Theories
    Linguistic Units
    Narrative Structure
    Phonology
    Prague School
    Semiotics
    Sentence Structure
    Syntagmatic Relations
    Syntax
    Text Structure

Student Teacher Communication
Use Classroom Communication

Student Teacher Relationship
DC 84730
HN Added, 1992.
UF Teacher Student Relationship
RT Adult Child Interaction
    Classroom Communication
    Classroom Observation

Student Teacher Relationship (cont'd)
RT Instruction
    Interpersonal Behavior
    Interpersonal Communication
    Students
    Teacher Attitudes
    Teachers

Students
DC 84750
HN Prior to 1992 this concept was indexed under terms representing specific levels of educational institutions, eg, Elementary School, Secondary School.
NT College Students
    Elementary School Students
    Secondary School Students
RT Academic Achievement
    Classroom Communication
    Classroom Observation
    Education
    Educational Activities
    Student Teacher Relationship
    Teachers

Stuttering
DC 84850
HN Formerly (1973-1991) DC st9.
UF Stammering
BT Disorders
RT Articulation Disorders
    Respiratory System
    Speech Pathology
    Speech Therapy

Stylistics
DC 84950
HN Formerly (1973-1991) DC st11.
NT Phonological Stylistics
RT Cohesion
    Discourse Analysis
    Foregrounding
    Form (Language Structure)
    Language Patterns
    Language Usage
    Lexicon
    Literary Criticism
    Literature
    Phraseology
    Rhetorical Figures
    Statistical Analysis of Style
    Text Analysis
    Textual Criticism
    Word Frequency

Stylometrics
Use Statistical Analysis of Style

Stylostatistics
Use Statistical Analysis of Style

Sub Saharan Africa
DC 85200
HN Added, 1992.
BT Africa
NT Angola
    Benin
    Botswana
    Burkina Faso
    Burundi
    Cameroon
    Cape Verde Islands
    Central African Republic
    Chad
    Comoro Islands
    Congo

Sub Saharan Africa (cont'd)
- **NT** Djibouti
  - Equatorial Guinea
  - Ethiopia
  - Gabon
  - Gambia
  - Ghana
  - Guinea
  - Guinea Bissau
  - Ivory Coast
  - Kenya
  - Lesotho
  - Liberia
  - Madagascar
  - Malawi
  - Mali (Country)
  - Mauritania
  - Mauritius
  - Mozambique
  - Namibia
  - Niger (Country)
  - Nigeria
  - Reunion
  - Rwanda (Country)
  - Sao Tome and Principe
  - Senegal
  - Seychelles
  - Sierra Leone
  - Somalia
  - South Africa
  - Swaziland
  - Tanzania
  - Togo
  - Uganda
  - Zaire
  - Zambia
  - Zimbabwe
- **RT** North Africa

Subject (Grammatical)
- **DC** 85300
- **HN** Added, 1992.
- **BT** Linguistic Units
- **RT** Agent Patient Relationship (Grammatical)
  - Agreement
  - Focus
  - Grammatical Relations
  - Noun Phrases
  - Passive Voice
  - Predicate
  - Relational Grammar

Subjective Meaning
- **Use** Connotation

Subjunctive
- **DC** 85350
- **HN** Added, 1992.
- **BT** Mood (Grammatical)
- **RT** Imperative Sentences
  - Subordination (Grammatical)
  - Verbs

Subliminal Speech
- **Use** Inner Speech

Subordinate Clauses
- **Use** Subordination (Grammatical)

Subordination (Grammatical)
- **DC** 85450
- **SN** A relation between two syntactic units (typically clauses) such that the pair has the same status/function as one but not both of the units; the unit that cannot assume the status/function of the pair is termed subordinate.
- **HN** Added, 1992.

Subordination (Grammatical) (cont'd)
- **UF** Dependent Clauses
  - Subordinate Clauses
- **RT** Clauses
  - Conjunctions
  - Coordination (Grammatical)
  - Embedded Construction
  - Linguistic Units
  - Relative Clauses
  - Sentences
  - Subjunctive
  - Syntax

Substantives
- **Use** Nouns

Substitution Drills
- **Use** Pattern Drills

Subvocal Response (1973-1991)
- **HN** DC su1.
- **Use** Inner Speech

Subvocalization
- **Use** Inner Speech

Sudan
- **DC** 85470
- **HN** Added, 1992.
- **BT** Arab Countries
  - North Africa

Suffixation
- **Use** Suffixes

Suffixes
- **DC** 85500
- **HN** Added, 1992.
- **UF** Inflectional Endings
  - Suffixation
- **BT** Affixes
- **RT** Prefixes
  - Word Formation

Suggestopedia
- **DC** 85600
- **HN** Added, 1992.
- **UF** Lozanov Method
- **BT** Teaching Methods
- **RT** Language Teaching Methods
  - Music
  - Second Language Instruction

Sumerian
- **DC** 85650
- **HN** Added, 1992.
- **BT** Language Isolates

Superficial Structure
- **Use** Surface Structure

Superlative Forms
- **Use** Comparison

Suprasegmentals
- **DC** 85750
- **SN** Phonetic features, such as stress, tone, and intonation, which extend over more than one speech sound in an utterance.
- **HN** Formerly (1973-1991) DC su2, Suprasegmental Analysis.
- **UF** Prosodic Features
  - Prosody
- **NT** Intonation
  - Juncture
  - Stress
  - Tone
- **RT** Accentuation
  - Articulatory Phonetics

Suprasegmentals (cont'd)
- **RT** Autosegmental Phonology
  - Mora
  - Morphology
  - Morphophonemics
  - Paralinguistics
  - Phonemes
  - Phonology
  - Pitch (Phonology)
  - Sentence Structure
  - Sound Change

Surface Grammar
- **Use** Surface Structure

Surface Structure
- **DC** 85850
- **SN** In many models of generative grammar, a level of syntactic representation that reflects the actual ordering of the elements of sentences.
- **HN** Added, 1992. Prior to 1992, see DC de3, Deep Structure and Surface Structure.
- **UF** S Structure
  - Superficial Structure
  - Surface Grammar
- **RT** Deep Structure
  - Extended Standard Theory
  - Form (Language Structure)
  - Function Words
  - Generative Phonology
  - Grammar Theories
  - Grammatical Analysis
  - Morphology
  - Morphophonemics
  - Passive Voice
  - Phonology
  - Phrase Structure Grammar
  - Sentence Structure
  - Syntax
  - Transformation Rules
  - Transformational Generative Grammar

Surgery
- **DC** 85900
- **HN** Formerly (1973-1991) DC su3, Surgical Treatment.
- **UF** Mastoidectomy (1973-1979)
  - Operations (Surgery)
  - Stapedectomy (1973-1991)
  - Surgical Treatment (1973-1991)
  - Tympanoplasty (1973-1991)
- **BT** Medicine
- **NT** Laryngectomy
- **RT** Esophageal Speech
  - Hearing Improvement
  - Prosthetic Devices
  - Therapy

Surgical Treatment (1973-1991)
- **HN** DC su3.
- **Use** Surgery

Surinam
- **DC** 85950
- **HN** Added, 1992.
- **BT** South America

Surveys
- **DC** 86000
- **HN** Added, 1992.
- **RT** Data Collection
  - Fieldwork
  - Interviews
  - Longitudinal Studies
  - Measures (Instruments)
  - Research Design

Surveys (cont'd)
RT   Respondents

Swahili
DC   86150
HN   Added, 1992.
UF   Kiswahili
      Komoro
      Pemba
      Tikuu
BT   Bantoid Languages

Swaziland
DC   86200
HN   Added, 1992.
BT   Sub Saharan Africa

Swearwords
Use   Obscenities

Sweden
DC   86250
HN   Added, 1992.
BT   Scandinavia

Swedish
DC   86400
HN   Added, 1992.
BT   Germanic Languages
      Scandinavian Languages

Switching (Language)
Use   Code Switching

Switzerland
DC   86450
HN   Added, 1992.
BT   Western Europe

Syllables
DC   86500
HN   Formerly (1973-1991) DC sy1, Syllable.
BT   Linguistic Units
NT   Nonsense Syllables
RT   Accentuation
      Consonants
      Intonation
      Length (Phonological)
      Metrical Phonology
      Mora
      Phonemes
      Phonology
      Phonotactics
      Stress
      Tone
      Vowels
      Writing Systems

Symbolism
DC   86600
HN   Added, 1992.
RT   Communication
      Imagery
      Literature
      Meaning
      Metaphors
      Mythology
      Poetics
      Poetry
      Rhetorical Figures
      Semiotics

Synchronic Linguistics
DC   86650
SN   Study of a language at a particular point in time.
HN   Formerly (1973-1991) DC sy1a.
BT   Linguistics
RT   Assimilation (Language Change)
      Descriptive Linguistics

Synchronic Linguistics (cont'd)
RT   Diachronic Linguistics
      Language Typology
      Language Usage
      Linguistic Theories
      Prague School

Synonyms
DC   86750
HN   Formerly (1973-1991) DC sy2, Synonym.
UF   Synonymy
BT   Lexicon
RT   Antonyms
      Meaning
      Semantics

Synonymy
Use   Synonyms

Syntactic Analysis
Use   Grammatical Analysis

Syntactic Borrowing
Use   Borrowing

Syntactic Change
Use   Grammatical Change

Syntactic Government
Use   Government (Grammatical)

Syntactic Processing
DC   86760
HN   Added, 1992.
BT   Language Processing
RT   Agrammatism
      Cognitive Processes
      Decoding (Cognitive Process)
      Grammaticality
      Natural Language Processing
      Neurolinguistics
      Psycholinguistics
      Syntax

Syntactic Relations
Use   Grammatical Relations

Syntactic Structures
DC   86770
SN   Patterns of co-occurrence of sentence elements; also termed constructions. Constructions may be continuous or discontinuous.
HN   Added, 1992.
UF   Constructions (Syntax)
RT   Clauses
      Grammatical Analysis
      Linguistic Units
      Morphemes
      Phrase Structure Grammar
      Phrases
      Sentences
      Syntagmatic Relations
      Syntax
      Transformation Rules

Syntagmatic Relations
DC   86780
SN   Inferred grammatical relations between sentence elements such that the elements can be treated as units in linguistic description. Syntagma include phrases but are not limited to them.
HN   Added, 1992.
BT   Grammatical Relations
RT   Grammar Theories
      Idioms
      Lexicology

Syntagmatic Relations (cont'd)
RT   Lexicon
      Linguistic Units
      Morphemes
      Neologisms
      Phonemes
      Phrases
      Sentences
      Speech Acts
      Structuralist Linguistics
      Syntactic Structures
      Syntax
      Tagmemics
      Text Structure
      Valence
      Word Formation
      Word Order

Syntax
DC   86800
SN   The specifiable relationships among sentence elements; the internal organization of sentences; the branch of linguistics concerned with sentence structure.
HN   Formerly (1973-1991) DC sy3.
RT   Agent Patient Relationship (Grammatical)
      Agreement
      Aspect
      Autolexical Grammar
      Case
      Case Grammar
      Categorial Grammar
      Clauses
      Clitics
      Cohesion
      Comparative Linguistics
      Comparison
      Conjugation
      Context Free Grammar
      Context Sensitive Grammar
      Coordination (Grammatical)
      Deep Structure
      Dependency Grammar
      Derivation (Morphology)
      Descriptive Linguistics
      Discourse Analysis
      Ellipsis
      Embedded Construction
      Extended Standard Theory
      Focus
      Form (Language Structure)
      Functional Grammar
      Gender (Grammatical)
      Generalized Phrase Structure Grammar
      Generative Grammar
      Government (Grammatical)
      Government Binding Theory
      Grammatical Change
      Grammar Instruction
      Grammar Theories
      Grammatical Analysis
      Grammatical Categories
      Grammatical Relations
      Grammaticality
      Idioms
      Inflection (Morphology)
      Language
      Language Patterns
      Language Typology
      Lexical Functional Grammar
      Lexicon
      Linguistic Units
      Linguistics
      Logic of Language
      Logical Form

Syntax (cont'd)
- **RT** Montague Grammar
- Mood (Grammatical)
- Morphemes
- Morphology
- Movement (Grammatical)
- Negation
- Noun Phrases
- Number (Grammatical)
- Opacity
- Paragraphs
- Parsing
- Person
- Phrase Structure Grammar
- Phrases
- Pragmatics
- Prescriptive Grammar
- Principles and Parameters Approach
- Redundancy
- Reference (Grammatical)
- Relational Grammar
- Relative Clauses
- Rule Ordering
- Semantic Analysis
- Semantics
- Semiotics
- Sentence Structure
- Sentences
- Stratificational Grammar
- Structuralist Linguistics
- Subordination (Grammatical)
- Surface Structure
- Syntactic Processing
- Syntactic Structures
- Syntagmatic Relations
- Tagmemics
- Taxonomic Approaches
- Tense
- Text Structure
- Transformation Rules
- Transformational Generative Grammar
- Universal Grammar
- Valence
- Voice (Grammatical)
- Well Formedness
- Wh Phrases
- Word Order
- Words
- X Bar Theory

Synthetic Languages (1973-1991)
- **HN** DC sy4, deleted 1992. See now Inflection (Morphology) or Artificial Languages.

Synthetic Speech
- **Use** Speech Synthesis

Syria
- **DC** 86950
- **HN** Added, 1992.
- **BT** Arab Countries
- Mediterranean Countries
- Middle East

Syriac
- **Use** Aramaic

Systemic Linguistics
- **DC** 87100
- **SN** A school of functional linguistics, developed principally by Michael Alexander Kirkwood Halliday during the 1970s; language is viewed as networks of interlocking choices made by a speaker during the speech act. Also known as systemic functional grammar, which is distinguished from functional grammar and lexical/functional grammar.

Systemic Linguistics (cont'd)
- **HN** Added, 1992.
- **BT** Linguistics
- **RT** Communicative Function of Language
- Functional Grammar
- Grammar Theories
- Linguistic Theories
- Sociolinguistics

Taal
- **Use** Afrikaans

Tacana Languages
- **Use** Ge Pano Carib Languages

Tachistoscopes
- **DC** 87150
- **HN** Formerly (1973-1991) DC ta1, Tachistoscope.
- **RT** Eye Movements
- Reading
- Reading Instruction
- Recognition
- Visual Stimulation

Tactile Perception
- **Use** Tactual Perception

Tactual Perception
- **DC** 87250
- **HN** Formerly (1973-1991) DC to3, Touch, Tactile.
- **UF** Cutaneous Sense
- Haptic Perception
- Tactile Perception
- Touch, Tactile (1973-1991)
- **BT** Perception
- **RT** Proprioception
- Reading Aids for the Blind
- Sensory Systems

Tadzhikskaya
- **Use** Tajikstan

Tagalog
- **DC** 87350
- **HN** Formerly (1973-1981) DC ta2. Reinstated, 1992.
- **BT** Malayo Polynesian Languages

Tagmemic Analysis
- **Use** Tagmemics

Tagmemics
- **DC** 87400
- **SN** A system of linguistic analysis originated by Kenneth Pike; grammatical, phonological, & lexical modes of language are distinguished; form and syntactic function are integrated in basic units termed tagmemes; discourse, not the sentence, is taken as the scope of analysis.
- **HN** Formerly (1982-1991) DC ta2a.
- **UF** Tagmemic Analysis
- **RT** Discourse Analysis
- Form Classes
- Grammar Theories
- Grammatical Analysis
- Language Patterns
- Negation
- Phonology
- Semantic Analysis
- Semantics
- Syntagmatic Relations
- Syntax

Tai Languages
- **Use** Kam Tai Languages

Taiwan
- **DC** 87600
- **HN** Added, 1992.
- **BT** Far East

Tajikistan
- **DC** 87610
- **HN** Added, 1992.
- **BT** Commonwealth of Independent States
- **RT** Union of Soviet Socialist Republics

Talmud
- **Use** Religious Literature

Tamashek
- **Use** Berber Languages

Tamil
- **DC** 87650
- **HN** Added, 1992.
- **BT** Dravidian Languages

Tanganyika
- **Use** Tanzania

Tanzania
- **DC** 87700
- **HN** Added, 1992.
- **UF** Tanganyika
- **BT** Sub Saharan Africa

Tasmania
- **DC** 87750
- **HN** Added, 1992.
- **BT** Australia

Taxonomic Approaches
- **DC** 87800
- **SN** Any approach to language analysis concerned with the segmentation and classification of linguistic data. Since 1957, chiefly used by proponents of generative grammar to refer to various nongenerative models of language.
- **HN** Formerly (1973-1991) DC ta3, Taxonomic Grammar.
- **RT** Form Classes
- Grammar Theories
- Language Classification
- Language Typology
- Linguistic Theories
- Phonemics
- Phonology
- Semantic Analysis
- Semantics
- Syntax

Teacher Attitudes
- **DC** 87840
- **HN** Added, 1992.
- **UF** Instructor Attitudes
- **BT** Attitudes
- **RT** Student Teacher Relationship
- Teachers

Teacher Education
- **DC** 87850
- **HN** Formerly (1973-1991) DC te1, Teacher Training.
- **BT** Professional Education
- **RT** Teaching Methods

Teacher Student Communication
  Use Classroom Communication

Teacher Student Relationship
  Use Student Teacher Relationship

Teachers
  DC 87860
  HN Added, 1992.
  UF Instructors
  RT Classroom Communication
      Classroom Observation
      Education
      Educational Activities
      Instruction
      Student Teacher Relationship
      Students
      Teacher Attitudes
      Teaching Methods

Teaching (Process)
  Use Instruction

Teaching English to Speakers of Other Languages
  Use TESOL

Teaching Language
  Use Language of Instruction

Teaching Machines (1973-1991)
  HN DC te2.
  Use Computer Assisted Instruction

Teaching Materials
  DC 87950
  HN Added, 1992.
  UF Educational Materials
      Instructional Materials
  NT Bilingual Teaching Materials
      Language Teaching Materials
  RT Computer Assisted Instruction
      Education
      Educational Activities
      Instruction
      Interactive Video
      Reading Materials
      Teaching Methods
      Visual Media

Teaching Methods
  DC 88150
  HN Added, 1992.
  UF Instructional Methods
      Teaching Techniques
  NT Language Teaching Methods
      Suggestopedia
  RT Classroom Communication
      Classroom Observation
      Education
      Educational Activities
      Educational Television
      Instruction
      Reinforcement
      Teacher Education
      Teachers
      Teaching Materials

Teaching Techniques
  Use Teaching Methods

Technical Language
  Use Scientific Technical Language

Technical Translation
  DC 88200
  HN Added, 1992.
  BT Translation
  RT Medical Language
      Scientific Technical Language
      Terminology

Teenagers
  Use Adolescents

Teeth
  Use Oral Cavity

TEFL
  Use TESOL

Televised Instruction
  Use Educational Television

Television
  DC 88300
  HN Added, 1992.
  BT Mass Media
  NT Educational Television
  RT Radio
      Videotape Recordings
      Visual Media

Television and Teaching (1973-1991)
  HN DC te3.
  Use Educational Television

Telugu
  Use Dravidian Languages

Temne
  Use West Atlantic Languages

Temporal Reference
  Use Time

Temporality
  Use Time

Tennessee
  DC 88400
  HN Added, 1992.
  BT Southern States
      United States of America
  RT Appalachia

Tense
  DC 88500
  HN Formerly (1973-1991) DC te4.
  BT Grammatical Categories
  RT Aspect
      Auxiliary Verbs
      Conditional Clauses
      Conjugation
      Form Classes
      Infinitives
      Inflection (Morphology)
      Modal Verbs
      Mood (Grammatical)
      Morphemes
      Morphology
      Syntax
      Time
      Verbs

Terminal Juncture
  Use Juncture

Terminology
  DC 88550
  SN Special words and phrases customarily used in a particular discipline, field, or occupation; also, vocabulary denoting items in a specified domain.
  HN Added, 1992.
  UF Jargon
      Specialized Vocabulary
  BT Lexicon
  NT Kinship Terminology
  RT Acronyms
      English for Special Purposes
      Language for Special Purposes

Terminology (cont'd)
  RT Language Standardization
      Language Styles
      Legal Language
      Medical Language
      Metalanguage
      Registers (Sociolinguistics)
      Scientific Technical Language
      Slang
      Technical Translation
      Words

Tertiary Education
  Use Higher Education

Tesnière, Lucien
  DC 88650
  SN Born 1893 - Died 1954.
  HN Formerly (1973-1991) DC te5, Tesniere.

TESOL
  DC 88700
  HN Formerly (1973-1991) DC te6.
  UF Teaching English to Speakers of Other Languages
      TEFL
  BT Second Language Instruction
  RT English as a Second Language

Test Validity and Reliability
  DC 88800
  SN Extent to which a test measures what it is intended to measure and/or its results are accurate, consistent, and stable.
  HN Added, 1992. Prior to 1992 see Testing.
  UF Reliability (Tests)
      Validity (Tests)
  RT Measures (Instruments)
      Rating Scales
      Tests

Testing (1973-1991)
  HN DC te7.
  Use Tests

Tests
  DC 88900
  SN Instruments or methods used to measure ability, skill, achievement, knowledge, aptitude, or perception.
  HN Formerly (1973-1991) DC te7, Testing.
  UF Testing (1973-1991)
  BT Measures (Instruments)
  NT Achievement Tests
      Aptitude Tests
      Audiometry
      Diagnostic Tests
      Illinois Test of Psycholinguistic Abilities
      Intelligence Tests
      Language Tests
      Prognostic Tests
      Reading Tests
      Speech Tests
      Stroop Color Word Test
      Writing Tests
  RT Academic Achievement
      Education
      Test Validity and Reliability

Texas
  DC 88950
  HN Added, 1992.
  BT United States of America
      Western States

Text Analysis
- **DC** 89100
- **HN** Formerly (1973-1991) DC te9.
- **RT** Cohesion
  - Content Analysis
  - Context
  - Discourse Analysis
  - Literary Criticism
  - Manuscripts
  - Narrative Structure
  - Rhetorical Figures
  - Statistical Analysis of Style
  - Story Grammar
  - Stylistics
  - Text Structure
  - Textual Criticism
  - Word Frequency

Text Criticism
- **Use** Textual Criticism

Text Editing
- **Use** Word Processing

Text Processing
- **Use** Word Processing

Text Structure
- **DC** 89200
- **HN** Added, 1992.
- **RT** Cohesion
  - Narrative Structure
  - Readability
  - Reading Comprehension
  - Reading Writing Relationship
  - Rheme
  - Sentence Structure
  - Story Grammar
  - Structuralist Linguistics
  - Syntagmatic Relations
  - Syntax
  - Text Analysis
  - Writing

Textual Criticism
- **DC** 89210
- **HN** Added, 1992.
- **UF** Text Criticism
- **RT** Authorship
  - Computer Applications
  - Literary Criticism
  - Literary Language
  - Manuscripts
  - Paleolinguistics
  - Printed Materials
  - Statistical Analysis of Style
  - Stylistics
  - Text Analysis

Thai Languages (1973-1991)
- **HN** DC th1.
- **Use** Kam Tai Languages

Thailand
- **DC** 89250
- **HN** Added, 1992.
- **BT** Southeast Asia

Thematic Roles
- **DC** 89300
- **HN** Added, 1992.
- **UF** Semantic Roles
  - Theta Roles
- **RT** Agent Patient Relationship (Grammatical)
  - Case
  - Deep Structure
  - Functional Grammar
  - Government Binding Theory

Thematic Roles (cont'd)
- **RT** Incorporation (Grammatical)
  - Noun Phrases
  - Semantic Analysis
  - Semantic Categories
  - Semantics
  - Valence

Theoretical Linguistics
- **DC** 89450
- **SN** Branch of linguistics that attempts to establish general principles for the study of language. Use Linguistic Theories or the names of specific theories when dealing with individual theories or groups of theories.
- **HN** Formerly (1973-1991) DC th1a.
- **BT** Linguistics
- **RT** Applied Linguistics
  - History of Linguistics
  - Linguistic Theories

Therapeutics
- **Use** Therapy

Therapy
- **DC** 89500
- **HN** Added, 1992.
- **UF** Therapeutics
- **NT** Language Therapy
  - Psychotherapy
  - Speech Therapy
- **RT** Disorders
  - Drug Effects
  - Handicapped
  - Hearing Improvement
  - Medicine
  - Patients
  - Practitioner Patient Relationship
  - Prognostic Tests
  - Prosthetic Devices
  - Special Education (Handicapped)
  - Surgery

Theta Roles
- **Use** Thematic Roles

Thinking
- **Use** Cognitive Processes

Thorndike Lorge Frequency
- **Use** Word Frequency

Thought
- **Use** Cognitive Processes

Thought Language Relationship
- **Use** Language Thought Relationship

Threats
- **Use** Verbal Aggression

Threshold Level (Language)
- **DC** 89550
- **HN** Added, 1992.
- **RT** Fluency
  - Linguistic Competence
  - Second Language Learning
  - Thresholds

Thresholds
- **DC** 89600
- **HN** Added, 1992.
- **UF** Limen
- **NT** Auditory Thresholds
  - Visual Thresholds
- **RT** Measures (Instruments)
  - Perception
  - Sensory Systems
  - Stimulation
  - Threshold Level (Language)

Tibet
- **DC** 89700
- **SN** A province of the People's Republic of China.
- **HN** Added, 1992.
- **BT** Peoples Republic of China

Tibetan
- **Use** Tibeto Burman Languages

Tibeto Burman Languages
- **DC** 89800
- **HN** Added, 1992.
- **UF** Burmese
  - Tibetan
- **BT** Sino Tibetan Languages

Tigrinya
- **Use** Semitic Languages

Tikuu
- **Use** Swahili

Timbre
- **Use** Voice Quality

Time
- **DC** 89850
- **HN** Formerly (1977-1991) DC ti1, Time, Duration.
- **UF** Temporal Reference
  - Temporality
- **RT** Deixis
  - Length (Phonological)
  - Meaning
  - Semantic Categories
  - Semantics
  - Sound Duration (Phonetics)
  - Space
  - Speech Duration
  - Tense (Grammatical)

Time, Duration (1973-1991)
- **HN** DC ti1, deleted 1991. See now Time or Sound Duration.

Tiwi
- **Use** Australian Macro Phylum

Togo
- **DC** 90250
- **HN** Added, 1992.
- **BT** Sub Saharan Africa

Tone
- **DC** 90300
- **HN** Formerly (1973-1991) DC to1.
- **BT** Suprasegmentals
- **RT** Intonation
  - Juncture
  - Morphology
  - Morphophonemics
  - Phonetics
  - Phonology
  - Pitch (Phonology)
  - Sandhi
  - Syllables

Tone Sandhi
- **Use** Sandhi

Tongue
- **Use** Oral Cavity

Tongue Slips
- **Use** Slips of the Tongue

Topic and Comment
DC 90400
SN A fundamental division of sentences into two parts; one part (the comment) communicates information about the other (the topic). May also refer to topicalization (ie, the process of selecting a sentence component to function as topic).
HN Added, 1992.
RT Focus
Meaning
Predicate
Psycholinguistics
Semantic Analysis
Semantics
Topics

Topics
DC 90520
SN Subjects of actual spoken or written discourse or topics that are appropriate for discussion within a given speech community.
HN Formerly (1988-1991) DC to1c, Topic.
RT Conversation
Topic and Comment

Toponymy
DC 90550
SN The branch of onomastics that treats names of places (toponyms), rivers (hydronyms), and other geographical features.
HN Added, 1992.
UF Placenames
Typonomastics
BT Onomastics
RT Diachronic Linguistics
Etymology

Tosk
Use Albanian

Touch, Tactile (1973-1991)
HN DC to3.
Use Tactual Perception

Trace Theory
DC 90700
SN In government and binding theory, a trace is a postulated empty category at S-structure that marks the D-structure position of a constituent that undergoes movement; coindexed with the moved constituent, it functions as an anaphor.
HN Formerly (1973-1991) DC tr1.
BT Linguistic Theories
RT Anaphora
Generative Grammar
Government Binding Theory
Movement (Grammatical)

Trade Languages
DC 90800
SN Languages or dialects used for communication among speakers whose native languages are mutually unintelligible, typically in situations where the development of trade led to the spread of a trade language as a second language.
HN Formerly (1973-1991) DC tr1a.
UF Commercial Dialects
Lingua Franca
BT Language for Special Purposes
RT Borrowing
Business

Trade Languages (cont'd)
RT Business English
Creoles
Cross Cultural Communication
Indigenous Languages
International Languages
Language Contact
Language Use
Pidgins

Transfer (Learning)
DC 90850
SN The effect that an existing habit, skill, idea, or knowledge has on learning new skills or material.
HN Formerly (1973-1991) DC tr2, Transfer.
UF Negative Transfer
Positive Transfer
BT Learning
RT Generalization
Interference (Learning)
Interlanguage
Paired Associate Learning

Transformation Rules
DC 90950
SN In early transformational-generative grammar, operations performed on strings generated by a phrase structure grammar to yield other strings and thereby account for all possible sentences in a language.
HN Formerly (1973-1991) DC tr3.
UF Transformational Rules
RT Deep Structure
Grammar Theories
Movement (Grammatical)
Phrase Structure Grammar
Rule Ordering
Surface Structure
Syntactic Structures
Syntax
Transformational Generative Grammar

Transformational Generative Grammar
DC 91150
SN A revolutionary model of grammar introduced by Noam Chomsky in 1957 and elaborated during the 1960s as standard theory and during the 1970s as extended standard theory; its successor is government and binding theory. Language is defined as a set of sentences; the ability of a native speaker to generate the sentences of his/her language is accounted for by a sentence-generating model containing a phrase structure grammar and transformation rules.
HN Formerly (1973-1991) DC tr4, Transformational and Generative Grammar.
UF Generative Transformational Grammar
BT Generative Grammar
RT Deep Structure
Embedded Construction
Extended Standard Theory
Generative Phonology
Generative Semantics
Language Universals
Linguistic Competence
Linguistic Peformance
Movement (Grammatical)
Native Language

Transformational Generative Grammar (cont'd)
RT Native Speakers
Phrase Structure Grammar
Reflexivity
Rule Ordering
Surface Structure
Semantics
Syntax
Transformation Rules
X Bar Theory

Transformational Rules
Use Transformation Rules

Translation
DC 91200
HN Formerly (1973-1991) DC tr5, Translation and Interpretation.
UF Free Translation
Interpretation
Interpreting
Simultaneous Translation
BT Language Processing
NT Literary Translation
Machine Translation
Technical Translation
RT Applied Linguistics
Bilingual Dictionaries
Bilingualism
Communication
Cross Cultural Communication
Grammar Translation Method of Language Teaching
Languages
Translation Instruction
Translators

Translation Dictionaries
Use Bilingual Dictionaries

Translation Instruction
DC 91300
HN Added, 1992.
UF Translator Training
BT Instruction
RT Educational Activities
Translation
Translators

Translator Training
Use Translation Instruction

Translators
DC 91350
HN Added, 1992.
UF Interpreters
RT Translation
Translation Instruction

Transparency
Use Opacity

Trigrams (1973-1991)
HN DC tr6.
Use Nonsense Syllables

Trubetzkoy, Nikolai Sergeyevich
DC 91450
SN Born 1890 - Died 1938.
HN Formerly (1973-1991) DC tr7, Trubetzkoy.

Trustworthiness
Use Credibility

Truth
- DC 91500
- HN Formerly (1973-1991) DC tr8.
- RT Beliefs
  - Credibility
  - Entailment
  - Pragmatics
  - Presuppositions

Tucanoan Languages
- Use Andean Equitorial Phylum

Tungus Languages
- Use Altaic Languages

Tunisia
- DC 91600
- HN Added, 1992.
- BT Arab Countries
  - Mediterranean Countries
  - North Africa

Tupari Languages
- Use Tupi Languages

Tupi Guarani Languages
- Use Tupi Languages

Tupi Languages
- DC 91650
- HN Added, 1992.
- UF Tupari Languages
  - Tupi Guarani Languages
- BT Andean Equatorial Phylum

Turkey
- DC 91750
- HN Added, 1992.
- BT Balkan States
  - Mediterranean Countries
  - Middle East
  - Western Europe

Turkic Languages
- DC 91850
- HN Added, 1992.
- UF Kazakh
  - Kirghiz
  - Turkmen
  - Uzbek
  - Yakut
- BT Altaic Languages
- NT Turkish
  - Azerbaijani

Turkish
- DC 91900
- HN Added, 1992.
- BT Turkic Languages

Turkmen
- Use Turkic Languages

Turkmenistan
- DC 91910
- HN Added, 1992.
- BT Commonwealth of Independent States
- RT Union of Soviet Socialist Republics

Turn Taking
- DC 91950
- HN Added, 1992.
- UF Conversational Turns
- RT Conversation
  - Cultural Factors
  - Discourse Analysis
  - Dyadic Interaction
  - Group Communication

Turn Taking (cont'd)
- RT Interpersonal Communication
  - Language Patterns
  - Language Usage
  - Listening
  - Pauses
  - Politeness
  - Silence
  - Speech
  - Speech Acts
  - Speech Duration

Tuscanoan Languages
- Use Andean Equatorial Phylum

Twi
- Use Akan

Tympanoplasty (1973-1991)
- HN DC ty1.
- Use Surgery

Typography
- Use Printed Materials

Typology of Language (1973-1991)
- HN DC ty2.
- Use Language Typology

Typonomastics
- Use Toponymy

Ubangian Languages
- Use Adamawa Eastern Phylum

Uganda
- DC 92000
- HN Added, 1992.
- BT Sub Saharan Africa

Ugric Languages
- DC 92100
- HN Formerly (1973-1991) DC ug1.
- BT Finno Ugric Languages
- NT Hungarian

Ukraine
- DC 92200
- HN Added, 1992.
- BT Commonwealth of Independent States
- RT Union of Soviet Socialist Republics

Ukrainian
- DC 92250
- HN Added, 1992.
- UF Little Russian
- BT Slavic Languages

Umbrian
- Use Italic Languages

Unaided Recall
- DC 92300
- HN Formerly (1973-1991) DC un1.
- UF Free Recall
- BT Recall (Memory)
- RT Aided Recall
  - Encoding (Cognitive Process)
  - Retention (Memory)

Undergraduate Education
- DC 92450
- HN Formerly (1973-1991) DC un2, Undergraduate School.
- UF College Undergraduate Education
  - University Undergraduate Education
- BT Higher Education
- RT College Students

Underlying Structure
- Use Deep Structure

Ungrammaticality
- Use Grammaticality

Union of Soviet Socialist Republics
- DC 92500
- SN Established 1917, dissolved 1991. If appropriate, see Commonwealth of Independent States or names of individual republics.
- HN Added, 1992.
- BT Eastern Europe
- RT Armenia
  - Azerbaijan
  - Belarus
  - Commonwealth of Independent States
  - Commonwealth of Independent States Cultural Groups
  - Estonia
  - Georgia (Republic)
  - Kazakhstan
  - Kyrgystan
  - Latvia
  - Lithuania
  - Moldova
  - Russia
  - Siberia
  - Slavic Cultural Groups
  - Tajikstan
  - Turkmenistan
  - Ukraine
  - Uzbekistan

United Arab Emirates
- DC 92550
- HN Added, 1992.
- BT Arab Countries
  - Middle East

United Arab Republic
- Use Egypt

United Kingdom
- DC 92700
- SN England, Scotland, Wales, and Northern Ireland.
- HN Added, 1992.
- BT Western Europe
- NT England
  - Great Britain
  - Northern Ireland
  - Scotland
  - Wales

United States of America
- DC 92750
- HN Added, 1992.
- UF US
  - USA
- BT North America
- NT Alabama
  - Alaska
  - Arizona
  - Arkansas
  - California
  - Colorado
  - Connecticut
  - Delaware
  - Florida
  - Georgia (USA)
  - Hawaii
  - Idaho
  - Illinois
  - Indiana
  - Iowa
  - Kansas

United States of America (cont'd)
- NT Kentucky
  Louisiana
  Maine
  Maryland
  Massachusetts
  Michigan
  Minnesota
  Mississippi
  Missouri
  Montana
  Nebraska
  Nevada
  New Hampshire
  New Jersey
  New Mexico
  New York
  North Carolina
  North Dakota
  Ohio
  Oklahoma
  Oregon
  Pennsylvania
  Rhode Island
  South Carolina
  South Dakota
  Tennessee
  Texas
  Utah
  Vermont
  Virginia
  Washington (State)
  West Virginia
  Wisconsin
  Wyoming
- RT Midwestern States
  Northern States
  Southern States
  Western States

Units
- Use Linguistic Units

Universal Grammar
- DC 92800
- SN Any set of statements claimed to apply to the structure of all languages; chiefly used in the framework of Noam Chomsky's principles-and-parameters approach to designate a hypothesized single grammar, transmitted genetically, that accounts for the ability of all normal humans to learn and speak their native language.
- HN Formerly (1989-1991) DC un3. Prior to 1989, see Language Universals.
- BT Grammar Theories
- RT Language Universals
  Principles and Parameters Approach
  Psycholinguistics
  Syntax

Universals (Language)
- Use Language Universals

University Graduate Education
- Use Graduate Education

University Students
- Use College Students

University Undergraduate Education
- Use Undergraduate Education

Unknown Languages
- DC 92900
- HN Added, 1992.
- BT Languages
- RT Anthropological Linguistics
  Archaeological Evidence

Unknown Languages (cont'd)
- RT Diachronic Linguistics
  Indigenous Languages
  Language Death
  Origin of Language
  Paleolinguistics

Unpronounceable Words
- Use Pronounceability

UPE Programs
- Use Literacy Programs

Upper Class
- Use Social Class

Upper Volta
- Use Burkina Faso

Uralic Languages
- DC 92950
- HN Formerly (1973-1991) DC ur1.
- UF Samoyed Languages
- BT Languages
- NT Finno Ugric Languages

Urdu
- Use Hindi

Uruguay
- DC 93100
- HN Added, 1992.
- BT South America

Utah
- DC 93200
- HN Added, 1992.
- BT United States of America
  Western States

Uto Aztecan Languages
- DC 93350
- HN Added, 1992.
- UF Aztec
  Nahua
  Nahuatl
  Numic
  Paiute Languages
  Sonoran Languages
  Shoshone
- BT North Amerindian Languages
- RT Mexican Amerindian Languages

Utterances
- Use Speech Acts

Uzbekistan
- DC 93400
- HN Added, 1992.
- BT Commonwealth of Independent States
- RT Union of Soviet Socialist Republics

Valence
- DC 93500
- HN Formerly (1973-1991) DC va1.
- RT Case Grammar
  Dependency Grammar
  Nouns
  Sentences
  Syntagmatic Relations
  Syntax
  Thematic Roles
  Verbs

Validity (Tests)
- Use Test Validity and Reliability

Vedic Sanskrit
- Use Sanskrit

Venezuela
- DC 93550
- HN Added, 1992.
- BT South America

Verb Phrases
- Use Predicate

Verbal (1973-1991)
- HN DC ve1.
- Use Verbs

Verbal Abuse
- Use Verbal Aggression

Verbal Accounts
- DC 93630
- SN Informal descriptions, explanations, or interpretations of events
- HN Added, 1992.
- UF Personal Accounts
- RT Interviews
  Speech
  Writing

Verbal Aggression
- DC 93650
- HN Formerly (1981-1991) DC ag2, Aggression, Verbal.
- UF Aggression (Verbal) (1981-1991)
  Insults
  Threats
  Verbal Abuse
- BT Interpersonal Communication
- RT Interpersonal Behavior

Verbal Conditioning
- Use Conditioning

Verbal Learning
- DC 93750
- HN Formerly (1973-1991) DC ve2.
- BT Learning
- NT Paired Associate Learning
  Serial Learning
- RT Discrimination Learning
  Language Acquisition
  Language Arts
  Listening Comprehension
  Mediation Theory
  Memorization
  Nonsense Syllables
  Nonsense Words
  Psycholinguistics
  Rehearsal (Verbal Learning)
  Verbal Tasks

Verbal Mediation
- Use Mediation Theory

Verbal Paradigm
- Use Conjugation

Verbal Play
- Use Word Play

Verbal Slips
- Use Slips of the Tongue

Verbal Tasks
- DC 93800
- HN Formerly (1973-1991) ve3, Verbal Task.
- UF Language Tasks
  Lexical Tasks
- RT Judgment
  Language Processing

Verbal Tasks (cont'd)
- **RT** Reading
  Recall (Memory)
  Verbal Learning
  Word Recognition

Verbs
- **DC** 93900
- **HN** Formerly (1973-1991) DC ve1, Verbal.
- **UF** Verbal (1973-1991)
- **BT** Form Classes
- **NT** Auxiliary Verbs
  Infinitives
  Modal Verbs
- **RT** Adverbs
  Agent Patient Relationship (Grammatical)
  Agreement
  Aspect
  Case Marking
  Conjugation
  Gender (Grammatical)
  Imperative Sentences
  Incorporation (Grammatical)
  Mood (Grammatical)
  Number (Grammatical)
  Passive Voice
  Performative Utterances
  Person
  Predicate
  Reflexivity
  Subjunctive
  Tense
  Valence
  Voice (Grammatical)

Vermont
- **DC** 93950
- **HN** Added, 1992.
- **BT** Northern States
  United States of America

Videos
- **Use** Videotape Recordings

Videotape Recordings
- **DC** 94000
- **HN** Added, 1992
- **UF** Videos
- **RT** Films
  Music
  Television
  Visual Media

Vietnam
- **DC** 94100
- **HN** Added, 1992.
- **UF** North Vietnam
  South Vietnam
- **BT** Southeast Asia

Vietnamese
- **DC** 94150
- **HN** Formerly (1985-1991) DC ve4.
- **UF** Annamese
- **BT** Austro Asiatic Languages
- **RT** Kam Tai Languages

Virginia
- **DC** 94200
- **HN** Added, 1992.
- **BT** Southern States
  United States of America
- **RT** Appalachia

Vision
- **DC** 94300
- **HN** Added, 1992.
- **UF** Eyesight
  Sight
- **BT** Sensory Systems
- **RT** Color
  Eye Movements
  Reading
  Vision Disorders
  Visual Perception
  Visual Stimulation
  Visual Thresholds

Vision Disorders
- **DC** 94350
- **HN** Formerly (1973-1991) DC vi1.
- **UF** Blindness
  Partial Sight
  Visual Impairments
- **BT** Disorders
- **RT** Eye Movements
  Handicapped
  Reading Aids for the Blind
  Special Education (Handicapped)
  Vision

Visual Arts
- **Use** Art

Visual Imagery
- **Use** Imagery

Visual Impairments
- **Use** Vision Disorders

Visual Masking
- **Use** Masking

Visual Media
- **DC** 94550
- **HN** Formerly (1977-1991) DC pi1aa, Picture, Visual Media.
- **UF** Pictorial Images
  Picture, Visual Media (1977-1991)
  Pictures
- **RT** Art
  Films
  Imagery
  Reading Materials
  Teaching Materials
  Television
  Videotape Recordings
  Visual Stimulation

Visual Perception
- **DC** 94600
- **HN** Added, 1992.
- **UF** Depth Perception
- **BT** Perception
- **RT** Color
  Discrimination Learning
  Dyslexia
  Eye Movements
  Language Processing
  Letter Recognition
  Lipreading
  Stroop Color Word Test
  Vision
  Visual Stimulation
  Visual Thresholds

Visual Stimulation
- **DC** 94700
- **HN** Formerly (1973-1991) DC vi2.
- **BT** Stimulation
- **RT** Auditory Stimulation
  Color
  Masking

Visual Stimulation (cont'd)
- **RT** Tachistoscopes
  Vision
  Visual Media
  Visual Perception
  Visual Thresholds

Visual Thresholds
- **DC** 94800
- **HN** Formerly (1974-1991) DC vi3.
- **BT** Thresholds
- **RT** Vision
  Visual Perception
  Visual Stimulation

Vocabulary (1973-1991)
- **HN** DC vo1.
- **Use** Lexicon

Vocabulary (Specialized)
- **Use** Terminology

Vocabulary Instruction
- **DC** 94850
- **HN** Added, 1992.
- **BT** Instruction
- **RT** Educational Activities
  Language Instruction
  Lexicon
  Native Language Instruction
  Pronunciation Accuracy
  Reading Instruction
  Second Language Instruction
  Second Language Reading Instruction
  Spelling Instruction
  Words

Vocal Cords
- **Use** Phonation Structures

Vocal Folds
- **Use** Phonation Structures

Vocal Quality
- **Use** Voice Quality

Vocal Register
- **Use** Voice Quality

Vocalic Harmony
- **Use** Vowel Harmony

Vocations
- **Use** Occupations

Vocative Case
- **Use** Case

Vocoids
- **Use** Vowels

Voice (Grammatical)
- **DC** 94950
- **HN** Formerly (1973-1991) DC vo2.
- **UF** Active Voice
  Causative Voice
  Middle Voice
- **BT** Grammatical Categories
- **NT** Passive Voice
- **RT** Auxiliary Verbs
  Morphology
  Nouns
  Syntax
  Verbs

Voice (Phonological Feature)
Use Voicing

Voice Disorders
DC 95150
HN Formerly (1973-1991) DC vo2a.
UF Dysphonia
Hoarseness
Spastic Dysphonia
BT Disorders
RT Articulation Disorders
Cleft Palate
Handicapped
Laryngology
Muscular Disorders
Phonation
Phonation Disorders
Respiratory System
Speech
Speech Pathology
Speech Tests
Speech Therapy
Voice Quality

Voice Frequency
Use Fundamental Frequency

Voice Qualifiers
Use Voice Quality

Voice Quality
DC 95200
HN Added, 1992.
UF Register (Phonology)
Timbre
Vocal Quality
Vocal Register
Voice Qualifiers
RT Age Differences
Phonetics
Pitch (phonology)
Singing
Speech
Voice Disorders
Voice Recognition

Voice Recognition
DC 95250
HN Formerly (1973-1991) DC sp8,
Speech Recognition by Machine
RT Acoustic Phonetics
Computational Linguistics
Computer Applications
Neural Networks
Speech
Speech Perception
Speech Synthesis
Voice Quality
Word Recognition

Voice Synthesis
Use Speech Synthesis

Voicing
DC 95400
SN Vocal cord vibration accompanying
the production of an obstruent (stop,
fricative, etc); a coarticulation, phonetically distinct from voice (phonation), which is used in the production
of vowels and resonants. Also, in
phonology, the distinctive feature
consisting of this coarticulation, or
the opposition between its presence
and absence.
HN Added, 1992.
UF Voice (Phonological Feature)
RT Articulatory Phonetics
Consonants

Voicing (cont'd)
RT Distinctive Features
Phonation
Phonation Structures
Phonemes
Phonology

Volgaic Languages
Use Finno Ugric Languages

Volksschule
Use Secondary Education

Voltaic Languages
Use Gur Languages

Volume (Acoustics)
Use Intensity (Acoustics)

Von Restorff Effect (1973-1991)
HN DC vo3.
Use Learning Processes

Vowel Harmony
DC 95450
SN In phonology, a pattern of vowel dis-
tribution characterized by shared
distinctive features among vowels in
adjacent or nearby syllables.
HN Added, 1992.
UF Vocalic Harmony
RT Morphophonemics
Phonology
Vowels

Vowel Identification
Use Sound Identification

Vowel Perception
DC 95600
HN Added, 1992.
BT Speech Perception
RT Letter Recognition
Vowels

Vowels
DC 95650
HN Formerly (1973-1991) DC vo4, Vow-
el.
UF Monophthongs
Vocoids
BT Phonemes
RT Articulation
Consonants
Diphthongs
Formants
Length (Phonological)
Nasalization
Orthographic Symbols
Phonetics
Phonology
Syllables
Vowel Harmony
Vowel Perception

Vulgarisms
Use Obscenities

Vygotsky, Lev Semenovich
DC 95700
SN Born 1896 - Died 1934.
HN Added, 1992.

Wakashan Languages
Use North Amerindian Languages

Wales
DC 95750
HN Added, 1992.
BT Great Britain

Washington (State)
DC 95850
HN Added, 1992.
BT United States of America
Western States

Wechsler Intelligence Tests
Use Intelligence Tests

Well Formedness
DC 96100
SN The conformity of an utterance, sen-
tence, or other linguistic production
to the language/grammatical system
by which it is generated.
HN Formerly (1973-1991) DC we2, Well-
Formedness.
RT Fluency
Form (Language Structure)
Government Binding Theory
Grammar Theories
Grammaticality
Linguistic Competence
Linguistic Performance
Sentence Structure
Syntax
X Bar Theory

Welsh
DC 96200
HN Added, 1992.
UF Cymraeg
BT Celtic Languages

Wernickes Aphasia
DC 96250
HN Added, 1992.
BT Aphasia
RT Brain
Brocas Aphasia

Wernickes Area
Use Brain

West Atlantic Languages
DC 96350
HN Added, 1992.
UF Baga
Ful
Fulani
Temne
Wolof
BT Niger Congo Languages

West Germany
Use Germany

West Indies
Use Caribbean

West Virginia
DC 96400
HN Added, 1992.
BT Southern States
United States of America
RT Appalachia

Western Europe
DC 96450
HN Added, 1992.
BT Europe
NT Andorra
Austria
Azores
Baltic States
Belgium
Canary Islands
Channel Islands
Cyprus

Western Europe (cont'd)
- **NT** France
  - Germany
  - Gibraltar
  - Greece
  - Ireland
  - Italy
  - Liechtenstein
  - Luxembourg
  - Madeira
  - Malta
  - Monaco
  - Netherlands
  - Portugal
  - San Marino
  - Scandinavia
  - Spain
  - Switzerland
  - Turkey
  - United Kingdom
- **RT** Eastern Europe

Western Samoa
- **DC** 96550
- **HN** Added, 1992.
- **BT** Polynesia

Western States
- **DC** 96600
- **HN** Added, 1992.
- **NT** Arizona
  - California
  - Colorado
  - Idaho
  - Montana
  - Nevada
  - New Mexico
  - Oklahoma
  - Oregon
  - Texas
  - Utah
  - Washington (State)
  - Wyoming
- **RT** United States of America

Wh Phrases
- **DC** 96650
- **SN** Phrases containing or consisting of an interrogative pronoun, adverb, or adjective (eg, who, what, where, which).
- **HN** Formerly (1989-1991) DC we5.
- **UF** Wh Questions
- **BT** Phrases
- **RT** Government Binding Theory
  - Interrogative Sentences
  - Movement (Grammatical)
  - Noun Phrases
  - Syntax

Wh Questions
- **Use** Wh Phrases

Whispering
- **DC** 96850
- **HN** Formerly (1973-1991) DC wh1.
- **BT** Speech
- **RT** Articulatory Phonetics
  - Inner Speech

Whistle Language
- **Use** Nonverbal Languages

White Noise
- **Use** Noise

White Russian
- **Use** Belorussian

Whites
- **DC** 96870
- **HN** Added, 1992
- **UF** Caucasians
- **NT** Anglo Americans

Whole Language Approach
- **DC** 96900
- **HN** Added, 1992.
- **BT** Language Teaching Methods
- **RT** Language Arts
  - Language Experience Approach
  - Literature
  - Reading Instruction
  - Reading Writing Relationship
  - Second Language Instruction
  - Written Language Instruction

Whorfian Hypothesis
- **Use** Linguistic Relativity

Wisconsin
- **DC** 97100
- **HN** Added, 1992.
- **BT** Midwestern States
  - United States of America

Wittgenstein, Ludwig Josef Johan
- **DC** 97200
- **SN** Born 1889 - Died 1951.
- **HN** Formerly (1973-1991) DC wi1, Wittgenstein.

Wives
- **Use** Spouses

Wolof
- **Use** West Atlantic Languages

Women
- **Use** Females

Word and Letter Association
- **DC** 97250
- **HN** Formerly (1973-1991) DC wo2.
- **UF** Letter and Word Association
  - Letter Association
  - Word Association
- **BT** Associative Processes
- **RT** Free Association
  - Letter Recognition
  - Reading Ability
  - Words

Word Association
- **Use** Word and Letter Association

Word Blindness
- **Use** Dyslexia

Word Borrowing
- **Use** Borrowing

Word Classes
- **Use** Form Classes

Word Discrimination
- **Use** Word Recognition

Word Formation
- **DC** 97400
- **SN** Process by which new words are created, including derivation, inflection, compounding, etc.
- **HN** Formerly (1973-1991) DC wo2b.
- **NT** Derivation (Morphology)
  - Inflection (Morphology)
- **RT** Acronyms
  - Affixes
  - Compound Words

Word Formation (cont'd)
- **RT** Conjugation
  - Form Classes
  - Lexicon
  - Morphemes
  - Morphological Change
  - Morphology
  - Neologisms
  - Redundancy
  - Roots (Morphology)
  - Syntagmatic Relations
  - Word Structure
  - Words

Word Frequency
- **DC** 97450
- **SN** The frequency of occurrence of specific words in speech or in written texts.
- **HN** Formerly (1973-1991) DC wo3.
- **UF** Thorndike Lorge Frequency
- **RT** Computational Linguistics
  - Computer Generated Language Analysis
  - Context
  - Language
  - Lexicon
  - Mathematical Linguistics
  - Speech
  - Statistical Analysis of Style
  - Stylistics
  - Text Analysis
  - Word Recognition
  - Words
  - Written Language

Word Games
- **DC** 97600
- **HN** Added, 1992.
- **UF** Acrostics
  - Crossword Puzzles
  - Language Games
- **BT** Word Play
- **RT** Problem Solving
  - Second Language Instruction

Word Meaning
- **DC** 97700
- **HN** Added, 1992.
- **UF** Lexical Meaning
- **BT** Meaning
- **RT** Ambiguity
  - Connotation
  - Context Clues
  - Homographs
  - Homonyms
  - Homophones
  - Implicature
  - Lexical Semantics
  - Lexicon
  - Polysemy
  - Semantic Analysis
  - Semantic Features
  - Semantic Fields
  - Semantics
  - Synonyms
  - Words

Word Order
- **DC** 97800
- **HN** Formerly (1973-1991) DC wo3a.
- **RT** Case Marking
  - Clauses
  - Functional Sentence Perspective
  - Grammatical Analysis
  - Grammatical Relations
  - Inflection (Morphology)
  - Language Patterns

Word Order (cont'd)
- **RT** Linguistic Units
  - Markedness
  - Phrases
  - Sentences
  - Syntagmatic Relations
  - Syntax

Word Play
- **DC** 97950
- **HN** Formerly (1973-1991) DC wo4, Word Play (Games).
- **UF** Puns
  - Riddles
  - Verbal Play
- **NT** Word Games
- **RT** Humor
  - Rhetorical Figures

Word Processing
- **DC** 98150
- **HN** Added, 1992.
- **UF** Text Editing
  - Text Processing
- **RT** Computer Applications
  - Computer Software
  - Data Processing
  - Machine Translation
  - Writing

Word Recognition
- **DC** 98200
- **HN** Formerly (1973-1991) DC wo5, Word Recognition and Discrimination.
- **UF** Word Discrimination
- **BT** Recognition
- **RT** Associative Processes
  - Context Clues
  - Context Effects (Perception)
  - Decoding (Reading)
  - Familiarity
  - Lexicon
  - Nonsense Words
  - Reading Comprehension
  - Reading Processes
  - Semantic Memory
  - Semantic Processing
  - Verbal Tasks
  - Voice Recognition
  - Word Frequency
  - Words

Word Structure
- **DC** 98300
- **HN** Added, 1992.
- **UF** Bracketing
  - Lexical Structure
- **RT** Compound Words
  - Morphological Change
  - Morphology
  - Phonology
  - Word Formation
  - Words

Words
- **DC** 98400
- **HN** Formerly (1973-1991) DC wo1, Word.
- **BT** Linguistic Units
- **NT** Compound Words
  - Nonsense Words
- **RT** Accentuation
  - Acronyms
  - Clitics
  - Dictionaries
  - Etymology
  - Form Classes
  - Lexical Functional Grammar

Words (cont'd)
- **RT** Lexical Phonology
  - Lexicon
  - Metrical Phonology
  - Morphology
  - Phraseology
  - Semantics
  - Syntax
  - Terminology
  - Vocabulary Instruction
  - Word and Letter Association
  - Word Formation
  - Word Frequency
  - Word Meaning
  - Word Recognition
  - Word Structure

Working Class
- **Use** Social Class

World English
- **Use** English as an International Language

Writing
- **DC** 98550
- **HN** Formerly (1973-1991) DC wo6.
- **BT** Language Arts
  - Literacy
- **NT** Basic Writing
  - Creative Writing
- **RT** Authorship
  - Cohesion
  - Communication
  - Handwriting
  - Language Processing
  - Orthography
  - Paleography
  - Paragraphs
  - Prose
  - Reading
  - Reading Writing Relationship
  - Rhetoric
  - Sentences
  - Story Grammar
  - Text Structure
  - Verbal Accounts
  - Word Processing
  - Writing Disorders
  - Writing Processes
  - Writing Systems
  - Writing Tests
  - Written Language
  - Written Language Instruction

Writing Disorders
- **DC** 98650
- **HN** Formerly (1973-1991) DC wr1.
- **UF** Agraphia
  - Dysgraphia
- **BT** Disorders
- **RT** Aphasia
  - Dyslexia
  - Handwriting
  - Language Pathology
  - Language Therapy
  - Learning Disabilities
  - Reading Deficiencies
  - Writing

Writing Instruction
- **Use** Written Language Instruction

Writing Processes
- **DC** 98700
- **HN** Added, 1992.
- **UF** Composing Processes (Writing)
- **RT** Language Processing
  - Learning Processes
  - Reading Writing Relationship
  - Writing

Writing Reading Relationship
- **Use** Reading Writing Relationship

Writing Systems
- **DC** 98800
- **HN** Added, 1992.
- **UF** Cuneiform
  - Hieroglyphics
  - Pictographs
  - Script Systems
- **BT** Written Language
- **NT** Alphabets
  - Ideographs
- **RT** Graphemics
  - Orthographic Symbols
  - Paleography
  - Phonemic Transcription
  - Phonetic Transcription
  - Printed Materials
  - Syllables
  - Writing
  - Written Language

Writing Tests
- **DC** 98850
- **SN** Instruments or methods used to measure writing ability, skills, and achievement.
- **HN** Added, 1992.
- **BT** Tests
- **RT** Achievement Tests
  - Language Tests
  - Reading Tests
  - Writing

Written Language
- **DC** 98900
- **HN** Formerly (1973-1991) DC wr2.
- **BT** Language
- **NT** Orthographic Symbols
  - Punctuation
  - Writing Systems
- **RT** Alphabets
  - Colloquial Language
  - Discourse Analysis
  - Graffiti
  - Grapheme Phoneme Correspondence
  - Graphemics
  - Handwriting
  - Language Acquisition
  - Language Patterns
  - Language Usage
  - Literary Language
  - Literature
  - Manuscripts
  - Numerals
  - Oral Language
  - Orthography
  - Phonetic Transcription
  - Printed Materials
  - Prose
  - Reading
  - Spoken Written Language Relationship
  - Word Frequency
  - Writing
  - Writing Systems
  - Written Language Instruction

Written Language Instruction
- **DC** 99200
- **HN** Formerly (1973-1991) DC wr3.
- **UF** Composition Instruction
  - Expository Writing Instruction
  - Writing Instruction
- **BT** Instruction
- **RT** Basic Writing
  - Communicative Competence

Written Language Instruction
(cont'd)
RT   Creative Writing
     Educational Activities
     Handwriting
     Language Teaching Methods
     Native Language Instruction
     Oral Language Instruction
     Second Language Instruction
     Story Grammar
     Whole Language Approach
     Writing
     Written Language

Written Language Spoken Language
Relationship
Use Spoken Written Language Relationship

Wyoming
DC 99250
HN Added, 1992.
BT United States of America
     Western States

X Bar Theory
DC 99400
SN A system of generative linguistic analysis that was created to regulate phrase structure; the rules of phrase structure grammar are more constrained, and more categories of phrases are recognized. Within the noun phrase, intermediate categories larger than the noun but smaller than the phrase are established.
HN Added, 1992.
UF X Theory
BT Grammar Theories
RT Extended Standard Theory
     Generative Grammar
     Government Binding Theory
     Incorporation (Grammatical)
     Syntax
     Transformational Generative Grammar
     Well Formedness

X Ray Technology
Use Radiography

X Theory
Use X Bar Theory

Yakut
Use Turkic Languages

Yemen Arab Republic
DC 99550
Use Republic of Yemen

Yiddish
DC 99650
HN Added, 1992.
BT Germanic Languages
RT German

Yoruba
DC 99700
HN Added, 1992.
BT Kwa Languages

Young Adults
DC 99730
HN Added, 1992.
BT Adults
RT Adolescents
     Adult Language
     College Students

Youth
Use Adolescents

Yucatan (Language)
Use Mayan Languages

Yucatec
Use Mayan Languages

Yugoslavia
DC 99890
HN Added, 1992.
BT Balkan States
     Eastern Europe
RT Bosnia Herzegovina
     Croatia
     Macedonia
     Montenegro
     Serbia
     Slovenia

Yukon
DC 99900
HN Added, 1992.
BT Canada
RT Arctic Regions

Yupik
Use Eskimo Aleut Languages

Zaire
DC 99910
HN Added, 1992.
BT Sub Saharan Africa

Zambia
DC 99920
HN Added, 1992.
UF Northern Rhodesia
BT Sub Saharan Africa

Zimbabwe
DC 99940
HN Added, 1992.
UF Southern Rhodesia
BT Sub Saharan Africa

Zipf, George Kingsley
DC 99950
SN Born 1902 - Died 1950.
HN Formerly (1973-1991) DC zi1, Zipf.

Bibliography

Akmajian, Adrian, Demers, Richard A., Farmer, Ann K., and Harnish, Robert M. *Linguistics: An Introduction to Language and Communication. Third Edition.* Cambridge, Mass.: MIT Press, 1990.

Baldick, Chris. *The Concise Oxford Dictionary of Literary Terms.* Oxford: Oxford University Press, 1990.

Birch, David. *Language, Literature, and Critical Practice.* London: Routledge, 1989.

Booth, Barbara, and Blair, Michael. *Thesaurus of Sociological Indexing Terms. Second Edition.* San Diego, Calif.: Sociological Abstracts, Inc., 1989.

Bright, William, Editor. *International Encyclopedia of Linguistics.* New York: Oxford University Press, 1992.

Clark, John, and Yallop, Colin. *An Introduction to Phonetics and Phonology.* Cambridge, Mass.: Basil Blackwell, 1990.

Crystal, David. *The Cambridge Encyclopedia of Language.* Cambridge: Cambridge University Press, 1987.

Crystal, David. *A Dictionary of Linguistics and Phonetics. Third Edition.* Cambridge, Mass.: Basil Blackwell, 1991.

Ducrot, Oswald, and Todorov, Tzvetan. Translated by Catherine Porter. *Encyclopedic Dictionary of the Sciences of Language.* Baltimore, Md.: Johns Hopkins University Press, 1979.

English, Horace B., and English, Ava Champney. *A Comprehensive Dictionary of Psychological and Psychoanalytical Terms: A Guide to Usage.* New York: David McKay, 1958.

Fasold, Ralph. *Sociolinguistics of Language.* Cambridge, Mass.: Basil Blackwell, 1990.

Flew, Antony. *A Dictionary of Philosophy. Second Edition.* New York: St Martin's, 1984.

Garman, Michael. *Psycholinguistics.* Cambridge: Cambridge University Press, 1989.

Garnham, Alan. *Psycholinguistics: Central Topics.* London: Routledge, 1985.

Gleason, H. A., Jr. *An Introduction to Descriptive Linguistics. Revised Edition.* New York: Holt, Rinehart and Winston, 1961.

Greenberg, Joseph H. *The Languages of Africa. Third Edition.* Bloomington, Ind.: Indiana University, 1970.

Haegeman, Liliane. *Introduction to Government and Binding Theory.* Cambridge, Mass.: Basil Blackwell, 1991.

Hartmann, R. R. K., and Stork, F . C. *Dictionary of Language and Linguistics.* New York: Wiley, 1972.

Horrocks, Geoffrey. *Generative Grammar.* London: Longmans, 1987.

Houston, James E. *Thesaurus of ERIC Descriptors. 12th Edition.* Phoenix, Ariz.: Oryx Press, 1990.

Jeffers, Robert J., and Lehiste Ilse. *Principles and Methods for Historical Linguistics.* Cambridge, Mass.: The MIT Press, 1979.

Ladefoged, Peter. *A Course in Phonetics. Second Edition.* New York: Harcourt Brace Jovanovich, 1982.

Malmkjaer, Kirsten. *The Linguistic Encyclopedia.* London: Routledge & Kegan Paul, 1991.

Martinet, André. Translated by Elizabeth Palmer. *Elements of General Linguistics.* Chicago: University of Chicago Press, 1964.

Newmeyer, Frederick J. (Editor). *Linguistics: The Cambridge Survey. I. Linguistic Theory: Foundations.* Cambridge: Cambridge University Press, 1988.

Nicolosi, Lucille, Harryman, Elizabeth, and Kresheck, Janet. *Terminology of Communication Disorders: Speech-Language-Hearing. Third Edition.* Baltimore: Williams and Wilkins, 1989.

O'Grady, William, Dobrovolsky, Michael, and Aronoff, Mark. *Contemporary Linguistics: An Introduction.* New York: St. Martin's, 1976.

Pei, Mario. *Glossary of Linguistic Terminology.* New York: Columbia University Press, 1966.

Pei, Mario, and Gaynor, Frank. *Dictionary of Linguistics.* Totowa, N.J.: Littlefield, Adams, 1969.

Pullman, Geoffrey K., and Ladusaw, William A. *Phonetic Symbol Guide.* Chicago: University of Chicago Press, 1986.

Reber, Arthur S. *The Penguin Dictionary of Psychology.* London: Penguin Books, 1985.

Richards, Jack C., and Rodgers, Theodore S. *Approaches and Methods in Language Teaching: A Description and Analysis.* Cambridge: Cambridge University Press, 1986.

Sampson, Geoffrey. *Schools of Linguistics.* Stanford, Calif.: Stanford University Press, 1980.

Steible, D. *Concise Handbook of Linguistics: A Glossary of Terms.* New York: Philosophical Library, 1967.

Toolan, Michael J. *Narrative: A Critical Linguistic Introduction.* London: Routledge, 1988.

Voegelin, C. F., and Voegelin, F. M. *Classification and Index of the World's Languages.* New York: Elsevier, 1977.

Wales, Katie. *A Dictionary of Stylistics.* London: Longman, 1989.

Werner, Abraham (Editor). *Terminologie zur neueren Linguistik* (Modern Linguistic Terminology). Second Revised and Enlarged Edition. Tübingen: Max Niemeyer Verlag, 1988.